It Happened in
MANHATTAN

An Oral History of
Life in the City During the
Mid-Twentieth Century

Myrna Katz Frommer and Harvey Frommer

Berkley Books, New York

A Berkley Book
Published by The Berkley Publishing Group
A division of Penguin Group (USA) Inc.
375 Hudson Street
New York, New York 10014

PRINTING HISTORY
Berkley hardcover edition / October 2001
Berkley trade paperback edition / September 2003

Berkley trade paperback ISBN: 0-425-19166-4

The Library of Congress has catalogued the Berkley hardcover edition as follows:

It happened in Manhattan : an oral history of life in the city
during the mid-twentieth century /
[compiled by] Myrna Katz Frommer and
Harvey Frommer.
p. cm.
Includes index.
ISBN 0-425-18169-3
1. Manhattan (New York, N.Y.)—Social life and customs—20th
century. 2. New York (N.Y.)—Social life and customs—20th century.
3. Manhattan (New York, N.Y.)—Biography. 4. New York (N.Y.)—
Biography. 5. Interviews—New York (State)—New York.
6. Oral history. I. Frommer, Myrna. II. Frommer, Harvey.
F 128.5 .I85 2001
974.7'1'042—dc21
2001035938

PRINTED IN THE UNITED STATES OF AMERICA

10 9 8 7 6 5 4 3 2 1

For our family:
Jennifer and Jeff, Freddy and Michele, Ian and Laura

Contents

Part Two

Part Three

Acknowledgments

*F*iguratively as well as literally, Jeff Schock towers over everyone. Setting in motion the chain of events that led to this book's creation, Jeff was the constant throughout, providing key introductions, never-flagging interest and enthusiastic support. Laura Tucker, who sold the idea and was—to use her favorite word—"terrific," will always have a special place in our hearts. Mike Harriot, who so ably picked up the baton at the Vigliano Agency, is a most worthy successor. And David Vigliano is the agent extraordinaire that everyone told us he is. Linking up with The Berkley Publishing Group has been an invigorating experience. And working with our new editor, the ebullient and talented Martha Bushko, has proven to be a true delight—how wonderful it is to work with someone who is so responsive, enthusiastic, and caring.

For this book as with our other oral histories, we have depended so much on the kindness of others—friends and strangers who have become friends: Lou Aronica, who introduced us to the Vigliano Agency; long-lost cousin Kenneth Allisburg and Sid Darion, who lent us many wonderful photographs from their personal archives; Ron and Howard Mandelbaum of Photofest, who once again provided a wealth of visual material; Gilles Larraín, who allowed us the use of his photographic images that reveal, as he put it, "the landscape of the soul"; Laura Lehrman of Fern Berman Public Relations, who made some major introductions; Drazan Lapic, whose technological expertise keeps us connected; Bill Harris, for a thorough and terrific copyediting job; Christopher Mount; Caroline Katz Mount; Marshall Mount; Laura Skoler; Fiorenza Sigler; Sharon Telesca; Mark Ricci; Arthur Richman; Sylvia Portnoy; Brad Turner; Lois Roisman; Michele Cohen; Linda Kleinschmidt; Corina Copp; Brock Brower; and Kathy Hicks, whose introductions, feedback, and interest were of immeasurable help; our children Jennifer, Freddy, and Ian, who once again served as members of a captive audience, sounding boards, and staunch rooters. We thank them all.

This book is a pastiche, an impressionistic account of life in Manhattan over three fateful decades, as remembered and evoked by a select group of people. Some, like the doyenne of haute couture Pauline Trigère or the voice of New York Jimmy Breslin, we went after. Some came to us by accident, in the manner in which way leads on to way.

Their reminiscences and perceptions are woven into a narrative that describes how New York became a world capital in the wake of triumphant victory in the Second World War; how this ever diverse city was affected by new immigrants and in-migrants fleeing fascism from Europe from the South and Puerto Rico seeking opportunity; how the look of the city changed as soaring real-estate values led to tearing down the old and building up the new; how architectural treasures were saved from the finality of the bull-dozer's blow by community activists who were often "just a bunch of moth-ers"; how the Manhattan of the Industrial Age, Tin Pan Alley, ocean liners and B. Altman's disappeared; how New York City almost went bankrupt; how it survived and continues to be a symbol of hope and a destination for the best and brightest of us all.

Each encounter was a story in itself that has become part of our memory. We will always remember Margot Gayle, now in her nineties, becoming young again as she relived the battles fought to create the neighborhood we know today as SoHo; Alvin Reed slipping into the free and easy manner of his young manhood when he charmed a dance partner across a Harlem nightclub's floor; Andy Balducci remembering how he pleaded with his father to move their produce market across the street where they would have doors and a floor and a ceiling over their heads; Dorothy Wheelock, from her house on the village green of our little New England town, recalling the heady days when she was a features editor at *Harper's Bazaar*; Polly Bernstein, emerging from a fog of forgetfulness only months before she died to describe with passion and telling recall the underside of working in New York City; and all the other voices in this book who generously and openly shared memories with us.

How grateful we are to every one of them. Here is their story, at once intimate and general, particular and universal, of what happened in Manhattan during this transformative time.

Myrna Katz Frommer and Harvey Frommer
Lyme, New Hampshire

Cast of Characters

RABBI DAN ALDER is a rabbi of the Brotherhood Synagogue in Gramercy Park.

MICKEY ALPERT is a longtime press agent for theater, movies and nightlife.

KEN ARETSKY, the restaurateur, is an owner of Patroon and Butterfield 81. Previously he owned Oren & Aretsky and Arcadia, and ran the 21 Club.

HERMAN BADILLO is the Chairman of the Board of Trustees of the City University of New York. He was formerly a U.S. Congressman and Borough President of the Bronx.

ANDY BALDUCCI founded and owned Balducci's, the produce and gourmet emporium.

NINA BALDUCCI, the wife of Andy Balducci, was an owner of Balducci's.

ANNE BERG is an expatriate New Yorker living near Boston.

RUSSELL BERG is a college administrator living near Boston.

POLLY BERNSTEIN, who was a saleswoman in a New York department store, died in September 2000.

SAM BERNSTEIN is a retired furrier.

SID BERNSTEIN is a music promoter who arranged the first appearance of the Beatles in the United States.

JANE BEVANS is a Manhattan-based attorney and artist.

JIMMY BRESLIN, the Pulitzer Prize–winning journalist and author of *The Gang That Couldn't Shoot Straight*, is a columnist for *Newsday*.

ANDREW BUSHKO is Dean of University Life at Widener University in Chester, Pennsylvania.

JOHN CAMPI is a vice president of the *Daily News.*

FATHER PETER COLAPIETRO is pastor of Holy Cross Church on 42nd Street.

JOE DARION, the lyricist, librettist, and playwright who won the Tony Award for writing the lyrics to *Man of La Mancha*, died in June 2001.

MERLE DEBUSKEY is a longtime theatrical press agent.

JERRY DELLA FEMINA is the owner of an advertising agency and two restaurants bearing his name, and the author of *From Those Wonderful Folks Who Gave You Pearl Harbor.*

JOEL DORN is a producer of jazz albums who worked for Atlantic Records for many years and won four Grammy Awards.

STANLEY DRUCKER is the first clarinetist of the New York Philharmonic, an institution he joined in 1948.

JOEL EICHEL is an owner of Bigelow's drugstore in Greenwich Village.

MARK FEDERMAN, an attorney, is the owner of Russ and Daughters, the appetizing store on the Lower East Side founded by his grandfather Joel Russ.

BILL GALLO, the award-winning sports cartoonist, has worked for the *Daily News* for more than forty years.

MARGOT GAYLE is a nationally known authority on cast-iron architecture and founder of Friends of Cast Iron Architecture.

MICHAEL GEORGE is an art and architecture historian.

IAN JAY GINSBERG is an owner of Bigelow's drugstore in Greenwich Village.

ALAN GREENBERG is the Chairman of the Board and Executive Committees of Bear Stearns and Company.

DAVE HART is a longtime talent agent in the music business.

MONTE IRVIN, the baseball Hall of Famer, was one of the first black players on the New York Giants and a longtime star of the Negro Leagues.

JULIE ISAACSON was the International President of the Toy Union, AFL-CIO, and is a well-known figure on the sports scene.

JANE JACOBS is an urban critic who authored *The Death and Life of Great American Cities.*

ANDRÉ JAMMET, the owner, along with his wife, Rita, of the restaurant La Caravelle, was born in the Bristol—one of the grand hotels of Paris, which was built by his father.

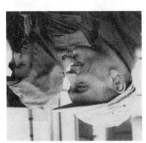

ELAINE KAUFMAN is the founder and owner of Elaine's, the restaurant and literary hangout.

THEODORE KHEEL is a longtime lawyer, arbitrator, negotiator and mediator who served three presidents and five New York City mayors.

HOWARD KISSEL is the senior theater critic for the *Daily News* and the author of *David Merrick: The Abominable Showman*.

LINDA KLEINSCHMIDT is a teacher and graduate student.

LEONARD KOPPETT, the only person named to the writers' wing of the Baseball and Basketball Halls of Fame, was for many years a sports columnist for the *New York Times*.

HILTON KRAMER, the author of *The Twilight of the Intellectuals*, is the cofounder and editor of the *New Criterion* and was for many years the art critic of the *New York Times*.

ELEANOR LAMBERT is the fashion publicist who invented the International Best Dressed List and the Coty Award

JACK LANG is a sports columnist who for many years wrote for the *Long Island Press*.

GILLES LARRAÍN is a landscape, portrait, and album-cover photographer whose subjects include many famous performers. He is the author of *Idols*.

KEN LIBO is an editor and writer, the coauthor of *World of Our Fathers* and *How We Lived*, and the author of *We Lived There Too*.

THEODORE LIEBMAN is a partner in the Liebman Melting Partnership, architects and planners.

SIRIO MACCIONI is the founder and owner of the restaurant Le Cirque 2000.

ELAINE MARKSON is a longtime literary agent in Greenwich Village.

ROBERT MERRILL, the Metropolitan Opera baritone, is also a star of the stage and television, as well as a recording artist.

RABBI JUDAH NADICH, rabbi emeritus of the Park Avenue Synagogue, where he served for thirty years, is past President of the Rabbinical Assembly.

HELEN O'HAGAN was the longtime Vice President of Public Relations and Special Events for Saks Fifth Avenue.

BARBARA PRINGLE was for many years the Executive Director of the Masters in Liberal Studies Program at Dartmouth College.

MAURICE RAPF wrote thirteen screenplays, including Disney's *Song of the South*. He founded the film studies program at Dartmouth College, and taught film history and production there for many years.

WALDO RASMUSSEN was head of the International Program at the Museum of Modern Art.

ALVIN REED, a former police officer, is the owner of the Lenox Lounge in Harlem.

CAROLE RIFKIND, an architectural historian, wrote *A Field Guide to Contemporary American Architecture* and teaches in the historic preservation program at the Architecture School of Columbia University.

TOM SLATTERY is Chairman of the Advisory Board of the United Restaurant and Liquor Dealers of Manhattan.

LACONIA SMEDLEY is a voice and music teacher and Harlem community activist.

JOHN TAURANAC is an urban and architectural historian and map designer whose books include an atlas of Manhattan.

MICHAEL TONG is the owner of the restaurants Shun Lee Palace and Shun Lee West.

PAULINE TRIGÈRE was a famed haute couture designer and a two-time Coty Award winner.

MARCIA TUCKER, founder of the New Museum, is an art critic, lecturer, former museum director, and comic.

JOAN WASHBURN is the owner of the Joan Washburn Galleries on 57th Street.

DOROTHY WHEELOCK was theater and features editor at *Harper's Bazaar* from 1940 to 1957.

MARGARET WHITING is a longtime nightclub singer and recording artist.

SAUL ZABAR is an owner of Zabar's, the Upper West Side food emporium founded by his father, Louis.

SID BERNSTEIN: I'm still a tourist in the city I was born and raised in. I'm a walker of the city streets. If I walk by a place and an aroma greets me, I go in there.

One day I walked past Dave's Luncheonette on the corner of Canal Street and Broadway. It had been there for years. This time I smelled chocolate, and I went in. It was their own bittersweet chocolate that they were making downstairs for their egg creams. I had one, and I was hooked. Dave's had their own recipe for egg creams. To the chocolate, they added very cold seltzer. Then they added the milk that softened the harsh seltzer taste and made it very mellow. They served it in a big, thick glass with a long spoon to mix the molecules. I didn't need a straw; that would take away from the taste.

Back then, garbage trucks used to stop, police and firemen would stop. It wasn't a hangout; it was more like a pit stop. For egg creams, it was number one.

Yonah Schimmel's on Houston and Allen Streets on the Lower East Side is famous for its knishes, but I loved its potato-nick—that's a potato pudding with a real firm crust. It was marvelous. How did I find it? Again, I smelled it. Yonah Schimmel started the business around 1910. He handed it down to his daughter, Mrs. Berger. Then her son took it over. Now a Russian guy owns it, but he keeps up the same tradition, uses the same recipes. Every ten to twenty years they repaint the store so it never looks like anything but an old store. But its knishes are world famous, more so than Mrs. Stahl's in Brighton Beach in Brooklyn.

One day I was walking down Houston Street near Yonah Schimmel's, and I smelled pickles in a doorway. I went in. Houston Street is a filthy street, but this store was white, immaculate, the counter was gleaming.

It was Russ and Daughters. When I first became a customer, one of Russ's daughters was still living. Her son Mark now runs it. They had chopped herring, which I love. And because the store was so neat, I felt I could trust the chopped herring. Then I saw the schmaltz herring. Every time thereafter when I went to Russ and Daughters, I'd have them slice one, and before I got to the street, I had at least one slice with a toothpick. By the time I got on the bus or back to my car to bring the food back to my family, I'd have knocked off half of it.

I go to Zabar's for the cheeses, I go there for the nova. I love it paper thin. Sam Cohen was a favorite behind the counter. I'd say, "Hello, Sam, *vus machts der* [how are you]?" and move on to the next clerk, who would slice it paper thin. Sam didn't have patience for me. I bothered him. He was more interested in the ladies.

Every few years Zabar's expanded—upstairs to the mezzanine, downstairs to the basement. Everyone who moves away comes there with the ice chest to stock up before they go home. The crowd is enthusiastic. I used to see Tony Randall there. He'd walk around, pick out his gefilte fish, wait for his sturgeon and nova, get a jar of sour tomatoes. I considered him a good shopper. What makes a good shopper? Someone who knows what he wants. Some of the tourists are like Alice in Wonderland: They just walk around staring, amazed.

Paolucci's, on Mulberry between Grand and Hester Streets—still my favorite Italian restaurant—is also run by the third generation. I like these generations. How did I discover it? Same way. Walked by and smelled a lot of garlic coming from up a stoop. It's a rustic, beat-up place. But the food . . . They made the best chicken cacciatore in New York City—wine and mushrooms, little bits of ham, green pepper. I used to love the house salad: anchovies, Genoa salami, roasted peppers, pimientos, lots of fresh tomatoes chopped up, lettuce of course. They've named the salad after me.

Some people say there was no food in New York before Henri Soulé. But the knockwurst was here, the herrings were here, the knishes were here. The cuisine Soulé brought to New York was for the Lutèce crowd, the moneyed crowd. But people without money could eat well too. At McGinnis on 48th and Broadway, you could get a roast beef sandwich that doesn't exist today on rye bread with seeds. Ratner's was great for its stuffed onion rolls. Better than the chopped vegetarian liver and the chopped eggs and onions, the vegetable soup, the lima bean soup, and the potato soup were the onion rolls. Their waiters were unique. Their Yiddish accents, their seriousness, their sense of humor and their style: "Joe, hurry up, bring it over." It was New York.

As a kid, I'd go to the Automat, dropping nickels into the machine. The vegetables were five cents when I first went there, then it became ten, then twenty-five. The bacon, lettuce and tomato sandwich on a nice *goyisha* white bread—I loved it. As I got older, the baked beans became a huge favorite of mine. And the mashed potatoes. You couldn't find them like that anywhere else. And the spaghetti—it wasn't Italian; it was a different quality. For my three vegetables, I'd have spaghetti, mashed potatoes and baked beans and let the juices mix with each other.

I have this dream of opening up my own restaurant, Sid's Place. I'd serve Dave's original egg cream—I have the recipe—McGinniss's roast beef, which was on a spit, the mashed potatoes and baked beans from the Automat, and my favorite Italian dishes. It would be a funky place where people could hang out and listen to music. We'd play Judy Garland and Beatles records, and Jacques Brel, whom I love, Sinatra, and Nat King Cole, and Tony Bennett. . . .

Part One

Chapter One

On the Sidewalks of New York

CURB YOUR DOG
VIOLATION
$25.
FINE

MICKEY ALPERT: Whenever I met kids who grew up in Manhattan, it was as if I came from Toledo, Ohio, or someplace in Iowa instead of the Borough Park section of Brooklyn. They seemed so much more sophisticated and more worldly than me. Their exposure was so much greater. They went to museums on a regular basis; I would only go to museums on school trips. They went skating in Central Park, to the movies "downtown." Even though geographically we were maybe ten miles apart, we were from different worlds.

JOHN TAURANAC: When I was a kid, my father was always being asked by proper suburbanites how he could think of raising my sister and me in New York City. My mother died when I was nine, and my father was a single parent before the phrase was even coined. He worked very hard to keep everything together. "Raising them in the city is paradise," he would tell his questioners. "It's home. It's where people should be."

"Raising [kids] in the city is paradise."

JANE BEVANS: I was born in 1940, the youngest of three kids. I lived with my mother and father, my sister and brother, my mother's father and my father's mother, and a maid to take care of all these people in a four-bedroom apartment at 310 West 79th Street. We had a postman who delivered the mail three times a day, walking up the street with a big letter case on his back. We had a German couple, Mr. and Mrs. Hoffman, living underneath us in apartment 5E. They were very rigid, and they scared me. Of course we were a bunch of kids jumping on their heads, which is why they were always screaming at us. Aside from them though, I wasn't aware of an influx of immigrants, even though many of my friends' parents and grandparents must have come from Europe.

I thought all the kids in the neighborhood were Jewish. Although there was Patsy, who was a year ahead of me. She was black. And there was Parvis Nafasion, who came from Persia. I had to teach him English. He lived on the eleventh floor of our building and his apartment smelled so bizarre. We used to race home from school together. If he got there first, he'd get in the elevator, push the eleventh floor, and then all the floors on the way down. I had to wait a long time.

We were the most integrated Jewish people ever to exist on the West Side. We had a Christmas tree. The first time I was in Temple was when Carol Dvorkin was bat mitzvahed in '52. For Passover we had a seder. We ate matzoh and matzoh ball soup and gefilte fish. But we also ate bread.

My father's mother's family came here somewhere between 1845 and 1860. My mother's father was Romanian. He had an accent and sat at the head of the table. I sat next to him. If I put my elbows on the table, he'd knock them off with his knife. My grandmother was the world's worst Jewish cook. She could cook a liver within an inch of its life; the tongue of your shoe didn't begin to describe it. Her apple pie was black on the bottom.

Every Sunday morning Grandma would send me to Zabar's, which was a tiny grocery store back then, to buy "stomach salmon" (we weren't allowed to say "belly lox"—that was too vulgar). On one side was the great smoked fish counter and on the other side was a counter where Mr. Zabar would put your purchase in a paper bag and total up the prices on it with a pencil. "Vadaya vant, honey?" he'd say to me. "Oh, you're Mrs. Apt's granddaughter. I recognize your voice; I recognize the 'stomach salmon.' Anything-gelse?"

Growing up on the Upper West Side

I remember when Grandma took my sister and me to see President Roosevelt. We were both dressed in the very same watch-plaid coats with hats to match, and standing on a stoop we waved our little American flags when we saw him ride by in an open car that went up Riverside Drive and onto the highway. It was very exciting. But I have no memories of when President Roosevelt died. It wasn't a big event in our house because my father was a Republican.

He was a CPA and when I asked him what that meant, he said he was a bookkeeper. For years, I had an image that he dusted books, and I didn't understand why he would go to the office every day and dust books. My mother also worked. She was in the fashion industry, and since she was the dominant one in the family, we lived in a house that was filled with fashion. Everything had to be beautiful. She was beautiful, five feet seven with brown wavy hair and green eyes like saucers. She always wore gorgeous clothes, the kind you would expect Katherine Hepburn to wear in the movies. I can picture her walking down the very long hall in our apartment in one of her creations, with stockings that had seams running up the back, four-inch high-heeled shoes, and a green straw pinwheel hat with cherries around it that practically filled the hall-way. People were always staring at her. They'd stop and ask me, "Is your mother Bette Davis?"

She loved to dress my sister and me. We were the first Barbie dolls. For my sixth-grade graduation, she designed my outfit and had it made at her factory. It was a red gingham blouse with elastic through the top so it went off the shoulders, and a three-tier red gingham skirt. For my sister's graduation, she made me a dress of pink polished cotton with colored polka dots.

When we were little, she bought our clothes at Best & Company on Fifth and 56th. I remember the feel of the place more than the way it looked. It was quiet; I had the feeling it was carpeted. Shopping at Best & Company was a solemn occasion for me, the closest thing I could imagine to going to a cathedral.

The first "Barbie dolls"

Our building was filled with children, and we played out on the street. I learned to ride a bike on the street; I scraped my knees roller skating on the street. We played Chinese American, which is a form of handball, against the wall of the building on the corner. We played hopscotch, ringalevio, capture the flag. We were on the street all day.

Or we were in Riverside Park. From 79th Street, the park goes south to 72nd Street and north beyond Grant's Tomb at 122nd Street. But my world stopped at 84th Street. There's a roadway in the park that goes down a big hill and up a big hill where we went sleighing, or bike riding, seeing how far you could get up the hill before you had to start moving your legs again.

The 79th Street entrance to the Henry Hudson Parkway from Riverside Park was my Cinderella castle. There were two staircases with wide stairs that led down to the harbor. At the bottom was this big rotunda that the cars went around, and out of the center was a fountain with water coming out. Under the roadbed were the railroad tracks where the Pennsylvania Railroad traveled. You could look in these grated windows to where the trains ran underneath. And then you came out in the park and there was the Hudson River, which was clean and pristine. On the other side there was nothing but the Spry sign. During that funny eleven, twelve, thirteen-year-old time when I wanted to be alone, Riverside Park was my garden. I would lie on the grass by myself for hours.

"Riverside Park was my garden."

We went to P.S. 9, a Dutch-looking building with gables on 82nd and West End Avenue. There were three rooms on each side of the hallway, and on the day that we had assembly the walls of the rooms slid back all the way to the end of the whole floor. So you stayed in your seats in your room and you were

The old people sat on the benches in the median along Broadway.

in the auditorium. I can still hear the sound of the walls as they moved. I remember my father coming to assembly when I was playing the part of an Indian in a play about Columbus coming to America. My father never came to anything so I was so excited he was there. I kept looking at him. He waved to me, and I waved to him, and I forgot my one line.

From the time I was seven, my sister Lee and I walked to school alone. It was a three-block walk along West End Avenue from 79th to 82nd Street. And after school we walked over one block to Broadway, our Main Street, to Benny's Candy Store, which was between 82nd and 81st on the west side of the street. Then we continued on Broadway to 79th, where we turned down the block and came home.

Benny's was a true candy store. It was very, very tiny with comic books on the right, candy on the left, and a soda counter in the back. We went there every day after school to get candy. Then we would stop to say hello to Grandma and Aunt Sadie, who sat on the benches in the median along Broadway at 79th Street. All the old Jewish people would sit there. Every day Aunt Sadie would say, "Ooh—you scared me!" and "Ah, you've grown so, I didn't recognize you." I used to wonder how much you could change or grow in a day.

Schraft's restaurant was on Broadway, a little farther uptown. I loved to go there; it was a very big deal. Ellen Cohen, a girl in my class at P.S. 9, used to go to Schraft's for lunch every day. Her parents were divorced, and, I gather, her mother didn't have time to make her lunch. One day she asked me to go with her.

When the waitress asked me what I wanted, I said, "It's all right. I have my lunch." She was very sweet. She obviously knew Ellen, and she brought me a milk to have with my lunch even though I had no money.

Afterward we raced back to school but were late. Our teacher, Mrs. Bow, asked Ellen why she was late. Ellen said, "The waitress was slow," and that was fine. The teacher asked me why I was late. I said, "Well, I went to lunch with Ellen."

"What did you eat?"

"I had my sandwich with me."

She lambasted me. "That woman has to earn a living. How can you bring a sandwich to a restaurant?"

She was so mean. I was humiliated in front of the class. I had no idea I had done something wrong.

But I got even with her. In those days, the teacher had a locker in the back of the classroom where she kept her coat and pocketbook and a little mirror. At the end of the day when she dismissed us, she'd open up her locker and put on her coat. I told everyone that when Mrs. Bow put her hat on I saw her wig slide off.

On Saturdays we went to the movies at either the RKO 81st Street or the Loews 83rd Street on Broadway. It cost twenty-five cents. We went in at 12:30 and were out at 5:30. The kids sat in the balcony with their matron, a woman in a white uniform who carried a flashlight. I can almost remember the music from the newsreels and the crisscross of the floodlights—the beauty pageant went this way, and the war went that way. Then came the cartoons and then the serials. And finally the double feature.

The Museum of Natural History was our museum. Every time we had to be occupied for the day, we were sent there. Grandma would say, "I'm not going to be home today. Take the girls to the museum."

"Do we have to go?" my sister and I would cry.

"Yes."

I thought it was the most boring place in the world with those stuffed animals in glass cases, the moles under the ground, the big bear over the ground, all the Indian exhibits. It was grimy and dark like so many of the buildings were in those days because they were heated by coal. One of the great sounds of my childhood was the coal going down the chute. But it made the city filthy. We were dirty. When we came in and were told, "Wash your hands for dinner," there was a good reason. You could see the coal dust.

Our world was circumscribed; there were places we were allowed to go and places we were not allowed to go. Broadway was the frontier. We never walked on Columbus Avenue; it was dangerous. My grandmother told me that. We had the sense the city was changing, heard that "those people" were coming in.

I led a very proscribed small-town life until I went to Joan of Arc Junior High School on 93rd Street. It drew from P.S. 9, which was west of Broadway, but also from P.S. 87, which was east of Broadway and picked up more of the Puerto Rican kids. Joan of Arc was a very integrated junior high school and a very rough place, like something out of *West Side Story*. There were kids who didn't speak English. The boys seemed much older and much more sexual than us. They dressed in black pants and white shirts and carried knives in their socks. There was a lot of pushing. You stayed out of the way. You went to and from school with your friends, traveled in packs.

But I was so happy there. I was twelve and on my own. My class was the first to graduate from P.S. 9 after the sixth grade, while my sister's class was the last to graduate after the eighth grade. Since we were a year apart, she stayed at P.S. 9 for the seventh and eighth grades, while I went on to Joan of Arc. So I was finally able to get away from my sister. I also had a bigger allowance than she did because I had to buy my lunch and take the bus to school. I was very little, but those were the two biggest years of my life.

Joan of Arc Junior High School, West 93rd Street

Nevertheless, I knew I didn't want to go on to Julia Richman High School. Word was out: you didn't want to go there. I decided to apply to the High School of Music and Art. I had done my first oil painting at the Albert Pels Art School on 71st Street and Broadway, where we used to go for art lessons on Friday evenings. When I was twelve and Lee thirteen, we transferred to the Art Career School in the Flatiron Building on 23rd Street. The best part was going up to the very top of the building, where you could go outside and touch both walls at once. I learned to draw a loafer there, which was kind of boring, but I also put my portfolio together for Music and Art High School.

They used to call Music and Art the Castle on the Hill because it looked like a Gothic castle up on 135th Street and St. Nicholas Terrace right next to City College. In addition to all the academics, students at Music and Art took three periods of art or music a day. There was a semiannual performance and a semiannual art show. There were orchestras, chamber music groups. You went to the fifth floor and it was as if you plowed into all these instruments from the harp to the cello, from the bassoon to the kettle drum. You walked past the art rooms and the smell of oil paint, pastels, clay would fill the hall.

Everyone at Music and Art was talented. It was a sexy group of kids, an artsy group. Kids came from all over the city, learned to go all over. The subway was the lifeline. I submitted my portfolio to Music and Art, and I got in. I was on my way.

HERMAN BADILLO: I came to New York as a young boy in 1941 on a boat called the *Marine Tiger*. It was very early on in the Puerto Rican migration but one of the last by boat. When I passed the Statue of Liberty, I cried like everybody else.

The town I came from in Puerto Rico had been decimated in a tuberculosis epidemic. My father died when I was a year old, my mother when I was five years old. What I remember most of all from that time is walking to the cemetery and going to funerals. When I arrived in New York, my aunt who brought me here was unable to take care of me because she didn't have a job. So she sent me to an uncle in Chicago. He couldn't take care of me either so he sent me to an uncle in California. I stayed there for about a year and a half. By then, my aunt had gotten a job and an apartment, and so I came to live with her on 103rd Street in East Harlem. I started school not knowing how to speak English, and my teacher didn't speak Spanish.

Painting at High School of Music and Art, c. 1957

Then we moved to the West Side. My aunt was a very gregarious woman. She'd walk down the streets, find some new immigrant and rent him a room in her large apartment. At any given time, we had six or seven tenants living in different rooms. I had learned to speak English fairly well by this time so I would give them orientation, look up in the Spanish newspapers where there were jobs. They would go out, get jobs, move into their own apartments, and my aunt would rent the room to somebody else. During the course of a year, dozens of people moved in and out. It got so that I felt I was personally witnessing the massive Puerto Rican immigration of the postwar years passing through my apartment.

It was a dangerous existence living on the West Side and going to junior high school on 127th Street and Broadway. The Puerto Rican kids had problems with the black kids. There were a lot of fights. Our school was one of the junior highs in West Harlem that fed into Haaren High School, a mixed school that drew from many neighborhoods. All the black and Puerto Rican boys went into the airplane mechanics program, where they learned how to make model airplanes, take apart internal combustion engines, do blueprints and mechanical drawings.

I was able to do the work, but I found it boring. Then I discovered the school newspaper and began doing interviews with people like Peggy Lee, who was just beginning her career. Before long, my interviews were front-page stories. Eventually one of the kids on the newspaper said to me, "Are you going to this school?"

I said, "Of course."

He said, "We don't see you in any of our classes."

"I'm in airplane mechanics."

"What are you doing that for?"

"I'm Puerto Rican."

"You don't understand," he told me, "you're taking a vocational course. You're obviously very bright, and you can write. You should be taking the academic courses so you can go to college."

I said, "I don't have any money for college."

"That's okay. You can go to City College, which is free."

I began attending the academic courses in Haaren High School, where the students were predominantly Jewish and Italian. I really shone. And everyone treated me very well.

That student changed my life. When I graduated from high school, my aunt wondered what I was going to do. I said, "Oh, I didn't tell you, but I've been admitted to City College."

ALVIN REED: We came from Eastover, a little town in South Carolina. My father wasn't an educated man, only went to third grade. Like everybody else, he farmed, didn't make any money. He heard from a friend there were jobs on the railroad in Richmond, Virginia. He went up, and my mother, sister and older brothers followed. Sometime after I and my younger brother were born, they heard there were better jobs up in New York. So my father came here, and two years later we all followed. That was 1945, when I was seven years old.

Once my father got to Harlem, a lot of his drive and ambition fell off. Back home, he didn't do anything but work and go home. The bright lights, the party life, the street life—that didn't exist down South. He got up here, he was chasing women, gambling, going to the pool halls.

Since he was a longshoreman and worked on the railroad, any time we applied for assistance they said, "No way, not with the money he makes." But he was a man who didn't bring his money home. So our mother, who had a college education, had to work as a maid. We were mostly on our own. We were poor, we didn't have any money. So we climbed up fire escapes, stole the empty bottles and cashed them in. We sold rags to the ragman, sold newspapers, shined shoes.

"Harlem was such a nice community when I was growing up."

Still, Harlem was such a nice community when I was growing up. The supers used to hose down the sidewalk every morning. They had a block guy, Mr. Bridges, who'd turn the fire hydrant on; everybody would sweep the debris into the street, and Sanitation would pick it up at the end. We had PAL teams. Mrs. Bouton, a lady on our block, organized games, had a basketball hoop put up. In the summer, she had the streets closed off so we could play. At Easter, we all got new outfits. It was beautiful, everybody coming out, sharp, walking to church. On Mother's Day, you'd wear a carnation in your lapel. A white one meant your mother's deceased, a pink one meant she's not feeling too good, a red one meant she's alive and healthy.

My mother went to Walker Memorial, the Baptist church on 116th Street. My brothers and I left the house like we were going to church, but most times we got lost on the way. The ladies of the church would come looking for us. Then we joined the Boy Scouts in the church and got a little more active.

We went to the Polo Grounds often, but we never paid. I mean, we were good. We'd climb the rocks outside and just wait. On the other side was a ramp the people walked across after they paid their admission. We'd wait till the coast was clear, hop over onto the ramp, and just start walking like everybody else. We'd go to the Colonial Pool—sometimes we paid, most times we didn't. We weren't bad kids, we didn't fight nobody. We were just trying to survive.

We knew all the cops. Johnny Jenkins was a famous black cop; everybody knew him, tough, no nonsense. He wasn't big, barely five feet eight, but he was big reputation-wise. Another tough, tough guy was Bumpy Johnson. We used to see him on 133rd Street every day, checking numbers and running his exterminating company, Palmetto Chemical. Bumpy was not a handsome guy. He was short with a short neck, bumps all over his face, a bald head. He was quiet, didn't talk a lot. But he was the sharpest dresser and the friendliest, most generous man. When he walked around, he'd smile at people. He gave out a lot of money.

The people who did the movie *Hoodlum*, which is about Bumpy, wanted me to tell them his history. They didn't keep histories of black hoodlums, I told them, especially one as tough as Bumpy. But what I do know is that a French-speaking lady named Queenie had started the numbers game right here in Harlem in the twenties. Everybody played it. The Mafia downtown, they wanted a piece of anything, but when they heard about it, they said, "Aw, penny game, penny-ante game." They didn't want any part of it. Until it got out she was making millions of dollars off this popular penny. Now they wanted to come up and get a piece. That's when Bumpy Johnson came in. He protected Queenie from the Mafia.

They didn't know what to do with this guy. When they came uptown and tried to bully people, they couldn't do it, not with Bumpy around. They'd come into a club, and everybody would get up to let them sit at the bar. Bumpy would come along and say, "Uh-uh. Wait a minute. You, get the hell out of that seat and let the lady sit there."

To us in Harlem, he was Robin Hood. For Christmas, at home I'd get either a pair of skates or a cap gun, and that was it. I couldn't wait to run over to Bumpy's fish and chips restaurant on our block where he kept all this stuff for the kids of the neighborhood: toys and pants and shirts and jackets. We would go in and take. When I graduated from elementary school and couldn't afford a jacket, I got one from Bumpy.

But there was a time when I was about nine years old when I actually ran from him. What happened was some kids on the other side of the street threw a stick with dog doo on it. I picked it up, threw it back diagonally, and Bumpy got it on the leg of his blue striped suit. He turned around, he looked, and I took off.

You know kids always have a little escape route. I lived at 121 West 133rd Street. But there was a way you could go into 123, go out the back through a little door, come around and get into my building. When we had little fights with the gang, I'd never run into my building. They knew where I lived. I'd run into that other building to get back home.

That's what I did now. I don't know how long I stayed in the house. When I came out, I went through the backyard onto the next block, afraid that Bumpy might see me. I did that for some time but never mentioned it to my father. I was afraid he would be hurt.

You see, I had heard that on top of his being nice, he was a guy you can't mess with, that you better stay out of his way. Later on when I talked about it, people said, "Oh, he wouldn't have hurt you. You were a child." That tough reputation—it wasn't for the children and the locals. But I didn't know.

Bumpy died three months after Martin Luther King's assassination eating a steak in Well's Restaurant on Seventh Avenue and 133rd Street. The headline in the *Amsterdam News* said BUMPY'S DEATH MARKS END OF AN ERA. The police lined Seventh Avenue because they heard the Mafia was going to come in there to take his body out and tear it to shreds. The Mafia probably didn't want him to die like that. It was so amazing—he, of all people, died of a heart attack.

Even though he was a gangster, Bumpy was a folk hero. But we also had a lot of good role models in those years. There were doctors, lawyers, school-teachers who lived in Harlem. When Jackie Robinson came up in 1947, were we happy. It was like when Joe Louis won. Every time we had a black figure do something, Harlem would jump.

And we needed those role models because it was rough. We got slapped around a lot; we got beaten. Once when I was around thirteen, fourteen, we were in a candy store, playing the jukebox. It was crowded, and I guess the owner felt we weren't spending money. He called the police.

A black cop came in and said, "Everybody out." I was all the way in the back drinking a soda. The people in the front were moving real slow, and I couldn't move any faster than they allowed me. "Move!" he said to me.

"I can't," I told him.

Well he kicked me square up my behind. There was blood. Then he shoved around some more guys. We talked about it outside and said let's go and make a complaint. So we go to the precinct; I had witnesses and everything. I told the lieutenant what happened. He said, "Okay," and he called the detectives. They came over, they took us in a room. They smacked us around. And then they brought us out back to the desk. The lieutenant asked, "Do you want to make a complaint?"

We said, "No." We didn't tell our parents; they would think we did something wrong. We didn't do anything about it. That kind of stuff was typical.

At the time of the Harlem riots, 1961, '62, I was a little rambunctious. I wanted to do some damage. I threw some bottles. There were some stores broken in. Yeah, I went in and took some things. I actually stood on the barricades talking to a black cop. "Man, you're on the wrong side of the fence," I said to him.

A lot of people don't understand black rage, all these little incidents that were done to you all these years, that were done to your mother, that were done to your father. Then when you get about eighteen, nineteen, twenty and things are not opening up, you remember them.

My mother thought a lot of white people, and she brought that into our lives. "You say hi to them and speak to them, be polite to them," she'd tell us. In my growing-up time, there were about three white ladies on our block, mixed marriages. We'd see white people at Count Basie's, Small's Paradise, and the other clubs. There were white merchants, and I had mostly white teachers. Still my view of white people was that they were rolling with money.

Then when I went to high school at Charles Evans Hughes, it was the first time I was out of Harlem, and the first time I was in the minority. The population was sixty-five percent white and thirty-five percent black. What was it like? Shock. I went into a shell, went to the back of the class. I didn't know how to study. "How do these kids do it?" I asked myself. I thought if you read something once, you're supposed to know it. No one ever told me you got to read things over and over.

Social-athletic club in Harlem

The white kids at Charles Evan Hughes dressed nice. To keep up with them, we wore ties, shirts, sports jackets, creases in our pants, shoes shined. I had three shirts, and I had to iron every night. My mother gave me thirty-two cents lunch money every day, but I ate milk and cake so I could put the money away to buy some shirts.

I was on the swim team and track team, but baseball was a sport the black kids weren't allowed to get into at Charles Evans Hughes. It was like "We're going to keep that one." I played with some of the kids in Central Park, and the kids said to the coach, "This guy is good. We need him; he's better than most of the guys on the team." I still couldn't even get a tryout.

Still, I have to say it was a nice mix at that school; there were no big problems. And what it did was inspire the black kids to do much better. We saw that the white kids were a little more educated than we were. They presented a challenge that made us very ambitious.

BARBARA PRINGLE: There was no way a black child growing up in New York City during that time could not be aware of race. I knew my mother, who worked as a seamstress in the garment district, considered herself lucky. The only black women they hired were West Indians. After my parents divorced, my father married a woman who had a math degree from Hunter College but was a civil service worker because she couldn't get a decent job in the private sector. And we knew black lawyers who had to work in the post office.

Yet, my family didn't have the rage of slavery. Both my parents came from Jamaica, and the people we associated with were middle-class families, professionals or businesspeople. It wasn't unusual for me to know blacks could be successful.

Throughout my childhood, every year I went to the circus at the old Madison Square Garden and to Radio City Music Hall for Christmas and Easter. Every Sunday my father took me to one of the museums. We went by bus, just the two of us. Sometimes we had something to eat at the Automat, where you could have a good meal and there was no racial thing. My father sent me for tennis lessons at the only private place blacks could play tennis in New York—a closed-in park that took up a square block on 148th Street and Convent Avenue near City College. I saw Althea Gibson play there.

Once a year my father, my aunts and cousin—six or seven of us—would get all dressed up and take a big Checker taxi to a restaurant called Frank's on 125th Street. It was Greek-owned and didn't have a single black waiter. That was where I learned to eat lobster. Then we'd go downtown to see a Broadway musical, sitting right up in front. And after that we went to a club. I saw all the black entertainers there: Cab Calloway, Count Basie, Lionel Hampton and, my favorite, Nat King Cole.

My father was one of the first managers of records for Hanover Trust on Canal Street. He was also a salesman at Klein's. Every day of his working life, he wore a suit, white shirt, and tie. He did not have a college degree, but he raised my sisters and me with the idea that education was the key to moving up in the world and worked two, sometimes three jobs to send us to private schools.

The first school he sent me to was the Modern School at 154th Street, which was a feeder for white private schools. Ethel Waters's daughter, W.E.B. Du Bois's granddaughter, a whole number of children who came from black professional families went there.

When I was thirteen years old, my father sent me to the Little Red School House and Elisabeth Irwin High School in Greenwich Village, where I stayed until the eleventh grade. It had only two black students, but I never felt strange. I made great friends. It was a very progressive environment; the kids were mostly from leftist families, and they talked a lot about the relationship between blacks and whites.

"There was no way a black child growing up in New York City during that time could not be aware of race."

At that time I was living on 141st Street with my father and stepmother. It was a schlep for me to go down on the subway, but it was great to go to school in Greenwich Village. There was such a sense of freedom. A lot of the students lived there, but many lived in the area from West 72nd to West 96th Street. This section was different from the West Side where I lived; it was white and wealthy. Uptown was comfortable and middle class, but it didn't compare to the buildings like the Beresford or the Dakota on Central Park West.

They all had separate elevators for passengers and service. The domestics, who were usually black, rode in the service elevator. When I was coming over, my friends had to tell their parents to let the elevator operators know I was to ride in the passenger elevator. Once I went to someone's house and they had a new elevator man. He said, "I think you have to go to that one."

I said, "Not me, dear."

I had plenty of awareness of black and white issues but very little personal experience. I had as many white as black friends. But one blatant racist inci-dent I will never forget occurred at the Barbizon Hotel. A bunch of us from Little Red planned to go swimming in their indoor pool. When we went up to pay, I was told, "You can't swim here." My friends and I were very upset, but we never spoke about it. I never even told my father.

Two of my friends at Little Red used to go to Florida for the winter break and invited me to come along. "You must be kidding," I told them. I wouldn't go farther than Philadelphia. I was terrified of the South. I knew about the white and black restrooms and drinking fountains. I was sure if I went there, I would be lynched.

On the other hand, when I was a freshman in college, I got a job around Christmastime at Lerner's on 125th Street and found it was the biggest racist store. They wouldn't let me touch the money. It infuriated me no end, and I got sick from being positioned right in the doorway in the wintertime.

JOHN TAURANAC: Both my parents were British and had originally come here as illegal immigrants through Canada. When I was born in 1939, they were living in Yorkville—a working-class neighborhood on the East Side that spread from 73rd up to the 90s. My mother was half Jewish, and when she saw the brown shirts goose-stepping up and down 86th Street, the heart of the neighborhood, she said, "We're getting out of here." So we moved to Montreal.

As soon as the war in Europe ended, we returned to a Yorkville that had greatly changed. All things Teutonic had been Swissified. Ultimately the German presence reappeared but it never became as strong as it had been. Other groups—Hungarians, Irish—had moved in.

My parents found an apartment on 79th Street and East End Avenue in the City and Suburban Houses, one of a group of model tenement houses that was put up at the turn of the last century. The rooms were tiny; there was a bathtub in the kitchen.

A company called Glauber was directly across the street from us. They were a pipe distributor for developers and made a tremendous clatter when the trucks were being loaded. But they also had the ideal wall with ridges for playing stoopball. You could hit the ball on the edge and have

All dressed up for a photo in Central Park, c. 1947

it go sailing in the air. Because 79th Street is one of the main crosstown streets, it is one hundred feet wide and great for street games like stoopball.

It was a generally idyllic life except for the fear we had of the 81st Street Boys. When we heard they were coming, we ran home with our tails between our legs. They were just kids like everyone else, probably no worse than the 80th Street Boys or the 82nd Street Boys, but we had this awe about them and were convinced we would be on the losing side of any encounter.

In 1948, Babe Ruth died at Sloan-Kettering, which was, in essence, right down the block. I felt the propinquity of his death was so great. That's when I became a Yankee fan, even though I didn't know much about baseball. But I came to my senses quickly and became a Dodger fan because of Jackie Robinson, who had played for the Montreal Royals in 1946 when we had lived in that city.

All the other kids on the block remained Yankee fans. They were also Irish. Come St. Patrick's Day, everybody wore green. One St. Patrick's Day I determined, as a good English Episcopalian, that I would wear a bright orange tie. My father dissuaded me, "No, that would not be a wise thing to do."

One day, a dispatcher at the 79th Street crosstown bus terminal on the corner decided we ought to have a baseball team. I don't know how it happened, but he managed to get us baseball caps with "AA" on them for "All American." Here we were, a bunch of immigrant kids, suddenly "All American." He'd get us on the bus for nothing—all the drivers would wink—and we would go over to Central Park and play baseball games that he arranged against other teams. Central Park was our backyard, a crosstown bus ride away.

"Central Park was our backyard, a crosstown bus ride away."

On Sundays after church, we would stroll with our father along the most exclusive streets, because what was the point otherwise? Frequently we'd go into Central Park around 67th Street, visit the statue of Balto, the dog who got the serum through to Nome, and continue the promenade to our typical Sunday afternoon destination: the Metropolitan Museum of Art.

Sometimes for Sunday outings we took the Third Avenue el all the way down to South Ferry, where we got on the Staten Island Ferry to Staten Island. Then we would turn around and come back. One of the virtues of riding on the elevated train was that it encouraged voyeurism; you were twenty feet away from people's windows. As a kid you always sat on your knees looking out the window. But when you were standing at the station and the train came in, the platform would shift. I was never confident the thing wouldn't collapse.

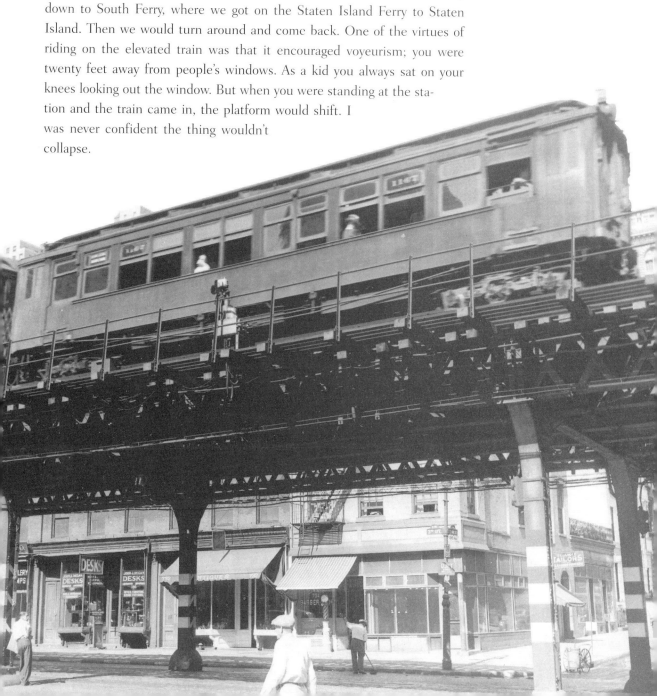

Third Avenue was still "Toid Avenue," then, a shadowy street under the el. In the movie *Lost Weekend,* Ray Milland searches for a pawnshop and a bar under the Third Avenue el. It was an understandable place for someone who was dispossessed and alienated to hide out. I remember visiting people who lived in the tenement apartments that lined Third Avenue. When the el went by, you could hear the china shaking in the cupboard. All conversation had to stop.

I had started school at P.S. 158 on York Avenue between 77th and 78th. Carved into the side of the building is "Avenue A," which is what the street was before they named it for Sergeant York following World War 1. But after my mother died, my father decided to send us to private schools because he felt our home life was tenuous at best. I went to Grace Church School on 10th Street and Fourth Avenue and my sister went to the Academy of Mt. St. Ursula in the Bronx, where she was probably the only Protestant in the school; my mother had attended an Ursuline school in Belgium when she was a girl and had liked the Ursuline nuns.

I began going to Grace Church School in the fifth grade, when they started teaching French. My very first day the teacher asked the class what "garçon" meant. I threw up my hand, proudly. " 'Garçon' means waiter," I said. "No," she said, "it means boy."

The summer of 1951 I went up to Grace Church Camp in Bear Mountain State Park for the month of July. August second was my birthday. That night I got sick. My father thought I had eaten too much ice cream and cake, but the next morning he called the doctor. It was polio. I was shipped to the Willard Parker Hospital on 26th Street, where all contagious cases were taken. It was a terrifying place. Across the hallway were kids in iron lungs. Fortunately, I had a very mild case. After a week or ten days, I was able to go home.

By the time school started in September, I was well enough to go back to school. We were assigned a paper on how we spent our summer vacation. I called mine "Look, I Can Run." It described what happened about a week after I was sent home: My sister and I were crossing York Avenue, and I was walking very slowly across the street. Suddenly the light changed. I had to either run or get run over. I ran. I reached the curb safely, turned to my sister, and cried, "Look, I can run!"

The paper came back with a bad grade. "I told you to write on something that had happened to you this summer," the teacher said.

In 1952 and '53, I was made "Optimus" at Grace Church. That meant you're in the honor room and your name is carved into the wall. I became an acolyte. And then when I was about fifteen, I learned that the minister did not know my name. Immediately, I became an apostate and turned my back on the whole thing. I felt they didn't think I was important enough.

My next school was Trinity on 91st between Columbus and Amsterdam. As a white middle-class kid, I had already learned to be street smart. If you ventured to 92nd Street, you were on enemy territory, somebody else's turf. I always wondered if the fear we had of the 81st Street Boys wasn't the same as the fear we had of the kids on 92nd Street.

Upscale hardly begins to describe Trinity. I remember going to a friend's apartment on Madison Avenue and 82nd after school. I assumed the nicely dressed man who answered the door was his father. It was the butler. And there I was, living on the top floor of a model tenement walkup.

I lost my scholarship to Trinity when I failed Latin and geometry, and my father then sent me to McBurney, a school on 63rd Street that was down the block from where Lincoln Center is today. J. D. Salinger went to McBurney. When Holden Caulfield in *The Catcher in the Rye* leaves the foils on the subway, he was on his way to a fencing match at McBurney. So McBurney lives on in fiction still. For me, it was much more haimish than Trinity, which was founded in 1709 and had this mantle of venerability.

While I was at McBurney, they were already starting to empty out the apartment houses that became the site for Lincoln Center. One day a place that had great hero sandwiches was gone. It was the death knell of the neighborhood.

FATHER PETER COLAPIETRO: Even though Manhattan was only a fifteen-cent train ride away from where I lived in the Bronx, it was a whole new world. I felt I had to dress up to go down there. I couldn't wear jeans and a polo shirt.

I was an eleven- or twelve-year-old, I knew what *Playboy* magazine was, but when I went into some of these stores on 42nd Street—wow! Ten or twelve of us used to come down to Herman's Flea Circus. It had an arcade with pinball machines, magic shows, and the famous Flea Circus. We would go to Rockefeller Center and see as many television shows as we could get into,

"When I went into some of those stores on 42nd Street—wow!"

getting there early to be first on line for shows like *The Price Is Right, The Match Game,* and *Truth or Consequences.* A warm-up person like Johnny Olson would ask the audience, "Anybody out there celebrating a birthday? anniversary? parole?" We got to know the routine. Once my kid brother and I got a pair of handcuffs. When Johnny Olson got to "Anybody celebrating parole?" we raised our hands handcuffed to each other.

I took a girl from Southport, North Carolina, to Radio City Music Hall. I was kind of smug. "She's never seen anything like this," I thought. A ticket to an afternoon show at Radio City was ninety-nine cents for the movie and the stage show with the Rockettes. I bought her a box of Mason Dots; the Bonbons were too expensive. This was the first time I was going to sit in the

A 42nd Street store featuring the Marilyn Monroe Publicity Calendar for fifty-nine cents!

orchestra. In the past, I had always sat in the balcony, where the cheaper seats were. We walked down the center aisle, I stepped aside to let her go into the row first, and before I entered, I genuflected: down on one knee, made the sign of the cross. Force of habit. Thank God she didn't see.

Afterwards we went to the Automat across the street, something she had never seen before. She asked me what Postum was. I didn't know what the hell it was, but it was always there. I showed her how to sit and stare at those revolving things until they turned and were filled up again. If you looked real hard, real close, as the turntable turned, you could see a flashlight and actually catch a glimpse of a person behind the wall.

"We went to the Automat across the street, something she had never seen before."

KEN ARETSKY: The Lower East Side was an interesting mix of people during my childhood: Jewish, Irish, Italian, and some Polish. There were no Puerto Ricans living in the area yet as I remember. The Chinese lived in Chinatown on the other side of the border, which was probably the Bowery. For the first twelve years of my life, I lived at 504 Grand Street in a three-bedroom apartment in the Amalgamated Dwellings, which was built by the Amalgamated Clothing Workers Union in 1930. It was one of the earliest co-ops in New York.

I went to P.S. 147 on East Broadway, where there were great teachers who were really involved with the parents. Once school was over, you played with your friends until your mother opened the window and called out, "Suppertime!" You played every imaginable game with a Spalding from stoopball to hit the penny. You were able to move around. Parents weren't on top of you all the time.

I was at a very formative age when the Subway Series were really happening. The three best baseball teams in the major leagues were in New York, and there were only sixteen teams. We ended up having a disproportionate number of Subway Series. I thought it was our given right; it never occurred to me somebody had to win something for this to happen. I can remember looking out my third-floor window and seeing the Yankees on a bus going down Grand Street. They were headed to the Williamsburg Bridge on their way to Bedford Avenue and Ebbets Field.

When my brother was twelve and I was eight, he used to take me every Saturday to triple-header college basketball games at Madison Square Garden. There were great players, great games. We'd go on the subway, stay the whole day, take the subway back to the Lower East Side, and stop off at Katz's Delicatessen for a hot dog before going home.

It was a great place to grow up, but it was a rough neighborhood. I saw gang wars, lots of them. After P.S. 147, I went on to P.S. 12 for the junior high school grades. My mother would give me fifty cents a day for lunch money, and

"The Lower East Side was an interesting mix of people during my childhood."

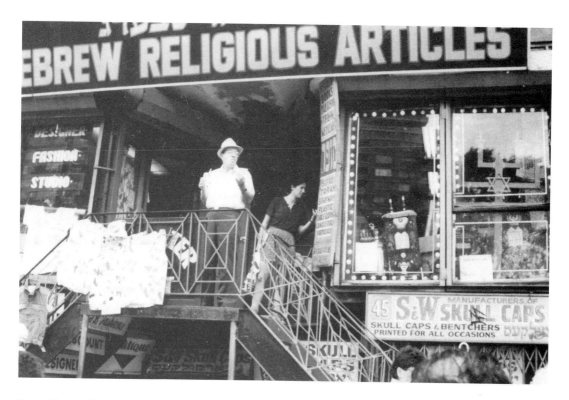

I would give this kid Tony Gallo twenty-five cents a day for protection. He was big, tough—he looked like a giant to me. And he really shook us down.

"How come you're losing so much weight?" my mother would ask me. I would never tell. But when you're eleven years old and you give somebody twenty-five cents a day so you don't get beat up, it teaches you something. If I have any street smarts, I learned them on the Lower East Side.

I used to go to the Eldridge Street Synagogue with my father. It was crowded with what seemed to me to be old, sad-looking people. The smell was unlike any place I knew, not offensive so much as it was frightening. The atmosphere was strict and very awesome. The rabbi was up on a platform. The women were upstairs. These were the years after the war, and a sense of peril, of something dangerous was communicated to me.

Still the neighborhood had a great beauty to it, a great sense of neighborhood. Orchard Street was filled with pushcarts with lots and lots of stuff hanging from them. That was where my mother bought my clothes. My grandfather was a barber. He had his own shop with two stools on Eldridge Street. I was the only kid who got a quarter whenever I got a haircut.

Sundays were elaborate days. In the morning, my father would go to Saperstein Brothers, an appetizing store off Essex Street, across the street from Gus's Pickles. Herman Saperstein lived two floors above us in apartment 5D. His son Michael was my age and we became great friends. Because we were neighbors, Herman Saperstein would cut us a better piece of sturgeon or salmon. My aunts and uncles would come over, my mother would make lox, eggs, and onions, and we would have a huge Sunday Jewish breakfast.

At night, we would walk over to Chinatown for Chinese food. What Jewish family didn't? We had a favorite place where the bartender knew me and always gave me a ginger ale with a cherry because I was afraid of the food. All I ate was some white rice while my parents and brother had the spare ribs and chow mein. Then we would walk back home, and everyone would sit in the living room and listen to *Name That Tune* and other programs on the radio. There was such a sweetness to it.

The neighborhood high school was Seward. I would have gone to Stuyvesant where my brother went had my parents not made the decision around that time to move out of New York to Long Beach. The Sapersteins, who became very wealthy from their appetizing store, had already moved to Neponsit. I was bar mitzvahed in Long Beach, but the whole Lower East Side came out for the occasion.

I became a Long Island boy—but I didn't. Long Beach was a beautiful place. You had the beach and everything; I had great friends there. But those first twelve years are the years that have stayed with me. I grew up on the Lower East Side, and there was something about that which was magical.

Chapter Two

I Want to Be a Part of It

**The High School of
Music and Art, a.k.a.,
the Castle on the Hill**

STANLEY DRUCKER: I think beginnings of people are the most interesting part, how they got started, how they became what they became.

MICKEY ALPERT: They still flock here. We still get the best and the
brightest. The names of the places change, the look changes, but it's the
same kind of experience.

STANLEY DRUCKER: When I was ten years old, Benny Goodman was the
rage. That was my inspiration. My parents bought me a cheap clarinet and
found a teacher who came to our apartment in Brooklyn to give me a weekly
lesson. There was not much music in the home. My parents were immigrants
who were just eking out a living. There wasn't much music in the elementary
schools, either. Once a week a string man would come in and conduct an
ensemble of a few violins, an alto saxophone, and me on clarinet. We all
played the melody line.

But things just developed from that point. I joined every kind of community group you could get into, going from one rehearsal to another. I got into
the National Orchestral, which had three rehearsals a week in Mecca
Temple—a Masonic building that today is City Center—and gave concerts at
Carnegie Hall. Leon Barzan, a famous conductor and educator who had been
the principal viola player in the New York Philharmonic under Toscanini, was
our conductor. His talent was in training orchestral musicians.

I went to the High School of Music and Art. It took an hour by subway, and then I had to walk up the hill. But each day there was new to me; everything was for the first time. We had different ensembles daily in addition to a very heavy academic program, which didn't interest me very much. I had been at Music and Art for a year and a half when I won a scholarship to the Curtis Institute in Philadelphia. I fully expected to remain there for a long time. But when I was sixteen, I auditioned for the music director of the Indianapolis Symphony and, to my great surprise, was offered a position. At that point, I went to Efrem Zimbalist, the director of Curtis, and asked what I should do. "You must take the position," he told me. "You can always come back." I never did.

While at Indianapolis, I played for Adolph Bush—the leader of a famous string quartet who hired me for an eight-week tour. At one point he recommended I play for William Steinberg in Buffalo. So I did, and at the age of eighteen, I became principal clarinetist of the Buffalo Symphony.

"On a weekend in 1948, I came down to Carnegie Hall."

While in Buffalo, I got the message that I should come to New York City and audition for Bruno Walter at the New York Philharmonic. I didn't know which chair it was, and I didn't care. On a weekend in 1948, I came down to Carnegie Hall. I walked into the Green Room, where a committee of principal players was seated. I recognized one or two of them.

The door opened, and Bruno Walter came in. That was the first time I saw him; he was a very dignified and serious-looking man. I wasn't scared though; I had won every audition I ever tried out for. He sat down at the piano; he had me play certain orchestral solos. Some discussion followed. I heard him say to the personnel manager, "He will become a valuable member of this organization."

Soon after I returned to Buffalo, I got a letter from the Philharmonic Society that offered me the position of assistant first and E-flat clarinet—the piccolo clarinet. What a big excitement that caused. There was a tremendous story and picture of me on page one of the *Brooklyn Eagle*. My father thought I was Joe Louis.

I really worked at it. I don't want to call it practice; I played every day. I never had the clarinet out of my hands. It wasn't a question of saying, Well, for a half hour I'm going to do this. I didn't work that way. My mind wasn't organized like that. I just played.

Every rehearsal at the Philharmonic was a master class for me. I knew how to listen, and so I was able to learn from the great players: John

Corleano, the concert master; James Chambers, the solo horn; John Wolmer, the solo flute; Leonard Rose, the principal cello—all legendary names. I would hear one of these great performers play a solo, and I'd hear something I never thought about before. Some of these players could make a fantasy out of one note.

When I first got to the Philharmonic, I thought the fact that I played in three other orchestras meant that I knew a lot. I was still eighteen years old, burning with ambition, and I thought I knew everything. I quickly found out I knew nothing.

ROBERT MERRILL: My mother, who had sung professionally, was interested in my having a singing career. She found a teacher for me, Samuel Margolis, whose studio was in the old Metropolitan Studio Building at 40th Street and Broadway. He was born in Europe and had taught there before coming to New York. The older generation of teachers was mainly from Europe. They came here because of the power of the Met. Going up there for my lessons, it was as if Caruso were singing in every studio.

In 1945, I auditioned for the Metropolitan Auditions of the Air and won. I was the youngest person at that time to have a Met debut in a major role. It was Germont in Verdi's *La Traviata*. For me, it was like being a baseball player coming from Brooklyn and playing at Yankee Stadium.

My debut was on a Monday night. My one and only teacher was there along with my mother, father, and kid brother, who took the subway from Brooklyn. My father was a tailor. He did not understand singing at all. He said it was not a profession. When he came backstage after the performance and people were congratulating me, he stood there in awe.

We took the subway back home to Williamsburg, Brooklyn. My mother had baked a cake. We sat around the kitchen table, drank tea and ate the cake. My father asked, "When do you work again?"

"Thursday night," I said.

"You see," he said and smiled, "I told you it is not a profession."

I had a job with NBC radio on a live program called *Music America Loves Best*, where I sang pop songs and an occasional aria with the NBC orchestra. On Sunday afternoons, the show was broadcast nationally. By chance, Arturo Toscanini tuned in. He told the man in charge of the talent on the show, "I like this voice. I want him to sing Germont."

I walked into the NBC studio for the first rehearsal expecting to see the entire cast. But only Toscanini was there, sitting alone at the piano. He looked up at me and stared for about five minutes. I was very young; Germont was the role of the father. Finally, he said, *"Avanti"* [come here].

I walked close to him.

"Are you a father?"

"No, Maestro. I am not even married."

He looked at me for another couple of minutes. Then he played my part, and I sang it with him. Afterwards he said, "All right, I make you a father." I sang the role again, this time for his historic broadcast with the NBC Symphony.

He was not a difficult person to work with if he liked you and thought you were serious about music. "Merrill," he would tell me, "I see you take a good breath."

HILTON KRAMER: I went to Syracuse University as an undergraduate, and it was during that period, either 1948 or 1949, that I made my first real

Looking north on Broadway from 115th Street. Columbia University is on the right.

visit to New York. A friend's father had taken a suite of rooms at a hotel for a long weekend. I saw the Matisse retrospective at the Museum of Modern Art, the Broadway production of *A Streetcar Named Desire*, and what I think was the first solo performance of Merce Cunningham at the 92nd Street Y. I was familiar with the Museum of Fine Arts in Boston and had been to the theater in Boston. Boston was a great city, but it wasn't New York. After that weekend, I knew if I went to graduate school, it had to be in New York.

In 1950, I came to Columbia to study literature and philosophy and stayed through the following fall semester. This was the period right after the war, the time of the GI Bill of Rights. My whole undergraduate and graduate school experience was very much shaped by that because there was a level of commitment on the part of these ex-GIs that raised the level of seriousness in the classroom.

At Columbia, I studied with Lionel Trilling, Mark Van Doren, Eric Bentley, Gilbert Highet, Ernest Nagel—it was a tremendous faculty in those days. Most of the courses were big classes with three to four hundred students. I didn't meet Lionel Trilling until much later because he was just a dot on the horizon giving a lecture, but his writing and lectures had a tremendous influence on me. Gilbert Highet especially stays with me.

He was a Scotsman with this marvelous accent who had been an undergraduate at Oxford, like all the aesthetes of his generation. You know how academics generally dress, but Gilbert was a fashion plate. His course was on the influence of Greek and Latin classics on later English and European literature. He was particularly funny about Joyce's *Ulysses,* which he loathed, although his edition of *Ulysses* was bound in black velvet. He generally loathed all of modern literature; compared to the Greek and Latin classics, he felt it was decadent.

In January 1951, I left New York because I had run out of money. When I came back in the fall of '52, I started looking around for a job in journalism and landed one on the night shift of the New York bureau of the Agence France Press, the big French news agency in the AP Building at Rockefeller Center. Then, in 1953, I published my first essay on art in *Partisan Review,* and as soon as I did, my phone began ringing with people asking me to write about art. I started reviewing exhibitions for the old *Art Digest,* a fortnightly that covered the art scene.

It became very convenient to be working on the night shift for the Agence France. I could see the exhibitions during the day and, since nothing ever went on in that office at night anyway, write my reviews at night. French journalists were lazy beyond imagining. They got what they needed out of the *New York Times* or the *Herald Tribune*. The only times I actually had to send anything to Paris on the teletype machine was when the sports editor was too drunk to send the scores.

I was supposed to work from four to midnight but it was French hours. One night I wandered in at six, and the general manager, whom I'd always heard spoken of but had never seen, and whom the French didn't regard as French because he was from Alsace, was there. The place was in an uproar. What happened? It was the day Joe DiMaggio married Marilyn Monroe.

One day I walked into the office of *Art Digest* and asked the general manager if there was a chance of a regular job there. It turned out one of the editors had just been fired that very morning. So I went to work for *Art Digest*, which became *Arts Magazine*. By the early sixties, I was freelancing and teaching part-time, and all the while the art world was getting bigger and bigger. Then one day in 1965, I got a call out of the blue asking if I'd be interested in coming to work as an art critic for the *New York Times*.

WALDO RASMUSSEN: I was born in a small town near Spokane, Washington. When I was fourteen, we moved to Portland, Oregon, as my father got a job working in the shipyards for the war years. I didn't want to move away from my extended family, but I came to Portland and discovered two things right away: the Portland Art Museum, which was the first museum I ever saw, and the Portland Symphony, which performed the first live concert I ever heard. That did it. The first show I saw at the Portland Art Museum had works by Mark Tobey and, of course, I had never seen art like that. But instead of being hostile, I was interested.

At Reed College I minored in art, and at the same time I worked at the Portland Art Museum. When I graduated in 1954, the director of the museum said I should leave and go to New York. He didn't fire me; he was promoting me in a sense. And so together with my wife, our sixteen-month-old child and a baby on the way, we set off with borrowed money and no place to live. Instead of going west, we headed east.

My wife and I had to move around a few months until we found an apartment on 83rd between Lexington and Third. Yorkville had Germans, Poles, Irish—all hating one another. We were a young couple with a child and soon another baby in a building filled with older couples who hated kids. I made sixty dollars a week; the rent was one hundred and twenty-five dollars a month, so it wasn't too easy. My wife was homesick; she had a very hard time at first.

But a friend from the Portland Museum who was now at the Modern helped me get a position there in a new program that sent American art abroad and brought in exchange exhibitions. And for me, being at the Modern was unimaginable. The abstract expressionists were there. Jackson Pollock, Willem de Kooning, Mark Rothko, Clyfford Still and Barnett Newman were showing at that time. Modern art had become my passion, and I was at the place I wanted to work in more than any other in the world.

CAROLE RIFKIND: I am a New Yorker born and bred—that is, if you count Brooklyn as being part of New York. My husband is Manhattan born and bred, and when we began dating in 1954, he was told by his parents that I was not a New Yorker. His father, a proper and gentle man, was very definite in letting his son know that he needed a passport to get across the Brooklyn Bridge.

As a kid living near the next-to-the-last subway stop on the local in Bay Ridge, I thought Manhattan was a very big deal. Brooklyn was isolated; Manhattan was where it was at. One of the most profound experiences for me was in 1947 when my sister took me to the Frick Museum. I saw a Rembrandt, and afterwards I remembered which Rembrandt it was. It was an experience that influenced all my life. Later on my sister went to NYU. She lived in the dormitory at Judson Hall, and every so often, my mother would send me into the city to bring her some money when she ran low. The movie *My Sister Eileen* was around that time. I identified my sister living in her Greenwich Village dormitory with the film.

Still, it was rare that I crossed that bridge to Manhattan until I transferred to Barnard after two years of college at Mt. Holyoke. It was that Frick experience. My interest was always in art and the history of art, and Barnard seemed like the place to go.

I couldn't get in the dorm because they had a perennial shortage of rooms for the New York City students. Neither Barnard nor your parents would let you live in an apartment—in those years women were very protected. And there was no way I was going to commute the hour and a half each way from Brooklyn. Fortunately I found the Parnassus Club, a protected residence for women on West 115th Street just west of Broadway. It was a six-story building run by Miss McMillan, who looked more like a madam in a whorehouse than a chaperone for a bunch of young women. But she ran a very tight ship. No young man ever got upstairs, and worse, each one was interviewed when he came in.

This was New York in 1954. The Parnassus Club was full of women who were attending the Juilliard School of Music, or the Fashion Institute of Technology, or Barnard School of General Studies. It was almost on campus, yet it was a world apart, a thrilling thing. You met terrifically diverse students, not just the academic grinds that you met at Mt. Holyoke. They were into the arts, fashion, music.

The neighborhood around Barnard was fairly seedy and getting worse. A lot of apartments were doubled up with Hispanic and black immigrants. Landlords were illegally allowing double occupancy. This impacted on

Columbia and Barnard. The campus was fine, but a few blocks out, especially to a girl of protected and limited experience, you felt wow!—this is something strange. You would hear stories about people taking the 2 train instead of the 1 train, getting off at 116th Street in Harlem and having to walk up through Morningside Heights Park to get back to campus. It was frightening.

But the entire scene was a tremendous learning experience because you got to appreciate the diversity and the energy of these people who were striving. The college was alive. It wasn't about grades; it was about learning and participating and being a part of things. As an art history major, I went with Professor Julius Held to the Metropolitan Museum of Art every week. He'd take us to auction houses, art galleries. He encouraged us to be participants in the art scene, not just academics. It was the time of abstract expressionism. I would ask him, rhetorically of course, what art I should buy—eighteenth-century Venetian or this or that—and he'd always say, "Buy from the New York School!"

"My interest was always in art and the history of art, and Barnard seemed like the place to go."

Teachers College,
Columbia University

On the other hand, the thinking was terribly paternalistic, patronizing. College was very in loco parentis in those days. They supervised your social life; they supervised your physical fitness. We had to pass a swimming test; they made us tread water for five minutes. It was very much a fifties scene— a timid, fearful time, and you felt that.

By my senior year, I was able to get a room on the fifth floor of the Barnard dorm on 115th and Broadway. My window overlooked Broadway, and to this day whenever I walk by, I look up at it. I would cross Broadway, amazed by the cacophony. I'd look uptown and see the geography of Manhattan Island, the heights of Morningside Heights. Nobody thinks Manhattan has any geography, but it does. I'd look downtown with all the traffic, and I felt Broadway went on forever and ever and ever.

Although affiliated with Columbia, Barnard has always had a separate identity. It's on the west side of Broadway, and Columbia is on the east side. They were two separate campuses, but the architecture was very similar. The whole Barnard-Columbia complex is a very powerful place, one of the great public places in New York City. It's a very strong, heavily designed campus, and it was homogenous—much more so than it later became—in terms of the uniform corner lines, the neo-Georgian classical buildings. The pattern of the campus, the repetition of open spaces in a very organized way with the quadrangles and courtyards, gave you a very strong sense of place. I felt very privileged being there.

ALAN GREENBERG: I showed up in Manhattan in March 1949 and went down to Wall Street looking for a job. At that time, all the firms in the investment banking industry were located there. It was a very impressive group of old-line firms, most of which have since gone out of business. The big ones had their own buildings.

One reason all the action was down there is that securities were moved back and forth physically. There were all these little guys with big briefcases running around, carrying securities from one firm to another. All the bookkeeping was done by hand.

But the whole street was dead. Everybody was starving. The volume of the New York Stock Exchange was one million shares a day.

People asked me, "Where are you from?"

"Oklahoma."

"Go back," they told me. "There's no future in Wall Street."

I went to maybe six firms, they all said no. It was a Wasp-oriented business. Some of them favored Ivy League applicants. But Bear Stearns was a partnership, and probably seventy-five percent were Jewish. There were about 125 people in the whole firm then.

They hired me as a clerk in the oil department for $32.50 a week. Oil wells were being drilled in Canada and west Texas, and my job was to put pins on a map. I felt lucky to get the job because Bear Stearns was making money despite the conditions. Still I fought very hard to get out of the oil department and become a clerk someplace else. When I became a clerk in the trading room, I felt at least I was in an area where I could grow.

JERRY DELLA FEMINA: We lived behind the Sea Beach subway in Brooklyn. I heard that train coming and going. The night I got married was the first time I slept away from the subway. Without the noise, I couldn't fall asleep.

My parents were Italian immigrants. Every morning my father would wake up at six o'clock, go to the 86th Street station of the Sea Beach and sell newspapers at the stand. At 7:30, the guy would give him four or five dollars, and he would take the train to Manhattan. He worked for the *New York Times* as a press operator in the composing room, but he probably never walked ten blocks in any direction in the city. I'd wait at the station for him at about 6:30 in the evening. He would kiss me, walk home and have his dinner. Then he'd go to work as a soda jerk at a candy store underneath the Culver Line el on Avenue U until eleven, twelve o'clock. He'd come home, go to bed, and start the day again. On weekends in the summer, he'd operate the rides in Coney Island. That was his life.

Our Italian neighborhood was a ghetto. Italian was the spoken language. People built this wall around them to keep the outside world from coming in. No one could get in, but no one could get out. They were content to be longshoremen, to lift things for a living. If someone got into trouble, he'd go to a Jewish lawyer. If someone got sick, he went to a Jewish doctor. You paid rent to a Jewish landlord. That meant in times of stress, you had to turn to someone Jewish, and that bred resentment. But my mom, instead of resenting, got me to understand there was a better way to live. She would take me along with her to Mr. Kahn's house on Buckingham Road in Flatbush to pay the rent. "Look at this. This is the way you want to live," she'd say to me. My mom always felt I could do something, be someone. So I had this work ethic from my father and "you-can-do-it" support from my mom.

Going to Manhattan was a way of climbing over the neighborhood wall. You could get on the subway and ten cents later you were on 42nd Street. It was safe then, and it was glittering, really shining. Manhattan seemed to me to be the realization of the dream, glamour, lights, intelligent people who wore suits and ties to work. I wanted to be a part of it.

By the time I was sixteen, I was working in Manhattan. I'd leave Lafayette High School at three o'clock, take the train, and head for the Mercury Messenger Service on West 23rd Street. I delivered messages until eight o'clock at night, wandering the streets because I was able to save a dime if I

walked instead of taking the subway or bus. Walking from place to place, I got to know the streets and neighborhoods. I got a feeling for the city that you just can't get otherwise. Once I delivered a message to 30 Beekman Place. I had never been there before. I said to myself, "Someday I'm going to live here because this is the most beautiful place in the world." Once I delivered to Ed Sullivan's apartment and got to see his wife. I went home and told my parents. Occasionally I'd get a tip. If someone tipped me a dollar, it was big-time stuff.

When I was seventeen, I got a job delivering advertising for the *New York Times*. They sent me to Lord & Taylor, Best & Company, Bergdorf Goodman. By the time I got there, the stores were closed. They'd let me into a side door, hand me the advertising, and I'd rush it back to the *Times*. Sometimes I made pickups at advertising agencies. One day I came into an agency, it was four, five o'clock, and I saw a guy with his feet up on the desk. Being a curious kid, I asked, "What does that guy do?"

"He's an advertising copywriter."

"Wow! A job where you put your feet on the desk and they pay you? How much does he make?"

"Thirty thousand dollars a year."

From that day on, I wanted to be in advertising.

In 1954, I got out of high school and began trying to break in as a copywriter. It took me seven years. In between, I worked as a shipping clerk; for a shirt company; for National City Bank, where my job was to carry this giant heavy satchel filled with canceled checks from 11 West 42nd to 10 Exchange Place.

Meanwhile just being in the city was magic. Everybody was young, excited and growing. There were so many opportunities. It was almost guaranteed that we would do better than our parents.

"Going to Manhattan was a way of climbing over the neighborhood wall."

LINDA KLEINSCHMIDT: In the spring of 1960, my freshman year at Lawrence College in Wisconsin, I decided I wanted to transfer to another school. But when August came around, and I wound up with no school to go to, my mother in her infinite wisdom said, "You are not taking this year off and hanging around the house. I am sending you to Katharine Gibbs in New York." I went kicking and screaming as I was not especially interested in going to a secretarial school to learn typing and shorthand.

Nevertheless, the next month I found myself at the Barbizon Hotel for Women on 63rd and Lexington, where the top five floors were appropriated as a dormitory for the Katharine Gibbs girls. The rest of the hotel was reserved for single women, supposedly from good families, who lived at the Barbizon because they kept an eye on you. Men could only come up to the second-floor level; they could never enter a young lady's room. There were curfews, and you were in deep trouble if you came back after the check-in time. Many of the residents were aspiring models or actresses; others were hoping for the ultimate secretarial job. Grace Kelly had lived there when she first came to New York and worked as a model.

Third Avenue and 42nd Street

I had a small single room with one window that looked out onto Lexington Avenue. It had a sink, but the bathroom and showers were down the hall. Every day a maid in a black-and-white uniform came and made up my room. A doorman let me in and out of the hotel. An elevator lady, who wore the kind of uniform that Shirley MacLaine wore in *The Apartment*, took me up to my room on the 17th floor. She knew all the Gibbs girls and would always speak to us.

The Gibbs girls were highly identifiable. We were required to wear a hat, white gloves, and shoes with one-inch heels. Our hair had to be cut short enough so that it did not fall below the collar of our jacket. And we always wore suits. I bought five wool tailored suits from Best & Company and a Chesterfield coat. We got all dressed up every day.

Five days a week, the Barbizon provided us with breakfast and dinner in the private Gibbs dining room on the second floor. We'd come down in the morning dressed in our suits, sit at a round table with white tablecloths and white cloth napkins, and be served our breakfast on china plates with silver flatware.

Then we'd either hail a cab or walk down to the subway on 59th by Bloomingdale's and take the IRT to Grand Central Station. Katharine Gibbs classes were held on the fourth floor of the New York Central Station Building. This was just when they were beginning to build the Pan Am Building right behind us. We took classes five days a week from 9:00 to 3:30 with an hour for lunch, two hours of stenography and transcription, an hour of something called business communication, and two hours of typing on a manual typewriter. While we typed, the teacher stood up in front and pounded a walking stick on the floor so we would type in time to her rhythm. Then she checked our work, never missing a typo or erasure.

All the teachers were women of the sort my father would call battle-axes. The first six weeks I was there I thought I was in basic training. But our business communication instructor, a six-feet-tall opera singer who had a master's degree in psychology, was probably the best teacher I ever had. She trained us to do the quarter fold with the *New York Times* so as to be able to read the newspaper on the subway without disturbing the person next to us.

The girls in the dormitory came from all over, a good number from the South. Quite a few were college graduates. But there were also girls who commuted from their homes in the boroughs of New York. Most of them had not gone to college and had the New York accent that needed refining. They were at Katharine Gibbs because they wanted to get a decent job. Being a

The
Gibbsonian
SPRING 1967

secretary then was a coveted job for a woman. For some, it meant getting in on the ground floor, from which it was possible to move up.

It was a kind of finishing school. They stressed good manners. You were expected to be professional, polite, and to know your job. We were taught never to let the phone ring more than three times. On the third ring you should be on that phone saying, "May I help you?" That was part of the image.

Lunchtime, we mingled with the midtown Manhattan crowd, although in our suits, hats, and gloves, everyone could tell we were Katie Gibbs girls. We would try to walk a few blocks away from the school, away from the teachers who were watching out for the girls who took off their hats or gloves. If you got caught, it meant a demerit.

There was this sense of "Here I am in Manhattan, all dressed up and going down Lexington or Park Avenue." I knew that East 63rd and Lexington was a high-class, big-name district, that Gypsy Rose Lee and Katherine Hepburn were my neighbors. At times it seemed like I was wandering around on the set of a movie, living in this hotel, getting dressed up every day. The Barbizon had a small drugstore with a little cosmetic area and a lunch counter. Every so often I'd have lunch there, a BLT on toast with mayo and a cherry coke. So New York. The people behind the counter would talk to me. "How's school? How is it going?"

When a girlfriend of mine turned eighteen, which was the legal drinking age then, we went to the Biltmore Hotel, sat down at the bar and had martinis with olives. It was a status thing. Standing-room tickets to see a Broadway show cost two bucks. From the back of the orchestra I saw Ethel Merman in *Gypsy*, Mary Martin in *The Sound of Music*, and Dick Van Dyke in *Bye Bye Birdie*.

It wasn't until much later that I realized that year in Manhattan was a crossroads moment. We Katharine Gibbs girls were learning on manual typewriters, but the IBM Selectric electric typewriter was coming out. Young ladies were expected to wear hats and gloves. Gentlemen still opened doors for us and lit our cigarettes. But all of that was beginning to change as well.

On a beautiful day in May 1961, I graduated from Katharine Gibbs. I was still very young, but I had learned a lot during my year in New York: how to fend for myself, how to get around on the subways and the buses, how to take in the life of the city. For me, there was a sense of wonderment and power that came from being a part of it.

There was a terrace on the 22nd floor that went all around the top of the Barbizon Hotel. The afternoon of my graduation day, I went up there and walked around the perimeter, looking out at the gorgeous New York City sky-scape, and I did not want to leave.

Chapter Three

If I Can Make It Here . . .

SAUL ZABAR: Henry Morgan was a humorist who lived on the Upper West Side and had a radio program. "Meet you in front of the cigar store," he'd always say. There used to be a cigar store on the corner of Broadway and 80th. Everybody passed by it. If you stood outside that cigar store long enough, you'd meet everybody you'd ever want to meet. Today, if you stand outside Zabar's, you'll probably meet everybody you'd ever want to meet.

My father, Louis Zabar, came to America from Ostropolia, a shtetl in the Ukraine, in 1923. At that time, there were public markets in Brooklyn where stalls could be rented. Almost immediately my father got a stall and went into the produce business. How he did it, I don't know. He didn't have any money. But he'd been very important to his father's business, and so he knew what to do. In the mid twenties, he married my mother, Lillian, who had come here earlier from the same town in the Ukraine, and then he got into the smoked fish business.

In 1934, when I was six and my brother Stanley was two, he heard about an appetizing counter that was available on the Upper West Side. It was in a Daitch Dairy, a fairly large store noted for its cheese. He rented the counter, and we moved to an apartment on Amsterdam Avenue and 81st Street.

After a few years, the owner of Daitch decided to sell. My father bought the store, probably on notes because he didn't have that kind of money. Now he owned an entire store, maybe twenty-five hundred square feet. The fish department was on one side, the cheese department was on the other side, and the grocery department was in the back.

East of Broadway to Columbus was Irish, but along Central Park West and from Riverside Drive to Broadway, from 72nd Street to about 86th Street, was an affluent Jewish area. The store developed a big charge account trade from the well-to-do people in the neighborhood, a lot of telephone orders and deliveries. George Gershwin, Fannie Brice, Babe Ruth were among the customers.

Then came the war period, and everything boomed. In 1941, my father moved his store down the block to the present Zabar's location at 2245 Broadway and 80th Street, the portion where the deli and appetizing departments are today. He was a very smart, very active businessman.

They had the Blue Laws then, which didn't allow retail establishments to be open for the full day on Sundays. We could only be open from nine to eleven in the morning and from four to seven in the afternoon. It was hard to get personnel to work those hours so Stanley and I had to come in. I worked in the

Saul Zabar minding the store, c. 1968

cheese department, where we sold sour cream and sweet cream by the dipper; butter, which came in blocks that we had to cut; Swiss cheese; American cheese; Munster cheese; a little bit of Brie; different cheddar cheeses.

In 1949, my father got very sick. I was a student at the University of Kansas at the time, but when I found out my father was sick, I came back to New York. He died the next year at the age of forty-nine. I thought I would spend a couple of years in New York and then go back to school. But that was not to be.

It's now the late 1950s. Stanley has graduated from law school and left the business to practice law. My father left his family comfortable. My mother has her own money; it isn't necessary for me to support her. My youngest brother, Eli, is provided for. I'm running the store, but I want to change my lifestyle.

Then one day Murray Klein appears on the scene. He was a survivor who managed to escape from the Germans and the Russians. After the war he wound up in a DP camp in Italy where he learned Italian and ran a business in the camp. He came to work for me as a stock man. He was so talented and capable that he soon became manager. After a while, he got married and went into business for himself.

This day he was passing by and came into the store. I said to him, "Murray, what are you doing?" He wasn't doing much. "Come on," I said, "join us." At first he said he didn't want to, but then he agreed.

Murray was really the founder of Zabar's as it exists today. He had a sense of humor; he liked to talk to celebrities. There was always something smart, but not offensive, coming out of his mouth. Murray was able to put everything together.

With Murray around, I became the outside buyer, doing the fish buying, the cheese buying. I was married by this time and had a family. I was able to take off on the weekends and do whatever I had to do by phone. Klein was the overall head.

Then my brother Stanley came back into the operation. He provided the more sophisticated aspects, like importing the cheeses from France, the olive oils. And we began servicing a new breed of customer who wanted the kinds of foods that were not generally available. Klein had briefly been in the housewares business, so he founded the mezzanine section and trained the people.

Now we're into the 1960s. The food revolution is taking place. We're becoming aware of European tradition, the cheeses, the breads. This is the

time of the so-called caviar
wars with the big department stores
like Macy's and Bloomingdale's, who had
very good food departments. They undercut us;
we undercut them. There was a lot of publicity. This was
also the time of David's Cookies. Everybody was baking cookies.

Zabar's had become a big family enterprise with a lot of interconnected people. By 1975, we had bought the surrounding buildings and broken through, and Zabar's was the property it is today. Why did it become the institution it became? You had a combination of three very smart people: me, my brother Stanley, and Murray Klein. I don't think my father ever dreamed this would happen.

MARK FEDERMAN: The day Japan formally surrendered to the United States on September 2, 1945, was the day I was born on Ludlow Street in

> "We began servicing a
> new breed of customer
> who wanted the kinds
> of foods that were not
> generally available."

Countermen at Russ and Daughters

the Lower East Side, about a block from the smoked fish store belonging to my grandfather, Joel Russ. He had come to this country from Galicia and soon afterwards got into the herring business. The Eastern European Jews had brought the taste for herring with them. Herring was a staple, and it cost pennies. They would pick one out, wrap it up in the newspaper of the day, which was generally the *Forward*, and with some onions and potatoes make a meal for a whole family out of it.

Originally my grandfather sold herring off a horse and wagon. Then he had a pushcart. In 1914, he opened up his own store on Orchard Street. By the early twenties, he had moved to the present location on Houston Street. In those days there were probably three or four of those kinds of stores on every block of the Lower East Side.

He had that Eastern European style typical of very bright, self-taught, hardworking people who put in fifteen hours a day, but had little patience.

No self-respecting Jew would ever buy a fish off the top of the pile. They wanted herring from the bottom of the barrel. My grandfather threw many a customer like that out of the store.

Grandpa Russ had no sons, but he did have three pretty daughters—Hattie, Ida, and Anne—and because of them the store prospered. As soon as they were in high school, they began helping out. You had these three good-looking teenage girls picking herrings out of barrels and slicing lox. Who was going to argue with them? Customers would fall in love with every piece of fish they laid on the counter. That freed my grandfather to do what he could do best: buy quality fish. Every morning, he drove his truck across the Williamsburg Bridge to be at the smokehouses in Brooklyn by four a.m., when the fish came out of the ovens.

The store became known for the quality of the fish and the three pretty daughters who sold it. People came from all over. The daughters met their husbands through the store. All three sons-in-law came to work in the business, and all the families lived together under the control of my grandfather.

When I was around five or six, Grandpa Russ moved everybody out to Far Rockaway. He thought the sea air would be good for our health. The whole deal then was to move out; nobody wanted to live on the Lower East Side. But as soon as we were old enough, all the grandchildren were brought into the store to work on a rotating basis. This was the late fifties, early sixties. They paid us what seemed like a lot of money, but we would have rather been playing ball with our friends.

We were never allowed to work behind the fish counter. They put us on the other side, behind the dried fruit, nuts, and candy. Somehow there was always a connection between all of that and smoked fish. There were chocolate halvah squares, orange and red marmalade with chocolate sprinkles, real apricot shoe leather, a confection of prune and apricot with marshmallow in

Grandpa Russ had no sons, but he did have three pretty daughters (from left to right): Hattie, Ida, and Anne.

Russ and Daughters celebrating

between wrapped in cellophane. You can't get that item anymore. The guy who made it died, and that was it.

At some point in the mid fifties, the middle daughter and her husband were having trouble getting along with my grandfather. They moved out to Long Island and set up their own smoked fish business. So by the time I started working in the store, it was basically Grandpa Russ, my parents, my aunt and uncle, and the kids who came in one or two at a time on the weekends. Although Grandpa Russ was not moving around too much by now, everyone was still afraid of him. Dressed in a three-piece tailored suit and a cane with a gold handle, he would sit in an old red leather chair near the candy counter, and watch everything. "*Nisht a zoy!* [Not like that!]," he would say; nothing positive ever came out of him. But it was his store until he died.

On Saturdays, Russ and Daughters would get very busy in the evening after the Yiddish Theater on Second Avenue let out. The audience, the actors, the producers—they all came to buy the bagels and lox and herring that Jews eat on Sundays. We had to stay open way past midnight, until one, two in the morning.

On Sundays, the scene was extraordinary. It was mobbed, and no one had come up with the idea of taking numbers yet. Everybody would cry, "I'm next, I'm next." And they all waited for their "see you's"—the particular person they wanted to wait on them. Be it my mother or my father or my aunt or my uncle, each customer had his or her favorite; they were in to "see you." This wasn't "Give me a quarter pound of nova" and you're out. This was like your special salesperson had a special chub in the back that she saved just for you.

Overall the Lower East Side was dead on Saturdays because the Jewish-owned businesses closed for the Sabbath. On Sundays, however, the area was teeming. I don't think my family ever shopped on Orchard Street. They were not from the shoppers; they were from the sellers, and besides, they had no time to shop. But Orchard Street was booming with the many little stores in the small buildings. The pushcarts were gone by this time—they weren't considered sanitary—but there was the big market on Essex Street with all the stalls. Because of its Jewish nature, the Lower East Side was exempted from the Blue Laws that kept businesses closed on Sundays. And that was what enabled the neighborhood to thrive economically. It was when the Blue Laws were abolished and the suburban malls stayed open on Sundays that the Lower East Side started to decline.

My parents inculcated in me the feeling that the Lower East Side was not a neighborhood to live in, and that the smoked fish business was not one to be in. They worked very hard, put in long hours on their feet in a place that did not have good heating or refrigeration. Every night the showcases had to be taken apart, and all the food had to be put away in the back. I remember them scrubbing, moving things around.

They were into survival. It wasn't glamorous. They didn't have a chance to sit down, much less sit back. They figured they would raise their kids and educate them so that they would not have to go into this business. We all went on to college. I became a lawyer.

By the mid seventies, my aunt and uncle had retired. My father developed a heart condition and thought of selling the store. It was a down time for the city. Russ and Daughters continued to do business because of its loyal Jewish clientele, but the customers had all moved from the neighborhood. The vibrancy was not what it had been. We were in a flat period, and there seemed to be no light at the end of the tunnel because of the changed demographics. The political powers of New York basically abandoned the Lower East Side, which was receiving new immigrants that the city was not paying attention to.

Nevertheless, it was at this time that I decided to take over the store. My work as a trial lawyer had become all-consuming. I'd come home at night, my wife would be talking about the kids, and my mind would be on what I'd be doing at the trial the next day. Now I thought I would give up my job at the fancy firm and still practice law privately on the side. As it turned out, the first day I came into Russ and Daughters as its owner was the last day I practiced law.

I bought out the other family members because I knew I couldn't have anybody telling me what to do from afar. But for a while the question seemed to be what was going to last longer, the business or me. I didn't have a clue as to what was going on. Here I am, this cocky lawyer telling the old Jewish countermen I inherited how to run the business. There was a virtual war. On top of that, fish is the most demanding, finicky product in the world. And

the customers are the most demanding in the world. They take your kishkas with every sale. "I want you to slice it like this, not too thin, not too thick; give me a half of a quarter of a pound." And for years the neighborhood was the pits. I treaded water for quite a while. But I was afraid of changing anything, afraid the ghosts of Christmas past would get to me.

What kept me going was holding on to my grandfather's mentality: Keep your eye on the register, make sure your customers are happy, give them quality. Limit yourself to one store. Survive.

I maintained the Russ and Daughters obsession: one slice at a time, nothing pre-packaged. Today they call it the "slow-food" movement. I run the store pretty much the same way my grandfather and his daughters and their husbands did. We sell the same products, even the dried Polish mushrooms that they used for sauces and mushroom and barley soup. Once they were a cheap staple. Today we sell them for $150 a pound. They're impossible to come by, and there is little market for them. The rest of the world becomes homogenized; this store stays the same. We try to be historically consistent in the look, the food, the service. But I did get my own counter people, who are nice to the customers. And they can cut salmon with the best of them.

ANDY BALDUCCI: I was born in Greenpoint, Brooklyn, in 1925. When I was two months old, my mom said, "Let's go back to Italy and get the boys baptized." So my mother, my brother and I went back to her hometown below Naples.

NINA BALDUCCI: Andy's mom was the only girl in a family of six children, and when she got married, her mother made my father-in-law promise not to take her only daughter away from her. He tried to find a business in Italy. But he had had a taste of America and simply had to come back. After Andy was born, however, his mother returned with her boys to Italy and stayed for fourteen years.

ANDY BALDUCCI: All during that time, Pop went back and forth. Each time he went to Italy, he would leave a fruit market he had built up to one of his brothers or a cousin. In Italy, he was not too successful. It was during the Mussolini era, when it was very difficult for anyone who had immigrated to get permits, licenses. Finally in 1939, the family came back to the United States.

I began working for my father's younger brother, Frank, in his fruit market on Main Street in Flushing. As I got a little older, my uncle made me the manager of his other store in Jackson Heights, which had once belonged to my father. Lo and behold, World War II broke out. I was drafted, served in the navy, and participated in the invasion of Normandy, where I was wounded. But then it's 1945. I'm back, safe and sound as could possibly be, happy to be working for Uncle Frank again.

One day when we came back from the market, my uncle said, "Andy, I want to drive you home."

"Any problems?"

"No, I want to talk to your father."

At that time, my father had a little ice business. He was carrying ice up flights of stairs in a burlap bag. "Louie," my uncle says, "David Yekes (of Yekes and Eichenbaum, one of the wholesale houses in the Washington Market) told me there's an open-air market in Greenwich Village looking for a good operator. Andy likes what he's doing and he shows very good enthusiasm for the product and the market. You know the business. Let's go take a look at it."

Andy and Nina Balducci in front of their Greenwich Village store

So the three of us went to see the property. The block was city owned and could never be developed other than light-duty stores because of the subway underneath. It started with a newsstand that went down Sixth Avenue and rolled around Greenwich Avenue all the way up to Christopher Street. There was also a little grocery store and a bakery.

We look at the market: a thirty-foot front, approximately twenty to twenty-five feet deep, a tin roof, a dirt floor, no doors, no windows, no heating, no bathroom, no basement—nothing but flies because when you attempt to sell fruits, especially in the summer, and you don't move the product fast enough, the sugar in the fruit turns to molasses.

Gus Klopstock owned the lease for the entire block. He was a wonderful man, a reformed alcoholic, a reformed gambler, and a Christian Scientist. He lived in the penthouse at 1 Christopher Street, where he had every kind of parrot you could imagine. He looks at the place with us, sees nothing but flies. "Will twenty-five dollars a month be all right?" he asks. "The first six months are free."

I put up the name: "Balducci Produce."

Pop said, "What is this 'Produce'? Why don't you put 'Balducci Fruit and Vegetables'?"

"Pop," I said, " 'Produce' is a little better."

It doesn't take us long. Inside of a year, we've chased away all the flies, put in a concrete floor, put a bathtub in the back room to wash the produce, made a little office in the back with a refrigerator. Mr. Klopstock arranges for us to be able to use the bathroom in the grocery store two doors down.

We buy a little truck. Every day we drive in from Little Neck to Manhattan. Mama's at the register, Pop's very content to have his lunch on an empty apple box. We're busy from six or seven in the morning until eleven at night because the Village has early people, midday people, late people. The store is open around the clock. Pencil on the ear, brown bag. That's the action.

After a while, we move from Little Neck to an apartment at 9 Christopher Street, right around the corner from the store, on the fourth floor of a walkup. It was my mother, my father, me, and my sister, Grace, who was a little girl then.

The business wasn't new to me. I'd been in Flushing with one trade, in Jackson Heights with another. The minute we opened, I recognized the trade we had, and that's what we went after. These people were looking for high-quality merchandise: mushrooms, a nice bunch of radish, a beautiful bunch of grapes, an artichoke, an expensive apple—nineteen cents a pound—red Delicious, golden Delicious, each individually wrapped.

One day, my Uncle Mauro's son Charles said, "Andy, maybe I could raise mushrooms for you."

I said, "Great, Charlie."

We subsidized his operation in Tough Kenamon, Pennsylvania. It became the world's center of mushroom growing and canning. Every night, Charlie would load up his pickup truck with pearl-white mushrooms, the champignon type. He'd be at the store by six in the morning. We're selling the most gorgeous mushrooms, thirty-nine cents a pound. People are coming from all over the city, Brooklyn, Jersey. They're buying not by the pound but by the three-pound basket for a dollar.

We didn't know what income tax was, what social security tax was. The small open-air markets operated on cash; the wholesale market was cash. But after a while, I said, "Pop, I want to pay by check." I did all the entries in the book, made out the checks for what we bought each week and sent them to the market.

The only problem was my father didn't believe in banks. He literally put his money under the mattress. So once a week, I would be called by Mr. Pinto, the president of Manufacturers Hanover on Sixth Avenue and Waverly Place. "Andy, you need three hundred dollars to cover the checks."

One day Mr. Klopstock came to me. "Andy, I got myself in a little bit of trouble. I could use twenty thousand dollars. I'll give you the lease I have with the city for collateral."

I said, "Sure, let me ask my father."

His intention was totally honorable. But my father didn't believe, or he didn't have the foresight, and he turned Mr. Klopstock down. The way we were brought up, the father is the boss. The only one above him is God. So my father's word was final.

The little baker on the corner, a Jewish fellow, gave Mr. Klopstock the twenty thousand dollars. Lo and behold, the day comes they find Mr. Klopstock dead of a heart attack. The baker gets the lease for what has become a very valuable location. From twenty-five dollars a month in the late 1940s, we were paying fifteen hundred dollars a month by the late 1960s.

Now the baker's lawyer comes in and says, "Andy, your lease will be up in a month or two. Be prepared to pay forty thousand dollars a year." That was

more than double. Meanwhile, my father, who didn't begin paying taxes until the late 1950s, turned sixty-five and wanted to get the money he paid in social security taxes back. The accountant told me, "Andy, your father's on the phone every night. He wants to retire. He wants to get that seventy-nine dollars a month."

When the forty-thousand dollar lease came up, that was the last thing Pop wanted to hear. "What are we going to do?" he asked.

Directly across Sixth Avenue was 69 West 9th Street, a twelve-story apartment building that I watched go up. It had a beauty parlor, a watch repair shop, a stock brokerage that took up the two center stores, and a Japanese import shop. It was 1970, the stock market wasn't doing much. The stock brokerage firm closed, and the two center stores, thirty-three hundred square feet, were available for thirty-six thousand dollars a year.

"Pop," I said, "it's time we got off the sidewalk. It's time we got doors, Pop, a bathroom, a basement. It's time to go *dalla stalla alle stelle* [from the stable to the stars]."

I went to the bank. By now, Mr. Pinto had retired. The new president was Ed Corliss. "Ed," I said, "I want to build a store across the street. I need about two hundred thousand dollars."

He took me downstairs to the office of Manufacturers Hanover where the vault was. "It's a great idea, Andy, it's a good thing. But how do I substantiate two hundred thousand dollars? You never put any money in the bank. We have to keep asking you to bring money in to cover the checks."

I said, "I'm not going to put the two hundred thousand dollars in my pocket. I'm going to use it to buy fixtures. Take a mortgage on the fixtures." On that strength we got the money.

The day we were going to sign the new lease, my father called me up at four in the morning. "Please don't take me to the lawyer with you," he said. He didn't want to move.

By this time, Pop and Mama—together with my brother, who was a doctor, and his family—were living in a beautiful two-story brick-face house in Flushing that Pop bought for thirty-five thousand dollars cash. My brother had told my father, "If something goes wrong, you may risk the roof of your house." Pop got scared.

Up to this point, my father had been the sole owner of everything. But now I formed a new corporation with the names of myself; my wife; my sister, Grace; and her husband, Joe. We were the new owners of Balducci's.

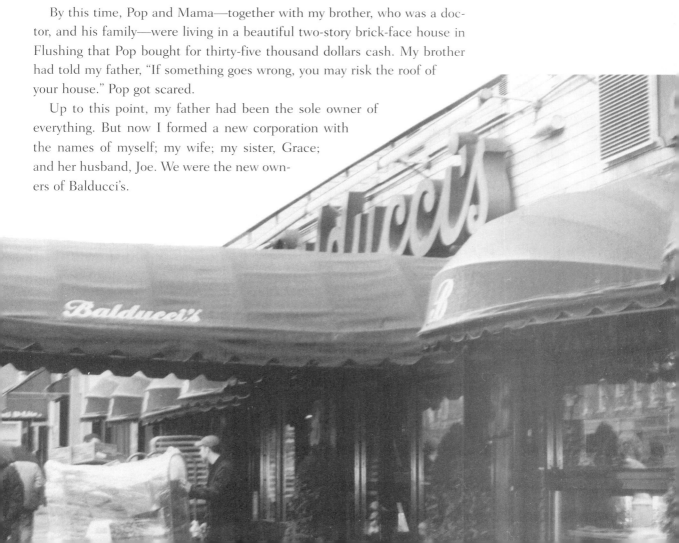

In our hearts nothing had changed. Mama was still the cashier. All the money still went to Flushing. Pop and Mama still went to Italy three months every year. Pop got a new car every other year. But now the business technically was owned by four younger people.

And it was no longer Balducci Produce, but Balducci's. We realized that the same clientele that needs a beautiful artichoke, a beautiful mushroom, a nice bunch of grapes needs a slice of prosciutto, a good piece of fish or meat, a good piece of bread, a nice dessert. Through the years, our customers had to go down the street for one thing, to Little Italy for something else, to Ninth Avenue for something else, even to Brooklyn for different specialties. The table was getting more and more sophisticated as people began to travel. Italy, in particular, became the paradise.

NINA BALDUCCI: The grand opening was Thursday, March 24, 1972. The night before, nobody slept. All our vendors were helping us stock the shelves. In the morning, Channel 7 News was there to photograph the event. Mom and Pop came up in a limo. They walked up a red carpet, and Mom cut the ribbon. Grace and I were the cashiers, and we did a real bang-up business from eleven in the morning until ten at night.

We started with what we knew best, beautiful fruits and vegetables, which remains our mother department, a lot of dried fruits and nuts in the front window. We had a simple deli with the Italian cold cuts, some cheeses and smoked fish. We had olive oil, vinegar, preserves. It was very, very simple.

When the beauty parlor on 9th Street and Sixth went out in 1974, we took over that space and expanded the deli, cheese, smoked fish department. We also built Mom a kitchen so she could prepare items like eggplant parmesan and her tomato sauce, which we sold in the deli. A few years later, the Japanese store went out, and we took over that space. "This is the time we're going to complete the table," Andy said. And that was when we opened the fresh fish and meat departments.

I always do my own shopping. One afternoon I was going around with a cart when Andy's cousin Charlie called to me. "Nina," he said, "would you like to meet Lauren Bacall?"

"I'd love to."

She saw I was shopping, got herself a cart, and fell right in step with me. "I want to see what you and Andy eat so I can get the same thing," she said.

ANDY BALDUCCI: We came up with a very beautiful shopping bag because we wanted people to walk out with something nice. It cost us more than the twenty-five cents we charged as an accommodation. One day when there was a long line at the register, a customer in the front began haggling. She didn't want to pay for the shopping bag. Suddenly someone at the back of the line yelled out, "Get that lady the hell out of there. Throw her out of the store."

I take a look. It was Jack Nicholson. "How the hell do you put up with that nonsense?" he said to me.

Balducci's have sprung up all over the country. They're not called Balducci's, but it's the same idea. People came, they looked, they went back home and tried to do the same thing. You think about the energy that goes into a business like this. Washington Market was one kind of energy. Balducci Produce was another kind of energy. Balducci's is yet a different energy focused on a sophisticated market, a complete table.

JERRY DELLA FEMINA: I married very young and was doing two, three jobs, living my father's life. Christmastime I would get work at Macy's or Gimbel's to supplement whatever salary I had. One year I went to Macy's for my annual job and they said, "Everyone has to take a test from now on." I went into this room with fifteen to twenty other guys, took the test, and failed. I have a learning disability; I was never able to take a written test. That was a real down point. But even then I never lost the faith that it was going to happen for me. The image of the copywriter with his feet on the desk I had seen when I was delivering messages for the Mercury Messenger Service stayed with me.

I got a job in the mail room at Ruth, Reuff, and Ryan, in the Chrysler Building. Their clients included Pontiac, Kentile, Arthur Murray Dance Studios, and Bon Ami with the little yellow chick—"Hasn't scratched yet" was their motto. Most of the guys who worked there were wealthy kids from Harvard, Princeton, Yale. They wanted a career in advertising, and the mail room was the traditional way to start.

I used to run around with the advertising plates in the one suit I owned, a heavy, winter, dark brown suit that I got from Korvette's for twenty-two dollars. The texture was pretty much that of a rug. My choice was freeze in the winter or swelter in the summer. I went for sweltering.

After a while, I got promoted into the production department, and my salary was raised to twenty-one dollars a week. They told me it was the second promotion in the history of Ruth, Reuff, and Ryan from the mail room. "Who was the first?" I asked.

"David Mahoney. Today he's the head of Good Humor Ice Cream."

"You mean all I can look forward to is selling ice cream?" I said.

I was a wisecracker. Being verbal has always been my compensation for my learning disability.

I decided to make up ads for how advertising agencies could sell their agency to clients. What I did was go down to the magazine stores on 42nd Street and Sixth Avenue where you could get old copies of *Photography Annual*. I cut out the best photographs, figuring I might as well have the best photographers working for me, wrote appropriate headlines to go with them, signed them JDF, and sent them to an agency called Daniel and Charles. Finally Daniel Karsh, the head of the company, said to his secretary, "Who the hell is this JDF and what does he want?"

I got in to see him.

"I'm going to give you a chance," Karsh said.

"You don't have to pay me," I told him. "All I need is a telephone so I can call my wife."

"No, I feel obligated to give you a token salary of fifty-two hundred dollars a year. Is that okay?"

I bit my lip. "It's okay."

"Are you sure it's enough?"

"Yes, it's fine."

I went down the elevator, walked out in front of 185 Madison Avenue, and let out a gigantic scream. It was the most any Della Femina in history had ever made.

For the first six months that I worked at Daniel and Charles, I didn't read a magazine. I didn't want to lose the edge, whatever I had that was fresh. The first ad I did was for Hahn Brothers Movers. It appeared in the *New Yorker*. The headline said " 'Oops!'—We haven't had cause to use this word in thirty years. We use other words, words like 'Watch that cabinet,' 'Be careful with that table,' 'There's been more padding on that painting.' As a result of these words, we never said 'Oops.' We won't either. Yet we charge no more than moving firms who advertise in less sophisticated magazines."

Within a year, I was a copy chief. I kept getting raises, and then I became almost like the son of Charles Goldschmidt, one of the partners. It got to the point where I could do no wrong. I wanted to get more out of the job than being the favorite. So I left.

This was the time of the creative revolution, the big change that took place in the advertising industry in the fifties, early sixties, when young men coming out of the army started to establish themselves. It was a changing of the guard. Prior to that, advertising was a Wasp business. If you were Italian they let you work in the production department. I remember going for a job at J. Walter Thompson, and the man looked at my little portfolio and said, "Well, you're very good. You could probably get a job here but they don't want to work with people like you." It took a few years before I understood what he meant.

If you were Jewish, the only accounts you were allowed to have were garment industry accounts. Grey was the first agency that broke away from that. Then a writer named Bill Bernbach spun off with two guys, Max Dane and Ned Doyle. Dane and Bernbach were Jewish; Doyle was Irish. They produced

A big change took place in the advertising industry in the fifties, early sixties.

intelligent advertising, as opposed to singing cigarette packs and such that treated people as if they were dumb. They had a sophisticated sense of humor. At first the old agencies made fun of Doyle, Dane and Bernbach. But as this new firm took account after account away from them, they realized that this was a real thing. By the time they figured it out, it was too late.

Advertising came to be more about words and about young Italian and Jewish guys from Brooklyn, Queens and the Bronx working in an industry they never thought they could work in before. We weren't the Wasps going to 21. We ate at our desks. We worked day and night, dreaming of what to do. Not many marriages succeeded in those days of the creative revolution; we were married to our business. One day we were poor kids with no prospects, and the next day we were creative mavericks, people who were breaking down barriers in a growing business. We all became friends.

In 1967, with absolutely no money and no prospects, I started an agency with another Italian kid. Della Femina and Travisano opened an office at 625 Madison Avenue and quickly ran out of money. We were down to our last eleven thousand dollars. We owed a lawyer who wanted a piece of the agency in return for his work; we owed the landlord. We figured we had a month and a half to go. I turned to my partner and said, "We're gonna die if we wait for the month to go by. Let's take all the money and throw a party."

We invited everybody in advertising to L'Etoile, a restaurant on 59th Street. It was the ultimate crapshoot; it was Brooklyn. Everybody from the business came, including potential clients. People were talking to each other and said things like, "Yeah, I've been considering them," and "They look like they're doing well." We got three accounts as a result of that party, and we were in business.

I started appearing on television shows. Part of our pitch was nobody knows the city like we do. There are a lot of people with a lot more talent, there are a lot of bigger agencies. But I've become a kind of symbol for Manhattan.

I have some favorite ads: "The magic is back" for the New York Mets; Joe Isuzu, the guy who tells lies about his cars; the Blue Nun ads. Before I had my own agency, I saw Jerry Stiller and Anne Meara in a small nightclub in the Village. Afterwards, I went up to them and said, "One of these days I'm going to use you in a commercial." We did it around 1971. These two people are shopping, and he says, "May I suggest a little Blue Nun?"

I came from people who were beyond schleppers, who worked the way people built the pyramids, lifting heavy things. I loved not lifting things. I loved getting paid for thinking. I loved being able to move to 30 Beekman Place, where I had once delivered messages.

Wherever I go, I'm in a place where I used to deliver messages for the Mercury Messenger Service. Like the Fred French Building on Madison Avenue. I delivered many a message there. Later on, when I was looking for a copywriter's job and had an interview uptown, I stopped off there on a day when it was three degrees, and I was walking to save the bus fare, going into building after building to warm up. When I got into the lobby of the Fred French Building, I was shaking. I was so cold I wanted to cry. But I went on and finally got to the interview, where the man wouldn't see me because I was late.

That was a turning point in my life. I realized I would never be afraid of anything again. It was cold, but it wasn't that bad. That was when I started sending ads to Daniel and Charles and got my first copywriting job. I'm still part of the four jobs my father had, his work ethic, the way he and my mother lived, all that.

SID BERNSTEIN: I was in the music business, a fast, high-blood-pressure business. In the mid fifties I started taking courses at the New School just to get away from the craziness. They had some amazing lecturers, one of whom was Max Lerner, who was a featured political columnist in the newspaper *PM* and later on the *Post*. I signed up for his course: America as a Civilization.

As part of the course, Max Lerner suggested we read British newspapers. I read the *Manchester Guardian*. Naturally I was attracted to the news about the musical scene in England, and that's how I learned about this group of four young musicians from Liverpool. Every week the font of the stories about them got bigger and bigger. I had not heard their music; all I knew is what I read. But it was like I got a whiff of this new act, and I felt I had to bring it to America.

In February 1963, I contacted their manager, Brian Epstein, and told him I wanted to arrange for the Beatles to come to New York in May or June. But he wanted to wait until they had a hit record so there would be no chance of their playing to an empty house. I booked the concert for February 12, 1964. It seemed to me Lincoln's birthday would be a good date.

I don't think I had ever been to a classical concert, but I knew all the great symphony orchestras and all the great basso profundos and sopranos performed at Carnegie Hall. So I figured that would be a good place, something different. At that time it cost three thousand dollars to rent Carnegie Hall. I took a gamble and put down a five-hundred-dollar deposit. The lady who arranged the Carnegie Hall bookings asked me, "Who are these four young men whom you're so excited about?"

I said, "Mrs. Satescu, they're an incredible group."

When she heard "group," she thought a chamber group, a string quartet. After the show, she told me, "Never come back again."

Some time later, Ed Sullivan was changing planes at Heathrow Airport, where he saw a crowd of kids waiting for a plane. They were shouting, "Long Live the Beatles!" "We Love the Beatles." He understood this was a phenomenon and booked them. Then he found out an American promoter already had a date on them.

Leonard Bernstein at the Beatles concert, Carnegie Hall

Sullivan called me and said, "I understand you're presenting the Beatles in America." I told him I had Lincoln's birthday at Carnegie Hall. So he booked the previous and following Sunday, and then the Sunday after that. With Sullivan booking them, the word got out.

My tickets were sitting there gathering dust until October 1963, when the Beatles' records hit. By February, they had the first five of the top one hundred hits, Carnegie Hall had sold out, and I was a celebrity.

I met them for the first time at the Waldorf-Astoria. They were lovely kids, unassuming, bewildered, amazed, laughing at the crowds downstairs outside the window.

The Beatles playing at Carnegie Hall was a breakthrough event for rock 'n' roll. It took it out of the local clubs to a bigger arena. It was a breakthrough event for Carnegie Hall as well; they had never done music like that before. After Carnegie Hall, I took the Beatles to Shea Stadium, and that changed the face of the rock 'n' roll concert.

I had acted on intuition. Sometimes I have hunches that I take long-shot chances on. I do have one regret though, and that is never having told Max Lerner that he was the spur that brought the Beatles to America.

GILLES LARRAÍN: I was born in Indochina. As my father was a diplomat, we moved to various places. During the 1950s, we lived in New York and I attended the French Lycee on 95th and Fifth Avenue. Then I went to Paris to study architecture at the School of Beaux Arts.

In 1963, I was in Mexico studying some structures for my thesis. The only way I could document them was through landscape photography, and in taking the photographs, I began to realize I was asking questions: What does this mean? How has time affected the sculptures and the decorations on the carvings? How does perspective and light affect the image?

By 1968 I was living in a loft in SoHo and working for an architectural firm. But while I had enjoyed the study of architecture, I found the actual practice to be eighty percent business, twenty percent design. I didn't like the office work; I didn't like working in groups where business is the purpose.

The big hangout at that time was Max's Kansas City on Park Avenue South and 18th Street, where there was a remarkable melting pot of artists, writers, and musicians. Norman Mailer was around. The Andy Warhol crowd was there, Leonard Cohen, Roy Lichtenstein, Frank Stella, Robert Rauschenberg,

Coquettes featured in *Zoom*.

Jasper Johns. They were great artists, breaking new frontiers, opening new doors. But at Max's Kansas City, they were just buddies drinking at the same bar. You spoke to them, you learned from them.

It was at Max's Kansas City that I met the Coquettes, a theater group of 150 transvestites from San Francisco. They were so outlandish and far out and funny that I decided to photograph them. I had them come to my loft in groups of twenty. The playwright Harvey Fierstein, who went on to write *Torch Song Trilogy* and *La Cage aux Folles*, was one of them. They arrived wearing feathers, boas, all kinds of extravagant outfits. They were so visually amazing, it was like a living theater. Liberace would be considered quiet in comparison. Afterwards I invited people to view projections of the photographs. We played "Imagine" by John Lennon continuously. It was a perfect soundtrack.

The magazine *Zoom* published twenty-six pages of these photos. I got many, many letters—some were asking how I could photograph such people. Then I put the photos together into a book called *Idols*.

These transvestites were my first subjects, and this experience of photographing them led to my leaving architecture for photography. I began going to museum exhibitions and saw amazing prints that will stay with me forever. I bought equipment and lights, and built a studio and darkroom in the building I had bought. I had never studied photography. I had to teach myself from books and looking.

I have the need to meet with people, to learn from them, but my activity I need to do alone. When I go to my darkroom, I can spend days and days there printing. Taking the photo is the tip of the iceberg; the printing is the iceberg.

From documenting the edge of society, I moved to social portraits of friends, celebrities, as well as landscapes and record album covers. Columbia Records sent Miles Davis to me to be photographed. It was the beginning of August, very, very hot and humid. My air conditioner was broken. He came in and said, "Are you Gilles?" in that hoarse voice of his.

I said, "Yes, Mr. Davis, I'm Gilles."

He said, "I have five minutes."

"Well," I said, "I don't know what we can do in five minutes, but are you thirsty?"

"I'm always thirsty."

So he came down to my studio. I had some good wine and tapas. I put on a record of a flamenco singer, an older woman, a gypsy from Seville. I knew he liked flamenco because of his record. And he said, "What is this music? Why do you have it on?"

"Because I love flamenco. I play the guitar."

He said to me, "Go get your guitar."

I said, "Go get your trumpet."

He sent his guy to get his trumpet from his limousine, and we made some flamenco music together.

I have done many portraits of Miles and other celebrities. But they are not about fashion or looking good. It's about having a moment with a person in front of me where I can go into a conversation with that person and reach the landscape of the soul.

New York helped form me as an artist. If I had been elsewhere, I would not have had the opportunity to become what I did. I left Paris because it was not alive enough for me. It was too bourgeois, too contained in its habits, in its ways of beauty, of antiquity. There was not enough energy, enough free-dom to move around. For me at that time in my life, I needed to see new horizons, new spaces. New York had that. There was a vibrancy not limited by culture, by arrondissement; everything was fluid, nothing was fixed—not class, not even sexual orientation.

Part Two

Chapter Four

Puttin' on the Ritz

PAULINE TRIGÈRE: When I came to New York in 1939, the food was something atrocious. Nobody cared about eating. The big change came about because of Henri Soulé, who was delegated by the French government to run the restaurant in the French pavilion at the 1939–1940 World's Fair. After the fair closed, he decided to stay here, and he opened Le Pavillon on 55th Street and Fifth Avenue. It was the most extraordinary restaurant in America, very chic. After the war, all of a sudden, French food became important, and New York became a city where you could eat as well as anyplace else.

Every good chef, every good waiter worked for him, and all those boys who were his waiters went on to become chefs at other great restaurants that opened up. It was like an explosion.

ANDRÉ JAMMET: People who were working at the French pavilion in the World's Fair were stranded here during the war and remained afterwards. There were also men from Brittany who got jobs on transatlantic ships and jumped ship when they came to America. One brought another over. They became Soulé's staff.

HOWARD KISSEL: When I first came to New York, the classy French restaurants were very snobbish, although in almost every case they were run by peasants from Brittany, which is the poorest region in France. But they had the Americans kowtowing to them in a way that was truly remarkable. They knew how to put the Americans in their place.

PAULINE TRIGÈRE: Henri Soulé was a peculiar man. If he didn't like someone coming in through his door, he would say, "I am sorry, I do not have a table."

SIRIO MACCIONI: He was very French, very superior. His attitude was: This is what it is, and you're lucky we allow you to come in. With all due respect to Mr. Soulé, his restaurant today would not stay open three weeks in New York.

Even the Colony, where I worked for ten years, had a little bit of that philosophy. When I first began, I would go around and ask, "Is everything all right?"

The owner took me aside. "At the Colony, everything is always all right."

HOWARD KISSEL: Once Harry Cohn—the head of Columbia Pictures, which owned the building on 55th and Fifth—came to dinner at Le Pavillon. Soulé didn't know who he was, and he put him back in Siberia. Cohn knew he was being slighted and got his revenge. He would no longer allow Soulé to store his wines in the cellar. So Soulé moved to 57th and Park, but he kept the restaurant space and gave it to his mistress, Madame Henriette Spalter. That became La Côte Basque.

ANDRÉ JAMMET: In 1958, Robert Meyzen, the manager of La Côte Basque; Fred Decré, the maitre d' of Le Pavillon; and Roger Fessaguet, the chef of Le Pavillon, came up with the idea of opening their own restaurant. They found a place on 55th Street that had been a speakeasy during Prohibition, which is why the bar was in the back. Nearby was a door that led into a hotel where Rockefeller and other wealthy people had apartments under false names. They'd slip through the door and pick up their liquor.

As they had a low budget, the three men planned a very nice, elegant bistro, with Fred and Robert in the dining room and Roger as the chef. They decided to call it La Caravelle, after the caravels *Niña*, *Pinta*, and *Santa Maria,* as a symbol of the discovery of America. On July 14, they had the walls painted with murals of Paris by Jean Pagès, who came to this country when he was hired as an illustrator by *Vogue* magazine.

Creating the restaurant was intimidating. They were coming from Mr. Soulé, who set the standard, and La Côte Basque was right down the block. Then just before they opened, there was some kind of argument between Ambassador Joseph P. Kennedy and Henri Soulé. Kennedy came to Fred and said, "Freddy, you open your place, we'll be there on the first day." And when the restaurant opened on September 21, 1960, the Kennedys were there. They backed La Caravelle morally and financially.

La Caravelle became a favorite of the Kennedys as soon as it opened in 1960.

Less than two months after La Caravelle opened, John F. Kennedy became president. The timing was terrific. He and Jackie came to La Caravelle often. It became the favored place, attracting dignitaries and celebrities. It was young, new and exciting. With connections to the White House, it became possible to import things like Dover sole and other special items that weren't available here.

At that time, the prix fixe dinner at La Caravelle was $7.50, lunch was $4.00 or $5.00, but a normal white wine like a Pouilly-Fuissé could be $7.00, $8.00. That was a lot compared to the price of the food. Pétrus, the renowned Bordeaux, was $15.00. It was not a wine that was in demand before La Caravelle, La Côte Basque, and Le Pavillon made it famous. They launched it in New York, promoted it, and made it a great wine. Who knows why. It was a quality wine that did well throughout the years, but perhaps also Soulé knew the people and wanted to do something nice for them.

After La Caravelle opened in 1960, Lutèce followed in 1961 and La Grenouille in 1962. Le Pavillon closed when Henri Soulé passed away, but a lot of other French restaurants appeared. The 1960s was a French invasion of the culinary scene in New York. There was enough business for all. La Caravelle was the first restaurant that bridged out from Le Pavillon. But everything came from Henri Soulé.

SIRIO MACCIONI: During and after the war, it was easy for French restaurants to open in New York because France was an ally. Italy, on the other hand, was the enemy. The Italian style was brought here by poor people who said, "Let's open a restaurant." In the early fifties, most of the Italian restaurants didn't even have a name. All they said was "Italian Restaurant, Northern Cuisine" or "Italian Restaurant, Southern Cuisine."

HOWARD KISSEL: Nobody valued Italian cooking because it was at its most basic, basic almost always meaning veal parmesan and spaghetti and meatballs. It was only into the sixties and early seventies that people began to distinguish between southern and northern Italian cuisine.

Around that time, I was working at *Women's Wear Daily*, and a big part of our coverage was chronicling who lunched where. Orsini's was one of the key places. The two Orsini brothers had started in a little take-out place that served northern Italian food, but by this time they had a beautiful restaurant on 56th between Fifth and Sixth. It was on the second floor with windows up near the ceiling, so when the sun streamed in it was like natural lighting to show you off. The thing about Orsini's is everyone knew the food was mezzo-mezzo, but it was the place to be seen.

One day a friend of mine who was very proud of her breasts (once she told me they weighed thirty pounds) was seated at a table at Orsini's that she regarded as much better than Mrs. Onassis's table. She remarked this to Mr. Orsini who, by the way, was a very handsome man. "In my restaurant," he said, "women are seated by cup size."

SIRIO MACCIONI: When I came to New York in 1956, the Colony on East 61st Street was one of the most famous restaurants in the city. It was the restaurant of society. The best people, like the Rockefellers, the Astors, came there. Fifty years ago there was Café Society, which meant a café where society met. They wanted good food but simple food. They didn't want to be impressed by a chef who would say, "I'm a three star, and you have to eat what I'm telling you."

Most of the haute cuisine French restaurants in New York around that time had a table d'hôte menu. If you asked for a smoked salmon, which is the easiest thing to serve, they would say five dollars extra. If you asked for a soufflé, which is the cheapest thing to make, that was five dollars extra too. The Colony was an a la carte restaurant. The owner, Gene Cavallero, was intelligent enough to keep it simple. He offered a cuisine that was a mixture of French and Italian. He had pasta on the menu, a rarity in those days. The food was served on beautiful, large plates.

I began working at the Colony not long after I came to New York. As I learned English, I began replacing the head waiters on their days off. One Saturday night, the maitre d' who had been there for many years died. All the assistants were clamoring to replace him, saying, "I was here the longest."

"Calm down," Cavallero told them. Then he turned to me. "You think you're good, don't you?"

I said, "Well, I don't know. It's up to you to judge." But I knew I was good.

"You can be in charge for the next couple of weeks. Do you want to try?"

I tried and I was good.

My first day on the reservation desk, the phone began to ring. "Mr. Onassis—the usual table."

"Mr. Sinatra—the usual table."

"The Duke and Duchess of Windsor—the usual table."

"Truman Capote—the usual table."

"Charles Revson—the usual table."

Cavallero comes in. "How's everything?"

"Okay," I said, "but would you mind to tell me what 'the usual table' means?"

He took me by the arm and showed me one table. "Everybody thinks that this is his table. But you want to be the maitre d'. It's your problem." And he walked out.

I made up my mind: first come, first served. It happened that the first to come was Frank Sinatra. "Okay, my boy," he said to me, "I'm going to tell your boss you're the best. But first I'm going to the bar. Keep my table."

I said, "Mr. Sinatra, no, please go to your table."

"What do you mean?"

Somehow I managed to convince him to go directly to his table. The next person who wanted that particular table was Onassis. He saw Sinatra and said to me, "You bastard. You gave him my table because he's Italian." Thank God those were the days of the three-martini lunches.

Then came the Duke and Duchess of Windsor. They looked right away at the table. I ushered them to a banquette. "Please, sit here, it's very comfortable."

The Duke said, "Don't judge for me what is comfortable. That is my table."

I got through that day using all of my charm, but I will remember it all of my life.

"My mentality in cuisine is real classical food but done in a modern approach."

At the end of the first week my name appeared in *Time* magazine. Henry Luce wrote, "The Colony, after forty years, has a new maitre d'. He's tall, he's elegant. It would be much better if he could speak English."

I worked at the Colony for ten years, and for all that time it enjoyed a big popularity, even as La Grenouille, La Côte Basque, La Caravelle—all the new generation that had started with Henri Soulé—opened. The Colony was more important from the point of view of society than Le Pavillon, even though Le Pavillon had the reputation for the food. It was classical, but heavy-handed.

One of the reasons the Colony closed is that the son was not that determined. We discussed my becoming a partner, but then the landlord wanted the space back. The rent went to five times what it had been. Meanwhile I received an offer from the Pierre, which was supposed to open a Maxim's of Paris in the hotel. That did not work out. Instead they opened another beautiful restaurant, La Foret, where I was the maitre d' and director. I was still very young.

In 1973, the Pierre was bought by a group from London. The place was making money which is unusual for hotel restaurants, but the new owners wanted to do something else. At that time, I was approached by William Zeckendorf, Jr., who was a twenty-five percent partner in the Mayfair House on 65th Street, a residential hotel. They were losing money; they asked me to manage the hotel. I said if I do something, I would like to have my own place. So we discussed and came to an agreement, and in 1974, for the first time, a private individual opened a restaurant in a hotel in New York.

I needed a name for my restaurant that would explain my mentality. To use my own name seemed presumptuous. Then I thought of the French expression *"Hier soir on s'est bien amusé. C'était un vrai cirque!"* ("Last night, we had such a good time. It was a circus!") And that is how I came up with the idea of "Le Cirque." It's an international idea. It suggests fun. I did not want a place that reminded me of going to church. Instead, I had a mural with monkeys.

My mentality in cuisine is real classical food but done in a modern approach. We started right away with beautiful plates. We offered broiled fish. In those days when you went to a French restaurant and asked for broiled fish, most of the time they said no. Then they started to do a broiled sole. But because they didn't have a grill, they would put the fish in the oven and mark it with an iron to give an impression, and for some reason, I don't know why, would put some paprika on top to give it color.

The most difficult person in those haute cuisine kitchens was not the chef—it was the saucier. He was usually a schizophrenic person who did not want to talk to anybody. I didn't believe in that. I believed in the Italian way: You cook the food, you add a little bit of lemon or wine, and that is the sauce. Why bother to buy good meat or fish, cover it with Sole Veronique, make everything look like a soufflé? Instead of a saucier, I had the chef put one, two more persons on, and when they are cooking they glacé the pan with cognac, wine, vinegar.

Elegance personified: Sirio Maccioni in front of the original Le Cirque

Making it happen at Le Cirque (from left to right): Pieter Schorner, patissier; Sirio Maccioni, proprietaire; Alain Sailhac, chef de cuisine

For dessert, they used to come around with a trolley with a big cake, fruit salad, chocolate mousse, and some floating island. At the beginning of the evening it was good. But once they began to cut . . . That was not my interpretation. I said we have to personalize; every dessert must be made to order. Most places had one pastry chef. I hired four.

Now as I was creating my own restaurant, I thought, Where is the best food in the world? And the answer was in an Italian home. It is the woman who goes to the market, who knows how to choose the products, who cooks the food. In Italy, people eat well at home. When they go out, it's to have a good time. That was my inspiration and my innovation. My philosophy is this: A good restaurant is good home cooking on a professional level.

When I opened Le Cirque in 1974, I had five kilos of beautiful white truffles sent to me from Italy. A famous lady journalist who was at the opening said to one of my assistants, "You better tell your boss that those potatoes are smelling very bad." Two years later, this same woman who didn't know what white truffles were wrote an essay on the subject.

John Canaday of the *New York Times* gave us two stars with the potential of four. A couple of years after, Mimi Sheraton came in and took away one star because she said I was presumptuous. People who are mediocre and vulgar like to bring everything down to the same level so they can understand. Now she tells me I am the very best thing that ever happened in New York.

In Tuscany where I was born, we say we are Italians, but first of all we are Tuscans. I'm joking but I'm not. We believe everything in Europe started from Tuscany: Dante, Raphael, Leonardo da Vinci. Any Tuscan farmer thinks he is a descendant of Leonardo da Vinci. It's presumptuous but not in a bad way.

MICHAEL TONG: How many New York restaurants can stay open for more than twenty years with the same owners? You can pick them, probably no more than ten: Le Cirque, Café des Artistes, Shun Lee. . . .

I came to the United States in 1963 as a student in hotel management. The summers of 1964 and 1965, I worked at the Chinese pavilion at the New

York World's Fair, where I became friends with chef T. Twang, who had been Nationalist China's ambassador to the United States. He had the idea to open a fine Chinese restaurant in New York City and asked me to be his partner.

We opened Shun Lee Dynasty on Second Avenue and 48th Street in 1967. Our cuisine was Yang Chow–Szechuan; Yang Chow is a town right next door to Shanghai that is famous for cooking. We were the first Chinese restaurant to pay attention to the décor. As a student in hotel management, I learned how important décor is.

At that moment in time, the Chinese restaurants in New York were places like Ruby Foo's or the House of Chan that served the old-fashioned Cantonese food: lobster Cantonese, egg rolls, spare ribs. It was not authentic, but it was

In the 1960s, the population of Chinatown was Cantonese—and so were the restaurants.

a favorite among the Jewish immigrants in Brooklyn and the Bronx, who would take their families to the neighborhood Chinese restaurants every Sunday. The kids grew up loving Chinese food, which is why our best customers are Jews.

Through the 1960s, the population of Chinatown was Cantonese. Not just Cantonese, but from a little village, Tai Sin. Everybody spoke the dialect from that village. If you didn't speak Cantonese, you could not survive in Chinatown; nobody would talk to you. Restaurant owners wouldn't give you a job; landlords would not rent space to you.

Then beginning in the 1950s, after the Communist Revolution, Chinese seamen jumped ship, sought political asylum, and stayed in New York. They worked underground for a few years, got together some money, and opened a few Chinese restaurants around Broadway and 125th Street, where the rent was cheaper and a lot of Chinese people, including students from Taiwan and Hong Kong, lived. These restaurants were all called Shanghai: Great Shanghai, Shanghai Café. . . . This was the beginning of Shanghai cuisine in New York, a new trend in Chinese food. Then it became a combination of Shanghai and a little bit of Szechuan, with things like chicken with peanuts and moo shoo pork. It was not really authentic but it was very new. However, it was all in that one area of the Upper West Side. Most New Yorkers didn't know about it.

In the late 1960s, 456 East Broadway opened with a chef from Taiwan. This was the first true Shanghai restaurant in Chinatown. After two years, the chef moved on to his own bigger restaurant, also on East Broadway, which became famous for spicy sauces.

Meanwhile at our new restaurant, I was out front while my partner was the chef. He didn't speak English well, but for all the years of our partnership, we had a very good relationship. He trained a lot of young chefs. They were in their twenties then. Today they are in their fifties, and they are still with me.

I became friendly with a gentleman who regularly ate at our restaurant. We would talk about Chinese food. After about three months, he told me he was Craig Claiborne, the restaurant critic of the *New York Times*. I didn't understand how powerful he was. In those days, people who opened Chinese restaurants didn't read the Friday "Going Out Dining Guide" in the *Times*.

One night he said to me, "Michael, my book is coming out."

"Really?" I said. "Which book?"

"The *New York Times Dining Out Guide*, and your restaurant's in there." He gave us four stars.

We began averaging 500 people a night, and we only sat 120 people. So as not to turn away business, we opened a second restaurant, Shun Lee Palace on 55th and Lexington. Two of our chefs were from Hunan and they were buddy-buddy with my partner. That was how we came to open Hunan on Second Avenue and 45th, the first Hunan restaurant in the United States. It was spicy but different, an instant success. Shun Lee was the pioneer not only for Szechuan and Hunan cuisine but for spicy ethnic food. Mexican, Thai, Indian cuisines were not popular until after people got used to the spicy tastes of Szechuan and Hunan food. Shun Lee means smooth sailing, and after the *New York Times* rating, it was indeed smooth sailing. Craig Claiborne put Shun Lee on the map.

Dorothy Wheelock, theater and features editor at *Harper's Bazaar*

DOROTHY WHEELOCK: I was theater editor and then features editor at *Harper's Bazaar* through the 1940s and most of the 1950s. It was the golden age of the magazine, when Carmel Snow ruled with impeccable instinct and an iron Irish hand as editor in chief, and Alexei Brodovitch, the courtly and paternalistic former White Russian cavalry officer, was art director.

Mrs. Snow was delicate and dainty with spindly legs always in high heels, white hair, a little turned-up nose, and a little tinge of Irish in her voice. But she was someone you'd pay attention to. She was intuitive and daring. She got the greatest people around her. She wanted the best features, the best stories, the best everything. You'd go to her with an idea, and she didn't want to know about any difficulty you were having, whether you couldn't get to someone or someone didn't want to see you. She wanted the piece whole. And when she got it, she was most appreciative.

Her mother was an Irish immigrant who worked as a seamstress in Chicago. So Mrs. Snow was brought up with clothes. She knew what you could pluck here and pluck there. She got her clothes in Paris from Chanel, Balenciaga, Dior, and after she'd worn them once or twice, she'd send them

Alexei Brodovitch, "the courtly and paternalistic former White Russian cavalry officer," was art director at *Harper's Bazaar*

around in a limousine to her friends. What wasn't taken, she'd let us have a go at. Before she showed up at the magazine offices at 572 Madison Avenue every morning, she had read all the newspapers and stopped at the church on Madison and 68th for a quick prayer. "Do you suppose I could stand this job if I didn't go to church every morning?" she'd say.

Photographs were beginning to be included in art, and I worked with Alexei Brodovitch choosing photograph assignments, attending sittings, and selecting the many images that appeared in the magazine. "Surprise me," he'd say when he sent someone out on a shoot. The photographers loved him.

Diana Vreeland was the fashion editor. She wasn't beautiful but made herself look so good that everyone was struck by her. She had jet-black hair and a wonderful fashion sense. A woman who went to school with her told me all the girls would ask her, "What should I wear?" "What color suits me best?" We would go to her apartment to watch her get dressed. It took an hour and a half; she was so meticulous.

There was a snobbism to *Harper's Bazaar*. The society girls' mothers would call Mrs. Snow and say, "Oh, can't you give my daughter a job?" The debutante daughters would say, "Oh, I'll do anything"—which means you can't do anything.

This famous horseman from Old Westbury asked Mrs. Snow to hire his daughter. "Now, Dorothy," she said to me, "take this girl in your office." Well, my God, what a pest she was. She'd get on the phone and call her boyfriend in Paris. After a week, I said, "I can't get any work done with that girl around. She doesn't know a darn thing. Why don't you give her to the Fashion Department?" At least the girls in the Fashion Department worked hard; they had to drag all the bags to the fashion fittings and shoots.

We had a shoot at Louise Dahl Wolf's studio with the poet Edith Sitwell, who was about to begin an American lecture tour. We were to photograph her in this robelike dress of red velvet trimmed with gold that she had made for the tour. Miss Sitwell was a very tall woman, and the dress was very heavy and queenly. She was sitting on a chair looking at herself in the mirror. "I'll get the dress on you, Miss Sitwell," I said. I stood on a chair behind her and slipped it over her head. Then I realized I had put it on backwards and pulled it off. As the dress came off, so did her hair. She was completely bald. But she was very nice about it and invited me to tea afterwards at the Ritz.

Dahl Wolf was a horrible person, although if she loved you, she couldn't do enough for you. Alexei Brodovitch liked Richard Avedon very much better than her, and she was very jealous. That was the time of the rise of Richard Avedon, who had showed up at the office, twenty-six years old, just out of the merchant marines. He was a little spot of a fellow, always hopping about.

Avedon had a marvelous studio. He always had music playing and would serve tea in dainty white cups. Fred Astaire was often featured in the magazine because he was social, and Avedon was so pleased to photograph him. When he saw Fred Astaire used a necktie in place of a belt, he began doing the same thing.

He was wonderful at fashion photography, retouched the models' faces so you could never see a wrinkle. When Anna Magnani was scheduled to be photographed, we went to see her at the Waldorf-Astoria. She came out with her hair all done up and said, "It's taken me forty-nine years to get these wrinkles. I don't want one taken out." (On the other hand, when we photographed Bea Lillie,

Picking pictures for
Harper's Bazaar

John Huston

Merle Oberon (left)

Veronica Lake (center)

she complained, "Not only did you not take the wrinkles out, you put some in that weren't there.")

We were guided and somewhat restricted by the Hearst organization, which was headquartered on 57th Street. *Harper's Bazaar* reported on important literary, artistic, and theatrical figures and events of the period and was geared to this upscale, Waspy elite audience. But the Hearst people wanted to appeal to the mass audience, to have the circulation of *Good Housekeeping*.

One time I had to take over for the literary editor, who was in the hospital, and I bought a poem to go as a filler in the last page of the magazine. Mrs. Snow called me into the office. "Do you know you have put a pornographic poem in this magazine? Look at this." She pointed to a line in "The Postures of Love" by Louis Comfit: "He kissed her nape."

"Mrs. Snow, *nape* means 'neck.'"

"Oh." It was 57th Street. They had called her attention to it.

Another time, I wanted to do a piece on this black actor who was performing in whiteface. "Why is it we never feature any of the black personalities?" I asked Mrs. Snow.

She said, "Dorothy, you write a note to Fifty-seventh Street and ask them if you can do it." I got a long memo back saying the Hearst organization has no restrictions on anybody at all. In fact, the memo went on to say, the front page of the *Journal American* yesterday had a picture of little black children playing on the streets of Harlem. "Mrs. Snow, they say it's fine," I told her.

"Dorothy, are you stupid?" she said. "Can't you read between the lines?"

Around 1957, Carmel Snow was fired. The Hearst people didn't like all the literature, all the features she brought in. They got a niece of Mrs. Snow's who'd been an editor at *Good Housekeeping* to replace her.

They called her over to 57th Street to give her the news. When she came back to the office, Diana Vreeland said, "Tell me this, did they ever mention me as a successor?" Mrs. Snow said, "Your name was never mentioned."

"Who cares if I'm editor of *Harper's Bazaar*?" Mrs. Snow said. "I don't." But she did. It was her life.

She died a few years later. There is no doubt that the firing led to her death. Her funeral filled St. Patrick's Cathedral. Every one of the Jewish garment manufacturers who depended on Mrs. Snow to tell them what was coming in from Europe so they would know what was going to be fashionable—they all showed up. Her husband, who was in his eighties, was escorted by their four children. In less than six months, he married one of his hunting companions, a hardy-looking woman with dyed black hair. Mrs. Snow's sister was quite put out. "I do think Palen could have waited a little longer," she said.

Diana Vreeland went off to *Vogue* and was there for ten years before she went on to the Metropolitan Museum of Art to take charge of costumes.

Alexei Brodovitch, who was fired at the same time as Mrs. Snow, got drunk, ultimately lost his mind. I went to see him afterwards at Riker's Island in a kind of sanatorium.

But I will never forget the pair of them, Alexei Brodovitch and Carmel Snow, inspired and ruthless partners who illuminated publishing history.

PAULINE TRIGÈRE: Before the war, Paris was the capital of couture. On Seventh Avenue, they were making clothes to wear, to be warm. The few designers, if I can call them that, had nothing to do with fashion, really. But during the war, women couldn't go to Europe, and so the few people who were making couture became famous. And in those years after the war, we discovered that we had talent right here. We learned we were almost as good, or as good, or better than the Parisians. Seventh Avenue became great just at this moment, and New York began to become the capital of the world of fashion. It was a revolution.

ELEANOR LAMBERT: Before the war, people in the garment industry feared that if war came, people would stop buying clothes, and so the International Ladies' Garment Workers' Union and the managers of dress businesses formed an organization to encourage women to buy dresses. They began an advertising campaign, but it proved to be rather banal, with messages like "Aren't you ashamed that you don't have a new dress?" Stores such as Saks Fifth Avenue and Bergdorf Goodman protested that this campaign was wasted.

"What do you think would work?" the organizers asked the store executives.

"You ought to do it with suggestions through publicity."

I was asked to handle the job as publicist, and that was how the Dress Institute began. We organized spectacular fashion shows for charity and invited fashion editors from newspapers and magazines all over the country.

Through these events, the names and the personalities of the fashion designers we showcased became known.

The war did happen, and the French designers were wiped out for that period. American manufacturers, who had forced designers to copy French designs, had to let them do their own thing. It was during this time that the Dress Institute had the opportunity to convince the consumer of the worth of the American designers. By the time the war ended, they were recognized as the equal of the French.

PAULINE TRIGÈRE: I came to New York from Paris in 1937 with my mother and brother, my husband and our two sons. I had a visitor's visa for six weeks. I've stayed for more than sixty years.

Soon after we arrived, my brother, husband, and I took one of those double-decker buses down Fifth Avenue. We got off at 57th Street, walked downtown until we came to Saks Fifth Avenue, and walked back up to 57th Street. I fell in love with the city. "I'm not going anywhere. I want to stay," I told my husband.

"You're crazy," he said. But that was the beginning.

My mother was a dressmaker and my father had been a tailor so I knew how to make clothes. I decided I could do something on my own, but my husband wanted me to be a hausfrau. So we separated. The question that's often asked of me is, "Did you want to become a designer?"

I say, "No. I had to feed two kids."

My mother took care of my small children, and I got a job at Hattie Carnegie as assistant to a designer named Travis Banton. He sketched, and I made his muslins. He got paid three hundred dollars a week, I got paid sixty-five. He dressed Garbo and all those people; he was eating lunch at the Colony and would come back to work completely drunk.

Pauline Trigère,
couturiere
extraordinaire

Then came the seventh of December, 1941. A week later, Hattie's brother came in and said, "We're closing the business."

I took over half of the loft, and that's where I started in 1942, together with my brother, Robert. The rent was fifty dollars a month. When the other half of the loft—which had been occupied by Carnegie's embroiderer—became available, I took it over too. Now the rent was one hundred dollars. I had nothing, no money, no nothing. I pawned the two diamond clips my husband had given me when my sons were born.

We made eleven dresses out of wool crepe. I was my own model and my own cutter. The dresses were ready in March, with a wholesale price of about forty dollars. My brother put them in a suitcase and went by bus to stores all over the country.

My first customers were Nan Duskin in Philadelphia, Becky Blum in Chicago, Elizabeth Quinlan in Minneapolis, Amelia Gray in Los Angeles, and Martha Phillips in New York. These were all women who owned their firms; they gave their breath to their business. They knew their customers: if they are married, if they go dancing, if they have careers. Then we started selling to Saks Fifth Avenue and Bergdorf Goodman, also B. Altman, Lord & Taylor, Bonwit Teller.

ELEANOR LAMBERT: I had proposed to Coty—the French perfume company, which was one of my clients—that it sponsor a fashion award honoring American fashion. But the idea was turned down. Then Coty added some American executives, and Grover Whelan, who had worked in the administration of New York City mayor John Hylan, became its head. We connected.

"You know we're having a terrible time at Coty," he told me. "It's gone down so much from the days when it was the best perfume company in the world, cheapening, cheapening, cheapening. Our fragrances, which had been so eminent, are being sold in drugstores. What can we do that shows we belong in fashion?"

I thought of my original idea and told Mr. Whelan about it. "This is exactly what I mean," he said.

The first Coty American Fashion Critics Awards ceremony was held at the Metropolitan Museum of Art on January 22, 1943. We had a big by-invitation-only audience and a jury of fashion editors. The winner that year was Norman Norell; Lily Dache and John Fredericks won awards for hat design.

PAULINE TRIGÈRE: In 1949, I got my first Coty Award. I was the youngest one to win. In 1952, I won my second Coty. That was the same year that we moved to the beautiful, fabulous building—550 Seventh Avenue. Later on, Bill Blass, Oscar de la Renta, Donna Karan would all be in this building.

My brother and I were at 37 West 57th when we heard there was a terrific place available in 550 Seventh Avenue. In those days, you had to buy the lease. "Robert, let's not go," I said. "We haven't any money."

But we took the subway to 42nd Street, and we walked over to Seventh Avenue and 40th, and I saw that showroom, big, nice, with a platform like a stage. The rent was about four times what we were paying. And we had to pay twenty-one thousand dollars to the man to get the key. That night I couldn't sleep. Then I decided, young as we were, we should take it. I didn't know how we would pay the rent, but I knew we would.

The showroom and the designing room had air conditioning. The factory in the back had none. After a few months, the summer comes, and I see the people working at the machines with the sweat coming down on my clothes. We put in air conditioning. That August, one of the union representatives comes in. "You know you haven't paid the contractors."

"I know, I know. I have no money."

"Why don't you go to a bank and borrow some money."

"How?"

"There's a new bank on the corner at Thirty-ninth. They're only open a month, and they're looking for customers."

"A bank is looking for customers?" I said. I mean, I was so stupidly ignorant.

"I'll call the guy and make an appointment."

Soon after, a tall guy came into our showroom. "My name is Mr. McCarthy, Miss Trigère." He was the vice president of the bank. "Can I see the place?"

"It's nice and clean," I said. "We just moved in."

He looked all around, and then he said, "Do you have a statement?"

"A what? No, my brother takes care of that."

"Well, can you get one?"

"He's in San Francisco. I'll call him."

I walked him to the elevator, and he said, "It was nice meeting you, Miss Trigère. We'll see you next week with the statement. By the way, you really run a tight ship."

What does he mean by that? I wondered. It was such a peculiar expression.

The next week, I walked over to the bank with the statement. It was a very hot day. I was wearing a cute little beige suit and high heels, and as I crossed the street, my heels sank into the tar.

I go into the bank. Mr. McCarthy interrogates me like I'm in front of a judge. I answer the best I can. Finally he says to me "How much money do you think you need?"

"I don't know. Fifty thousand dollars?"

He said, "You'll never make it with fifty thousand. We'll give you seventy-five thousand."

I started to cry. It was my first loan. When I repaid it, he came to me and said, "Don't you need any more money? We can lend it to you." This bank became Marine Midland Bank, and Mr. McCarthy became a good business associate until he retired. I still get Christmas cards from him.

I always made clothes that women could wear at any time, classical things. I never made clothes to sweep the floor or show the *pupik* (navel). I only bought fabric that was the best and produced clothes made by the best workers I could get. I don't sketch. I drape and cut directly on the model with big scissors.

Fabric is my dictator. I would go to Paris every year to buy fabric, not to see the shows. We used to have our own shows—four, sometimes five a year. We could sit 150 people in my showroom by opening two doors. There used to be what we called market week when buyers from Chicago, San Francisco, Palm Beach would all come at the same time. They had a chance to see not only Trigère but all the New York designers. They would be invited, come to the showroom, sit down. I never was ready until the last minute, having to put a button on someplace. The models would come in holding a number, walk back and forth. Then the buyers would make appointments. That was it.

Two or three days later, the buyers would come back and see the racks: the evening clothes, the daytime clothes. We would have a model show the clothes again. Each buyer came to see the collection and buy directly.

In 1956, I put an ad for a model in the *New York Times*. About twenty women responded. One of them was black. I liked her style, I needed her, and I took her on. Well, it turned out I was the first one to engage a black model on Seventh Avenue. It was a revolution. A customer from Memphis told my brother, "I'm not going to buy any clothes modeled by a black."

"You don't have to," he said, and he escorted her out.

My brother always traveled around with the collection, but then somebody asked me to make a personal appearance. So I began traveling, and I learned Chicago was one customer, Atlanta was another one, Los Angeles yet another. When I went to Palm Beach for the first time and saw the sky—that was something. You think pink, pale green, not dark brown and black.

I got to know the Neiman Marcus brothers in Dallas. I became very friendly with Mr. Goodman of Bergdorf Goodman. When I say friendly, I mean I had him at my table when I gave dinner parties. I also became a very good friend of Adam Gimbel, who owned Saks Fifth Avenue. Adam loved to speak French, and he adored me. Sophie, who became his wife, made all those fabulous clothes.

HELEN O'HAGAN: Before the war, Sophie used to go to Paris and buy couture from designers. Saks would duplicate them, made-to-order. But once the war came, Sophie began designing herself. By the time the war was over, she was confident enough to continue her own work. She was the first American designer to appear on the cover of *Time* magazine because she went against Christian Dior's "New Look," even though she entertained him in her home.

PAULINE TRIGÈRE: I was not at all influenced by the "New Look." I continued doing the same thing. But there was a mood, some kind of feeling in the air when Dior started making the full skirts. New York copied the Dior skirt, but they made it half the size.

For a while, some houses depended on what they saw in Paris. They viewed the collections and bought two, three pieces. But then it stopped. The mood changed. You don't go to Paris to copy. Paris comes to New York to copy the sportswear.

Stars of the fashion scene (from left to right): Helen O'Hagan, Jerry Silverman, Sophie Gimbel, 1969

HELEN O'HAGAN: I came to New York from Charleston, South Carolina, in 1955, looking for a job as a photographer. I was visiting a friend of my father's who had a home in Sands Point and was renting a boathouse on her property to Slim Aarons, a photographer who worked for *Town and Country*. I called him. "Let me think about it," he said. But when I called him back, he said, "I have just the job for you. I just spoke with the Countess DeMun, who does publicity for Saks. She's desperate for someone." Grace DeMun interviewed me in Sophie Gimbel's couture salon, and I was hired on the spot as press assistant for a salary of sixty-five dollars a week.

Saks Fifth Avenue was one of the most elegant stores one could imagine. All the rooms were like beautiful drawing rooms in Europe. The walls of Sophie's salon had been painted by a Frenchman famous for painting interiors who mixed a special shade of blue he called Sophie-Blue. The salon had lovely sofas, French armchairs, and black lacquered coffee tables. And it was there, at 2:30 every afternoon, that Sophie showed to a clientele that included Mary Benny, the wife of Jack Benny; Marlene Dietrich; Estee Lauder; the Annenbergs; and Claudette Colbert. She had four models and two dressers who worked full-time, and workrooms that took up half of the tenth floor of Saks. In addition to the custom-made, Sophie did a ready-to-wear collection that was sold to other stores with the label "Sophie of Saks Fifth Avenue."

Saks was unique in that we had so many designers on the premises. There was Stephen Erklin, who did evening wear, and Miss Isabelle, who made custom sweaters with little diamond openings that showed the pattern of the dress they were worn over. There was also Tatiana du Plessix Liberman, the wife

Talking shop in the mid-1970s (from left to right): Calvin Klein, Helen O'Hagan, Paul Leblan, and Mildred Custin

of Alexander Liberman, editorial director for Condé Naste. Tatiana was a great friend of Sophie's and designed custom hats for her. We even had two children's-wear designers.

In those days, even in the ready-to-wear department, most of the clothes were kept in a back stockroom. The salons had tea stands and beautiful furniture. Women would come in, and the sales ladies would go in the back and bring out clothes to show them. It was not rack-city at all.

The designers would ship their garments to Saks without a label because you were not selling a particular designer, you were selling Saks Fifth Avenue. The "Saks Fifth Avenue" label was sewn on the side. Once I received a letter from a young ensign. He saved all his money to buy his wife a dress from Saks Fifth Avenue. At Christmas, he gave her this beautiful Saks box. She opened it, and there was a beautiful Saks dress, but no label.

I wrote back, "I'm sure you'll find the label sewn in the inseam. However, I will be more than happy to be sure you have enough labels." I sent him a box. She must have put one in every garment she owned.

Although he did not let them put their labels in the garments until the late sixties, Adam Gimbel was not against designers. Fifty percent of our garments came from designers in the garment center. Adam started out as Saks vice president when it opened in 1924. Less than a year after the store opened, Horace Saks, who was president, died, and Adam took over. He was a renaissance man, spoke French and German, was a great sportsman, and read three books a week, always one in a different language. And he had an eye like no one else. (He actually had only one eye; the other had been lost when he was a child.)

When Adam came into the store in the morning, he'd leave his coat and hat in the men's hat department on the first floor. At night, he'd walk down from his office on the eighth floor, stopping to check every floor on his way down. He prided himself on having the most beautiful, elegant store. "America's largest specialty store" was what he called it. Adam didn't want to hear about Saks 34th, which was a real cheap department store and had no relationship to Saks Fifth Avenue. Neither did Gimbel's, which was run by his cousin Bruce Gimbel, who also trained at Saks.

A few years after I arrived, Grace DeMun was let go. I went up to Sophie and said, "I don't know what to do. Grace wants me to leave with her."

She said, "You wait right here." She called Adam. I was in the fitting room, and I could see his feet going past. Then I heard him say, "You tell Helen I'm going to give her six months, and if she does the job, it's hers. She won't get an increase; she'll have to work for it."

And I did. I directed all the public relations; I produced and directed every fashion show. And when we started new stores in places like Chicago, Atlanta, Palo Alto, it was my job to go out in the market, meet the community, and open the store. I would have breakfast meetings with women—there weren't many working women in those days. A Saks Fifth Avenue in their city was so exciting to them. "Oh, we're going to get a little piece of New York," they'd say.

In the late 1950s, Saks buyers began going to the shows in Europe, buying couture, and copying them. They were line-for-line copies, often in the original fabrics. By the early sixties, Saks was including designer labels in their clothes. Adam had discovered Anne Klein. He was so impressed with her, he put in a boutique of her sportswear, the first sportswear boutique in the store.

Our buyers had the best eyes in New York. Nevertheless, every so often there'd be a big mistake. The midi skirt of 1969 was a bomb. Stores had racks of them. Employees were told, "We will let you buy them at cost if you wear them," but it didn't work.

After Adam and Sophie retired in 1969 (Adam died that same year), it was up to me to keep the Saks Fifth Avenue image in front of the public. I did it by always remembering what Adam wanted. Fifth Avenue is so important a part of the name. Any time a magazine wrote an article and referred to us as Saks, I wrote them: "The name is registered as Saks Fifth Avenue."

There were so many beautiful department stores when I first came to New York. I loved the feeling of B. Altman's, the high, high ceilings, the old-fashioned wide aisles. But that's gone along with Peck and Peck, Best & Company, Bonwit Teller. But Saks Fifth Avenue has carried on even to this day.

I was blessed to have known and worked with Sophie and Adam Gimbel. I spent my summer weekends with them, I traveled with them. It was a whole life. They helped form my taste. You'd go to a dinner in their beautiful town house on East 64th Street, the men in black tie, the women in evening dresses. And after dinner, all the ladies would get in the elevator and go up to Sophie's bedroom for their coffee while the men would have their coffee in the dining room and smoke their cigars.

"For the most part, I never changed my style." Helen O'Hagan

Helen O'Hagan with
Mme. Revillon of
Revillon Furs

I was a girl who hated fashion. I grew to love clothes because of Sophie. I'd sit and watch her fit, see a dress begin in muslin. The first Sophie suit I had was the most beautiful purpley blue and white tweed, hourglass waist-line, full tweed skirt. For the most part, I never changed my style. I found an old photo from Charleston. I'm in a pink buttoned-down shirt, a navy blazer, charcoal gray shorts. All that's changed is now I wear slacks.

HOWARD KISSEL: I first came to Fairchild Publications in 1967, working for the *Daily News Record*, which covered menswear and textiles. It was there that I became aware of this thing they put out called *Women's Wear Daily*. It had begun, I believe, in the teens when the ready-to-wear industry sprouted. As the women's-wear garment industry grew, *Women's Wear Daily* grew.

By attrition, I became editor of the arts page at *Women's Wear Daily*, and I soon realized it put me in the best place to observe New York. They were launching this magazine, *W*, and John Fairchild, I assume, came up with the brilliant idea of making *W* a kind of offshoot of *Women's Wear Daily*. Since there would be nothing in *W* that didn't come from *Women's Wear Daily*, they didn't have to pay us for something they used two times.

Women's Wear Daily reported on the movers and shakers related to the fashion industry. Pat Buckley was key; she was like the leader of the pack. There was also Mica Ertegun, the wife of Ahmet Ertegun—the head of Atlantic Records—and a very good friend of Jerry Robbins in the New York City Ballet. They were part of the upper crust. By focusing on and cultivating women like these, *Women's Wear Daily* made itself into an important thing to read.

These people we were writing about were dubbed the Cat Pack. They had the Cat Pack kiss, which is essentially the air kiss. There was the Cat Pack game, a board game where you advanced or retreated in society. *WWD* had this thing called "They Are Wearing," where a photographer would go out on the street to see what people were wearing. Once they had a photo showing Jacqueline Onassis in a short skirt with her knees crossed out—in other words, telling her she shouldn't be wearing something this short. It was all totally silly. We had fun because we didn't take ourselves seriously, but the rest of the press did.

A man named Peter Davidson Dibble set the tone for the publication; it was a very queenly style. We had a double-spread thing with editorial

comments and certain things would be in all cap letters, bold. It was very, very funny. There was a family named Crespi who did public relations in Rome. In the late sixties, the Crespis did something to irritate *Women's Wear Daily*, so the magazine devoted two pages to maligning the Crespis, saying they were having a terrible time marrying off their younger daughter. It got to the point where the Crespis sued for damages. The daughter, Pilar Crespi, was gorgeous; a few years later she was a fixture in society. They were not having trouble marrying her off. But that was *Women's Wear Daily*; they were constantly having feuds with people.

Then in the early seventies John Fairchild moved to New York and began seeing all these people we were making fun of. Since he wanted to get invited places, we had to suck up to them. Where *Women's Wear Daily* was outrageous in the sixties, by the seventies it had become much more establishment. We were invited to many places because people saw us as very chic. That was when the fashion designers were becoming celebrities in their own right.

I think John Fairchild is the godfather of contemporary journalism because a lot of the horseshit that you now see in the *Times*, especially in its "Styles" section, comes directly from what *Women's Wear Daily* did in the sixties and seventies. In an essay that appeared in something called *The Grand Street Reader* some years ago, a disgruntled *Times* reporter named John Hess said he knew the *Times*'s days were numbered when he saw a copy of *Women's Wear Daily* on Abe Rosenthal's desk every morning.

JANE BEVANS: My mother, Tami Apt, was a businesswoman, a designer, and probably the first traveling saleswoman who went around the country. Even though she always said, "I hate the rag business," I knew she loved it.

I went down to her place on 35th Street between Fifth and Sixth a lot. There was the showroom where the models came out in their beautiful gowns and outfits and walked and twirled around to show the buyers the garments. And there were the people in the back who were sewing and cutting on the machines. I worked in the garment center as a showroom model and a salesperson right out of high school. It seemed natural that I would go into the industry. College was not a subject in my household. But walking around in my underwear and in bathrobes in front of people all the time was very uncomfortable. It was only when I took charge of my life and said, "Wait, who wants to be part of this screwball world?" that I got out of it.

PAULINE TRIGÈRE: When I first moved to 550 Seventh Avenue, the tailors and sewers were mostly Polish, Hungarian, and Russian Jews; a few were Italian. I would walk out onto Seventh Avenue at noon, and nobody was speaking English. I learned Yiddish from hearing it spoken by the garment workers. Then over the years, slowly but surely, these people disappeared. They didn't want their children to be tailors or dressmakers; they wanted them to become lawyers and accountants.

SAM BERNSTEIN: When I came back from the war, a man in my brother-in-law's family recommended me to Schwartz, Rosenzweig and Schifmann, a shop on 29th Street that made fur trimmings for cloth coats. I was hired as a nailer. My job was to get ahold of the fur collar, stretch it, nail it on a board and wait till it dried out. It was a dirty job, and in the summer, it was unbearable. The showroom was air conditioned but not the factory. You sweated a lot over the skins.

We were working on beaver. Different places worked on different kinds of furs. Mink was the best, Alaskan seal was also high end. Most of the little shops like the one I worked in were in the twenties and thirties between Seventh and Eighth Avenues. They were owned by Jews, although more and more Greeks were coming into the industry. The bigger, more expensive places were on Seventh Avenue.

I took the Sea Beach Express in Brooklyn at seven o'clock every morning to 34th Street. Then I got off and took the local back one stop to 29th Street. I worked from 8:00 in the morning until 5:30 at night. At twelve o'clock, the shop chairman would ring a bell, and we stopped for lunch, which we always ate in the factory. Sometimes we took an hour; if it was busy, we took only a half hour and then started working again.

We punched in and out on a time clock. At the end of the week, they figured out how many hours you worked and paid you cash in a little brown envelope. But they always tried to cheat you, like if you worked thirty-seven hours, they'd pay you for thirty-five. And who dared to argue? It wasn't a union shop. They could fire a union man and hire a non-union man. I thought, What am I going to do if I lose my job? I was always afraid I wouldn't be able to make a living.

POLLY BERNSTEIN: The man that recommended Sam for the job used to collect the leftover pieces of fur from different shops and get Chinese people to piece them together into cheaper garments and quilt covers. There were a lot of Chinese immigrants in the fur district who did that kind of piecework. Everybody tried to grab work from everybody else. "How much do you pay? I'll work cheaper for you." They'd bring the pieces home in a bundle, make the wife and kids work at home.

I worked at home for a while, sewing collars for a small shop. Then I began doing piecework on 37th Street. I got paid per collar. One day, this man said to me, "What are you doing here, you dumbbell, working for nothing? Come with me, I'll give you a job that pays for your work." He didn't like the owner of the shop because he took advantage of poor people.

Through him I got a job in one of the big department stores as a saleswoman in the brassiere section. A department store was clean, the work was not manual. But it was the same idea. If the boss liked you, he let you be. But if he didn't, you were out of work. There were a lot of buyers who took advantage of the young salesgirls. One had about five girls. I remember a young woman who told him, "I love my husband, why do I need you?" But she ended up going with him. Everybody knew from ten to eleven she wasn't around.

SAM BERNSTEIN: I spent my entire working life in the fur district. Every spring there was the slack season, and there was no work. Those were very bad times. We tried to pick up piecework here and there. Later on there was unemployment compensation, which helped a little bit. By the time I retired in the mid 1970s, the industry was mostly Greek. The union was giving a small pension, but most of the shops were still not air conditioned.

I did think of going to evening college after the war on the GI Bill of Rights, but somehow it didn't work out. I was afraid I wouldn't be able to hold on to the job if I went to school. But I knew I didn't want my children to work in a factory. I wanted them to be professionals. When my son was accepted at City College, we were so proud and happy. I knew he wouldn't end up in a shop like me.

Chapter Five

Sanctuaries in the City

LACONIA SMEDLEY: Black people are very quick to pick up on a person's spirit. You can be beat down, left out, lynched. But when you come together, you're saying I am a child of God and I have worth. You can always resort to that space, that one feeling, that one idea that you can overcome. That's what you hear in our music all the time.

Although I was not a churchgoer, I visited the churches of Harlem because of the music. There were great voices in the choirs when I came to New York in the 1950s. Many of the singers were classically trained. They performed Handel's *Messiah*, Mendelssohn's *Elijah*, and Bach chorales like they did downtown.

The choirs also sang spirituals, the older songs from the time of slavery. Professor Edward Boatner, who led the thousand-voice National Baptist Convention Choir, was known for arranging the spirituals he had learned as a child. The slaves couldn't write but they composed collectively. It was the way they were able to express their feelings and communicate without the overseers knowing they were sending messages. Once I came into a church before services had begun, and I saw an

"Although I was not a churchgoer, I visited the churches of Harlem because of the music."

elderly woman sitting by herself and humming a pentatonic phrase in a minor key. People started to come in, and at first they were very quiet. Then they started humming along, and before you knew it, there was four-part harmony. It was very improvisational, the same kind of collective composing that had created spirituals.

FATHER PETER COLAPIETRO: Most Catholic boys growing up in the fifties and early sixties felt they would want to be a priest. It was "I wanna be a fireman," "I wanna be an astronaut," "I wanna be a priest." I went to the seminary from 1965 to 1970, but I didn't have a calling at that time.

I did get involved in programs under church auspices, however: Summer in the City, Full Circle. We were lower-middle-class kids from the Bronx who would go down to the projects and the Henry Street Settlement on the Lower East Side and work with the kids there. This was something you were supposed to do.

Almost all the people were Hispanic. They had nothing; the job situation was bad. There was so much misery in their lives, but when they got together they could really enjoy themselves. They would pool their money and roast a pig in the street. Drugs, of course, were a problem, although not as bad as it got to be by the mid seventies.

The summer of 1971, one of my buddies told me, "We're doing volunteer work for this priest, Bruce Ritter. He has these apartments and takes in kids, and we rehabilitate the apartments with Sheetrock and fix doors and stuff. Do you want to come down?"

I said, "Sure."

There were about thirty kids in apartments in an abandoned tenement on 7th Street between Avenues C and D in Alphabet City. They had another building across the street where they had their cooking facilities, and we would eat cafeteria style down there together. This was the forerunner of Covenant House.

Bruce Ritter was very affable, friendly. But he was a Franciscan. A Franciscan is supposed to live in a community, and he was living by himself in his own apartment. I didn't know if I liked this.

Covenant House did some great, great things. But once Bruce Ritter got into trouble because of accusations from a couple of kids, he left. All you got to do is make the accusations. A nun came in and she's built the place up. I

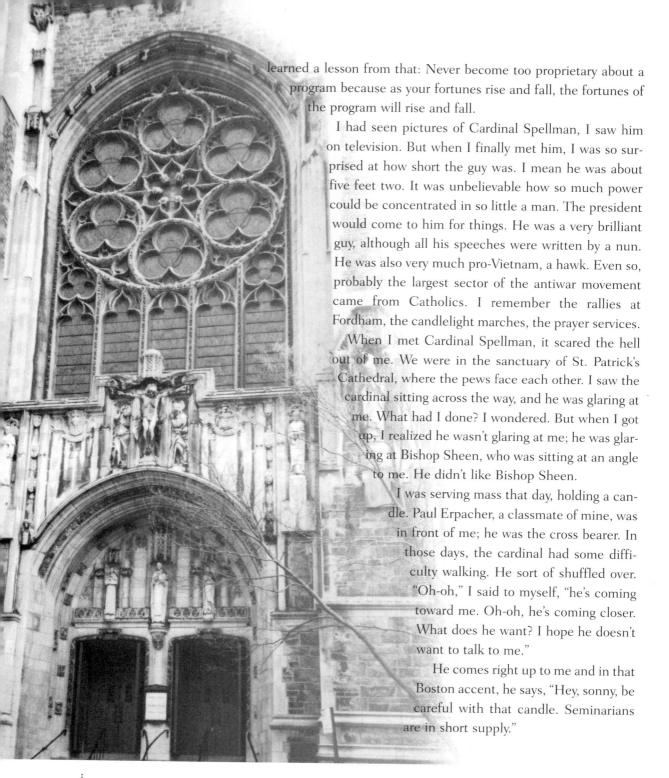

learned a lesson from that: Never become too proprietary about a program because as your fortunes rise and fall, the fortunes of the program will rise and fall.

I had seen pictures of Cardinal Spellman, I saw him on television. But when I finally met him, I was so surprised at how short the guy was. I mean he was about five feet two. It was unbelievable how so much power could be concentrated in so little a man. The president would come to him for things. He was a very brilliant guy, although all his speeches were written by a nun. He was also very much pro-Vietnam, a hawk. Even so, probably the largest sector of the antiwar movement came from Catholics. I remember the rallies at Fordham, the candlelight marches, the prayer services.

When I met Cardinal Spellman, it scared the hell out of me. We were in the sanctuary of St. Patrick's Cathedral, where the pews face each other. I saw the cardinal sitting across the way, and he was glaring at me. What had I done? I wondered. But when I got up, I realized he wasn't glaring at me; he was glaring at Bishop Sheen, who was sitting at an angle to me. He didn't like Bishop Sheen.

I was serving mass that day, holding a candle. Paul Erpacher, a classmate of mine, was in front of me; he was the cross bearer. In those days, the cardinal had some difficulty walking. He sort of shuffled over. "Oh-oh," I said to myself, "he's coming toward me. Oh-oh, he's coming closer. What does he want? I hope he doesn't want to talk to me."

He comes right up to me and in that Boston accent, he says, "Hey, sonny, be careful with that candle. Seminarians are in short supply."

St. Patrick's was always a sideshow kind of place. Because it was in Manhattan, it had all this pedestrian traffic. I remember all the movement, people walking around, walking around, walking around, and the strong smell of incense and beeswax from the burning candles.

In the back of the cathedral was a wax statue of Pope Pius XII in his white cassock. Apparently these clothes were a gift to Cardinal Spellman from the pope, who was a friend of his, and when the pope died in 1958, the cardinal had this wax statue of him cast. They protected it by putting it in a glass case because people would invariably try to destroy the thing, some looney bird would come along and try to knock the pope's head off.

Even as a kid, I knew Holy Cross Church was sort of an oasis on 42nd Street. It's the oldest church on 42nd Street from river to river, built in 1852; it caught fire and got rebuilt in 1867, then was redesigned in the 1880s by Louis Comfort Tiffany. What interested me the most was this big fluorescent cross that stands perpendicular to the front of the church. At first I didn't think it was a Catholic church. We don't do that—it's like Elmer Gantry. Still, you don't expect to see a church on 42nd Street with the buses, and the smells, and the noise. People pass by and say, "There's a church over there?" They come in and they're surprised to hear Gregorian chants.

We have a prayer called the Novena—*novena* means "nine"— where you say a particular prayer nine times, nine weeks in a row, nine days in a row. At the parish here, we had the Miraculous Medal Novena for peace, which is dedicated to Mary. During and after the war, through the seventies, the place would be packed. There'd be people out on the sidewalk. It would be broadcast over the radio.

Before I returned to the seminary in 1973, I worked as a bartender and ditch digger. There's nothing worse than digging a hole in the middle of a Manhattan street on an August afternoon when the temperature is ninety-five degrees and you're down ten feet in the ground, kissing a steam pipe. We worked very, very hard for $5.95 an hour. That was a lot of money back then.

All the men I worked with came from Calabria, Italy, and spoke very little English. They'd bring their lunch along. We had a coffee break at ten and a beer break at two, when you'd really be dragging. These guys would sit there, drink their Rheingold or Ballantine beer out of a quart brown glass, and it revivified them. Then they'd go back to work for another two hours.

We had a job downtown on Wall and Beaver Streets putting in sidewalk walls, big boxes where the transformers go. You couldn't get a machine down there because of the pedestrian and vehicular traffic. So this guy named John got down in that hole and steadily, steadily, for about four hours, dug that hole. Rhythmically, he didn't even appear to break a sweat. But I know it was hard work because he swung a shovel of dirt weighing at least ten pounds up ten feet. John was forty-eight years old but he looked like he was sixty. He had been doing this kind of work for years.

I did this kind of work for about six months. Later on, I would see those guys and say to myself "How the hell did I do that?" But as they say in Yiddish, *Mehabt machen a leiben* (You got to make a living).

I was ordained in 1976 by Cardinal Cooke. It's all a blur except for one point in the ceremony when we had the prayer of litany, where you mention a saint's name and say, "Pray for us, St. Michael," "Pray for us, St. Thomas." Traditionally people kneel for that. But the guys who were being ordained would lay prone on the floor of the cathedral. The only thing I remember is getting up after lying prone on the floor of the sanctuary and seeing condensation marks.

Cardinal Cooke wasn't as visible as Cardinal Spellman. He was more behind the scenes. He benefited from Spellman's power. I benefited from Spellman's method of fund-raising: You find out who has the money and you ask him for it.

HOWARD KISSEL: When the Reverend James Parks Morton took over at the Cathedral of St. John the Divine on Amsterdam and 112th in the early seventies, they resumed work on the building, which had stopped some time before. The thought was that they were going to work on the church instead of giving the money to the poor, but they would employ people from the neighborhood and teach them skills so that the church would become a community center. Reverend Morton's idea was that the church should be at the center of the community. He said, if there's a material emptiness, that is a vacuum the spiritual and artistic can fill.

JOHN TAURANAC: For my money, Grace Church at 10th Street and Fourth Avenue is the finest Gothic Revival church in the city. It was the first architectural commission of James Renwick II, who was a faithful member of the church until he died in the 1890s. He did everything except the deeper altar that is there now, which was done by Heins and LaFarge, the architects of the subway. In the late nineteenth century, Grace Church was the social church. Edith Wharton wrote about it. People bought pews like you buy a co-op.

Although I went to school at Grace Church, on Sundays we attended St. James Episcopalian Church on 71st and Madison, where I'd sit in my wool suit and scratch. In the late nineteenth century, the church had to decide whether to build St. James east of Park Avenue and be a church for "the people" or on proper Madison Avenue and be an upscale church for the rich. They opted for Madison Avenue, and in their little history they are perfectly straightforward about the decision that was made. I always felt absolutely ostracized there.

RABBI DAN ALDER: The Brotherhood Synagogue on Gramercy Park was originally a Quaker meetinghouse that is believed to have been one of the stops on the underground railroad.

In 1965, the Quakers, who had another meetinghouse nearby, decided to sell the building to a developer who planned to erect a thirty-story apartment house. But local residents were able to get the newly established Landmarks Preservation

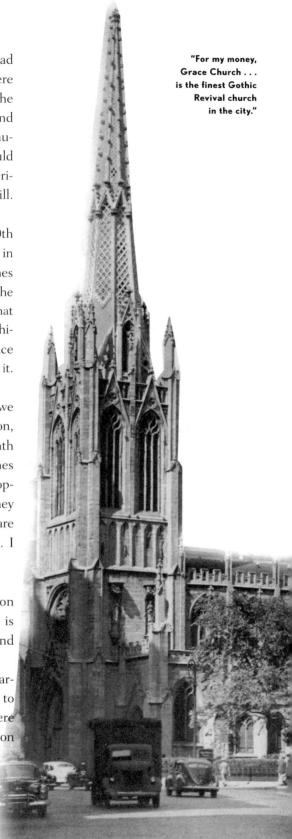

"For my money, Grace Church . . . is the finest Gothic Revival church in the city."

Commission to designate it a city landmark, and a group of neighborhood people bought it with the idea of turning it into a center for the performing arts. When that did not work out, they sold it to the United Federation of Teachers.

It's now 1974. The real estate market is down. The UFT finds the building unsuitable and puts it up for sale. Coincidentally the Brotherhood Synagogue, which has been without a home for a year, learns the building is available and is able to get it for a good price. But it's in a terrible state of disrepair. James Stuart Polshek, Dean of the School of Architecture at Columbia, and the contracting firm of Lawrence Held and Son volunteer their services. A wellspring of community support comes from non-Jews as well as Jews. The Epiphany Roman Catholic Church welcomes the Brotherhood Synagogue into the neighborhood. The Calvary–St. George's Parish Episcopal Church invites our rabbi, Irving Block, to preach at a Sunday-morning service. And on April 6, 1975, our Torahs are carried into the sanctuary.

The Brotherhood Synagogue in Gramercy Park, originally a Quaker meetinghouse, is believed to have been one of the stops on the underground railroad.

That was the beginning of the Brotherhood Synagogue in Gramercy Park. But the congregation's actual beginning took place some twenty-one years earlier in a Greenwich Village Presbyterian church. It was the vision of Rabbi Block, my predecessor, working with the Reverend Dr. Jesse Stitt, minister of the Village Presbyterian Church on West 13th Street. For two decades, they and their congregations not only shared a building, which was unusual enough in those days, but had a joint board and conducted cultural and social-action events together. It was a real covenant of brotherhood.

The Village Presbyterian Church was built in 1846 on land once owned by the Spanish and Portuguese synagogue Shearith Israel, the oldest Jewish congregation in New York. From 1949 to 1953, a congregation of Reform Jews rented space from the church until they were able to establish a synagogue of their own. But a very young Rabbi Block, who was involved with this congregation, had an idea of creating a new synagogue that would equally share a facility with a church in a true act of brotherhood, a notion that Reverend Stitt and his congregation embraced.

The union turned out to be quite simple. An ark was recessed into the wall of the church's altar, and above it "Love Thy Neighbor As Thyself" was inscribed. A sign on the gate outside the main sanctuary read "One House Serving Two Faiths." The building served as a synagogue on the Jewish Sabbath and holy days, as a church on Sundays and days of Christian observance. Members of both congregations attended each other's services. The rabbi and minister spoke to each other's congregation.

This joint venture tapped into a powerful feeling that arose after the Second World War with the birth of the United Nations, National Brotherhood Week, the National Conference of Christians and Jews. As a concept, brotherhood was pretty cutting-edge. And it was somehow fitting that people in Greenwich Village, who were generally more progressive, would take to this idea.

Still, Rabbi Block and Reverend Stitt were an anomaly—the rabbi and the minister who were friends. People were moved by the picture of the two of them standing side by side. Articles about them appeared in the *New York Times*. Invitations to tell their story came from all over.

The rabbi and minister appeared on television, not only religious programs but popular shows like *I've Got a Secret* and NBC's quiz show *The Big Surprise*, hosted by Mike Wallace. For their category, they picked religion—the rabbi

taking questions about Christianity, the minister about Judaism. They won ten thousand dollars, which they donated to the work of their congregations.

This beautiful arrangement began to unravel in the summer of 1971 when Dr. Stitt retired. He died several months later, and the Brotherhood Synagogue said Kaddish for him for the entire year. Sadly, the new minister appointed by the Presbyterian Minister's Council was a man who clearly did not share the same brotherhood values as his predecessor. By 1974, the situation had deteriorated so badly that the Jewish congregation left the premises. Ironically, the pastor resigned the following year, and soon after, the Presbytery of New York dissolved the Village Presbyterian Church and sold the building. In a fate not unlike that of the Quaker meetinghouse, this house of worship came up against landmark regulations, as it was located in a landmarked district. From the outside, it still looks like a Greek Revival church with six Doric columns. But inside, a sanctuary that seated eight hundred has been converted into apartments.

KEN LIBO: My rediscovery of my Jewish roots began when I came to New York in the early 1960s. I'm not a New York Jew by birth. Rather, I grew up in what I like to think of as an American shtetl. What is an American shtetl? It is usually a Jewish community in a town of maybe two thousand people that pretty much re-creates the warp and the woof of shtetl life in Eastern Europe. So I had an intimacy with Jewish life. I knew about the kosher butcher, I knew about the cheder, I knew about gefilte fish, which we had on Friday. Both of my parents were Yiddish speaking, and I felt as though I'd grown up in a never-ending Yiddish play in which there was no first act, no last act. You always came in the middle and people were always yelling at each other just as they did on the Yiddish stage.

I finished college, my navy career, and came to New York in the early 1960s. I wasn't sure what I wanted to do so I joined the international department of Bankers Trust and stayed there for four or five years. That was the time when banks were just beginning to open up to ethnic groups.

By the mid sixties, I realized I didn't have any talent for that kind of work. I began teaching at City College, where I met Irving Howe and became chief researcher for *World of Our Fathers*.

Something told me the place to begin researching was the secondhand bookstores on Fourth Avenue, which are now practically all gone. I would go there religiously, look through everything in their Judaica sections and find books that nobody knew about. Many were vanity press, but for our purposes they were invaluable because they described the life of the immigrant and children of the immigrant at the turn of the century better than anyone else. One of them in particular was by Sophie Ruskay, who wrote a wonderful book about what it was like to be a little girl growing up on East Broadway in 1910, what kind of games she played, what it was like in her house, what school was like. I found memoirs written by these Jewish political hacks who worked for the Irish politicos. They told what it was like to work for the Ahearn gang, which controlled Tammany politics on the Lower East Side until the 1930s, because the Jews knew if they voted for an Irishman they'd be better off than if they voted for a fellow Jew. Irving had given me a budget so I bought these books, which ranged from one to eight dollars. I would come home with fifteen at a time, and he was delighted with them.

There were maybe a dozen stores, all owned by Jews who were book lovers, carrying out the tradition of love of the written word from the sacred into the secular. Very few of them had college educations. The stores were very cramped, there were tens of thousands of books in each of them, but the owners knew where everything was.

Before coming to New York, I had a rather flip idea of my Jewishness. I was not terribly respectful of Judaism, no more than Alexander Portnoy was. I was rather resentful of my mother being overprotective. I was ashamed of my father, a *kleyner mentsch*, who—although he had mastered the mechanics of the English language—spoke with an accent. I wanted very much to be mainstream American. Israel was but a speck in the eye of world Judaism when I was born in 1937, so the attitude Jews have today about being Jewish, which came about largely because of the success of the State of Israel, is very different from the attitude I had when I was growing up, which was like that of the military: "Don't ask, don't tell."

Coming to New York with that kind of baggage, I discovered Jews predominate in New York. As Lenny Bruce said, "Even the *goyem* in New York are Jewish." I would go to Jewish restaurants like Ratner's from time to time and have the experience of being waited on by Jewish waiters who would give people a hard time.

"What kind of soup do you want, Mr. Fancy-Dancy?"

"Potato soup."

"You want to live to tomorrow?"

I hadn't been aware of this carrying on before. But I loved it. To me, this was life on the wing.

HOWARD KISSEL: An edition of *Fortune* that came out around 1960 entirely devoted to New York City included an article entitled "The Jewish Elan." We know the Luce magazines were not known for their philo-Semitism. So for *Fortune* to acknowledge the Jewish motor of New York was remarkable.

The Jews themselves were busy assimilating until the late sixties. Around 1969, the Jewish Museum on Fifth and 93rd, which had been a haven for avant-garde art and had little or nothing to do with Jews, held an exhibit on the Lower East Side. That was the busiest the museum had ever been. It was a big turning point, the first time the Jews stopped fleeing the legacy of the Lower East Side and embraced the notion.

Chapter Six

High Culture

or
"Who the Hell Is de Kooning?"

HIGH CULTURE

HILTON KRAMER: The thing I very quickly discovered when I came to New York in 1950, and which continued to both interest and baffle me all during the fifties, was the enormous role played by psychoanalysis. It seemed everybody I met in the academic world, in the literary world, in the art world, was in analysis. I couldn't understand how they could afford it because most of the people in those worlds didn't have any real money, and the going rate in those days was twenty-five dollars an hour. I knew people who went three or four times a week.

In the mid fifties I got to know the art critic Clement Greenberg. I knew he was in analysis, and one day when we both had had sufficient quantity to drink, I asked him, "How long has this been going on?"—meaning the role of psychoanalysis in the lives of educated people.

He said, "Well, that depends on whether you were in the army" (which he had been).

I said, "What do you mean?"

And he said, "Well, if you were in the war, it's been going on since 1945, but if you weren't in the war, it's probably been going on since the Hitler-Stalin pact in 1939."

Clem didn't elaborate; he tended to be very laconic. But he meant that quite seriously. When disillusion set in with Stalin, the Soviet Union, and Marxism, people switched from Marx to Freud or his followers. The bourgeoisie remained the enemy, but instead of class warfare, it became war between parents and children. Instead of fighting on the barricades, you were fighting on the couch, excavating the past and demonizing your parents.

Jackson Pollock was in analysis for years and years, first Freudian, then Jungian analysis. A lot of good it did him. I remember a breakup of a romance of my own with this girl I was quite mad for because of something I said about psychoanalysis. "All this time you've just been pretending to be well adjusted," she said.

Psychoanalysis was going on in other parts of the country, but the heart of it was in New York. Even though it happened much more in this country than in Europe, a lot of the analysts were European, and New York had a very European atmosphere in those days.

HOWARD KISSEL: A dear friend of mine left Vienna the day of the Anschluss and came to her brother, who had an apartment on 115th and Broadway. She still lives there with the family furniture they were somehow

> "New York had a very European atmosphere in those days."

able to bring from Vienna. I used to go to Vic and Katie's Viennese Restaurant
on the Upper West Side, which was run by a couple who came here in the
thirties; they served Wiener schnitzel and all those sorts of things.

And then there was the pair of sisters from Germany I became friends
with. The older was statuesque, so beautiful; the younger was a little *zaftig*
but more sensual. In March 1969, they asked me to be their escort to the
opera. If I would rent a tuxedo, they would pay for the tickets. I didn't get it
at the time, but afterwards I pieced together that the older of the girls was
being kept by a married man who had provided the tickets but for obvious
reasons wasn't able to go to the opera with her.

We saw *Il Trovatore*. It was one of the great performances: Leontyne Price
in her prime, Grace Bumbry in her prime, Placido Domingo in his first season, Zuban Mehta, who was sublime. Our seats were in the orchestra of the
old Met on Broadway between 39th and 40th, which was quite a thrill as I
was used to standing room for $1.75. The older sister wore a kind of linen
brocade gown that was just so elegant, and the younger a kind of Moroccan
pajamas, which was a little shocking as pants on ladies were not yet com-
mon. I was there in my tuxedo with my unruly hair, thinking I looked like a
young conductor.

As we marched up the stairs during the intermission, we were a very
impressive sight. We passed a woman, who was clearly from the upper rungs
of society, wearing a dress that came down like a bell with layers of chin-
chilla. She was engaged in conversation with someone, but as we moved in
her direction, she nodded at us. It was one of the most glamorous evenings
of my life.

STANLEY DRUCKER: When I joined the New York Philharmonic in 1948,
nearly all the musicians were European—German, Italian, French, Russian.
Outside of the Lewisohn Stadium concerts, there wasn't much summer
playing, and the musicians would go back to Europe just to soak up the
atmosphere. Musicians were very individual in those days. They were all
ethnics, characters; they had a certain personality.

HILTON KRAMER: Classical music was totally different in New York than in
any other place because of the sheer population of European émigrés. If you
went to Carnegie Hall or Washington Irving High School on Irving Place,

where they had wonderful chamber music concerts, a large percentage of the audience would come with musical scores that they would follow. There was a big central European—German, Austrian, Hungarian—element in that audience; they were properly dressed, musically sophisticated, and harsh judgers of performance. Many of the musicians had the same background. These were people who had gotten out of Europe when Hitler came to power, and it was a tremendous enrichment to the cultural world in New York.

The New School was actually founded in the twenties, but it really didn't get going until the thirties when it had all these émigrés. It was virtually an enclave for them.

The faculty at the Institute of Fine Arts at New York University was almost like a German enclave for a time and largely Jewish. Virtually the entire surrealist movement came to New York from Paris because of the Nazi occupation, and that emigration affected the emergence of what came to be called the New York School—the abstract expressionists. Jackson Pollock famously said, "It's been tremendously important for these European avant-garde artists to have come here because they spurred us on." If you look at what Pollock was doing in the thirties, he was a provincial artist.

Paris had been the art capital of the world, and when Paris was occupied by the Nazis, New York—much to the shock of American artists—suddenly found that if there was going to be an immediate future for modernist art in the world, it was going to happen here. And that has an effect on artists. They try harder; they no longer consider themselves underdogs. They feel it's their turn. The emigration had a very galvanizing effect on all those artists. Abstract expressionism would not have happened without the war.

WALDO RASMUSSEN: Because of the connection that was forged between European and American artists, American art became more radical, more open to different trends. The invention of that first generation of abstract expressionists was stronger than anything that was happening anyplace else in the world. It was heroic; it had heart and energy. In Pollock and Newman and Rothko there is a very definite sense of the tragic. There was a lot of tragedy going on with them, troubled lives.

JOAN WASHBURN: After *Life* magazine did some articles on abstract expressionist artists, people began to look at them seriously. *Life* was a great power at that time; it educated the American public to begin to look at their own artists.

HILTON KRAMER: *Time* and *Life* concentrated on Pollock because Clement Greenberg had said he might be the greatest American living artist. There was a magazine article called "Jack the Dripper," which had models in haute couture with Pollock paintings in the background. Still, the prices for his works didn't go ballistic until after his death.

Larry Rivers told a story about someone coming into the Artists' Club and announcing that a painting of Pollock's had been sold for eight thousand dollars. That was the end of the Artists' Club, Rivers said, because no one could imagine that one of their paintings could fetch that much money, and if there was that much money in circulation, there was nothing left to talk about.

The social circuit of the abstract expressionists revolved around the Cedar Bar. I was there a few times, but the food was atrocious and it didn't amuse me to see guys getting drunk and being violent to each other. That was part of the scene, Pollock tearing off the door to the men's room. To say they were Gauguin types is putting it in the best possible light.

I had a very strong friendship with Richard Pousette-Dart, who was the youngest of the abstract expressionists and the only one of those painters who had something resembling what I would call a normal life. He didn't have to revolt against anything to become an artist. His father was a painter and a writer, his mother a poet. He was a very happily married man. His two children are successful. When he died, I wrote in the *Times* that he was the only abstract expressionist who dressed up as Santa Claus to entertain his children at Christmas.

But he paid a high price for that. He raised his family in Rockland County. He didn't hang out at the Cedar Bar. Because he wasn't part of that social circuit, he was written out of many of the books of that time.

WALDO RASMUSSEN: When I began working at the Museum of Modern Art in 1954, it was the heyday of American abstract expressionism. The museum was still the original building then. It had not yet been enlarged so it had an intimate feel. But the collection was so broad that you could go from the work of the twenties and thirties, from great masterpieces like Matisse's, which were difficult but easier to respond to, up to the

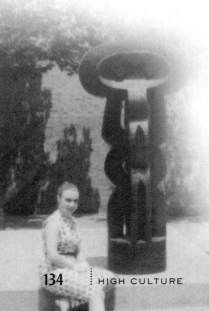

The garden at the Museum of Modern Art, 1958

abstract expressionists. The general public, though, came for Picasso—*Guernica* was the most famous picture in the world.

What I was most attracted to was the work of the second generation of the abstract expressionists, and somehow I felt a special connection with a number of the women artists—Helen Frankenthaler, Joan Mitchell, and Grace Hartigan. I got to know them through Frank O'Hara.

Before Frank came to work at the Museum of Modern Art, he was already part of the gallery world and a critic for *Art News*. He was also a wonderful poet. We met in 1955. He became the greatest friend of my life, and I loved him very deeply.

Frank's contemporaries, like Frankenthaler and Larry Rivers, were crazy about him. They had a snappy relationship, were very verbal, quick on the uptake with each other. I was quite shy, and some of the art scene was quite daunting to me. I remember going to a Frankenthaler show feeling kind of lost, swamped by it all. But Frank was a great help about that.

Taking the measure of André Derain's *Bathers* at MoMA

Although not a trained art historian, Frank was so brilliant that he could cope with the more scholarly exhibitions as well as the contemporary. He wasn't discerning and analytical; he was more an enthusiast. And we became conspirators in a mission to prove the quality of American art. It was the second generation Frank was mostly involved with, the younger artists who were just happening, whose pictures were so strange, they didn't look like anything recognizable.

He was small and skinny with a broken nose and a slightly nasal voice, tough, cocky, very funny, and more openly gay than anyone I had ever met, which kind of shocked me at first. He was also a great drinker. The Cedar Bar was his home away from home. Quite often we'd have drinks after work. After two martinis, I'd have to go home in a taxicab and breathe fresh air. But Frank could down quite a few.

He was wildly sentimental, a true Irish romantic with an appetite for all the arts, almost every kind of music. He didn't distinguish between high and low art. It could be a Laurel and Hardy movie or *King Lear*. He adored campy opera stars and movie stars. When James Dean was killed, he was absolutely crushed. He took James Dean as seriously as he took Mark Rothko.

The one artist I knew before I came to New York was David Smith, and the first work of art I ever bought was a Smith drawing, which cost $125. I paid it in installments of $10 a month when I had the $10. Frank and I were working on a great David Smith retrospective in 1966, but shortly before it opened in Europe, David was killed in an automobile accident.

A few months later, Frank was coming back from a bar on Fire Island where, ironically, cars are not allowed. I think he was blinded by the lights of the Jeep that hit him. The David Smith retrospective opened. I was in charge of it. But the two people I loved the most were not around to see it.

HILTON KRAMER: I think abstract expressionism will be seen as one of the last important developments in the history of modernist art. It's a movement that to me represents the end rather than the beginning of something. It followed in the footsteps of the European avant-garde. In a way, it is one of the final chapters in European modernism given a new lease on life with American energy and ambition. For one thing, it changed the scale of painting by abandoning small-scale easel painting for large-scale wall painting that isn't mural painting; it's still canvas stretched on a wooden stretcher. And that influenced everybody in the world.

Studying Picasso's *Les Demoiselles d' Avignon* **at MoMA**

The New York School, the abstract expressionists, succeeded in putting modern American art on the international map in a way that nothing prior to that generation of painters did. It was tremendously important, although I never believed Pollock was equal to Picasso or Rothko to Matisse.

When Picasso died, I was still working for the *Times*. It was a Sunday, and I was in Connecticut. I got a call from CBS news. "Mr. Kramer, you probably heard Pablo Picasso died."

I said, "Yes."

"Was he, in your opinion, the greatest artist of the twentieth century?"

"Actually, I think Matisse was."

"That's very interesting. We'll get back to you."

However, almost every critic I respect agrees. It was like the tortoise and the hare. Picasso made the most noise, but Matisse was the greater master.

JOAN WASHBURN: Although I studied art history in college, I never expected to end up in the art world. But after I graduated in 1951, I had a hundred dollars left over from a scholarship and used it to take a six-week course in shorthand. Afterwards I was so terrified I'd forget all I learned, I came to New York looking for a job and ended up in an employment agency where I was told, "We have a job for you in an art gallery. There won't be much social life, and you'll have to work for a woman." That was it. I started to work for Antoinette Kraushaar—answering the phone, taking letters—and I've been in the field ever since.

Antoinette's gallery was one of the oldest in New York. It had a complete range of art. Her family had been in the business since 1905 and managed to get through the Depression—which separated the men from the boys. She had a marvelous reputation and a lot of knowledge.

It was Antoinette who took me to my first opening, which was also the last exhibition at the old Whitney Museum on 8th Street. It was the John Sloan Memorial Retrospective, and Kraushaar Galleries had represented John Sloan for many years. Antoinette had the painting *Charma Running Red* by Sloan in her gallery for sale at six thousand dollars. One day someone came in, wrote a check out for three thousand dollars, and then ripped it up. Since I was alone in the gallery at that time and wasn't allowed to accept offers anyway, it didn't matter. Still, that painting today would be worth six figures.

I found it startling to come across modern art. At first I was totally confused. I had no background for it. But working for Antoinette, I learned what modern art was about and how to look at it while it was happening. It takes a while to fall in love with paintings of such a different nature.

That postwar period was a breakout time in art. At the same time, because of its small size, the art world was very immediate. Everything was on 57th Street. Kraushaar Galleries was at number 32. Curt Valentin, one of the major figures responsible for bringing European art here after the war, was in the building. There were dealers in old masters. You could see a Cezanne watercolor show at Knoedler's and go across to Betty Parsons and see Pollock or de Kooning. Charlie Egan was in business across the street. Exhibitions usually lasted three weeks. You could easily see everything by going between Park and Sixth Avenues along 57th Street. There weren't huge crowds, and people were fairly informed.

When Lou Pollock, the very much loved owner of the Peridot Gallery, died in 1970, Alan Gussow, one of the artists in that gallery, came to see me with the idea that I should take the gallery over. "Oh, no, I can't afford it," I said. "I have small children. I can't handle the hours."

A few months later, Alan came by again with Lou's cousin, who was a lawyer and accountant. "You really should take this over," he said. "We'll do anything we can to make it financially possible for you."

I hesitated, but then I went for it, and it was a rather seamless move because by then I had worked in the business for so many years. The difference was now I had to worry whether the paintings sold or not. The art business is the sport of kings, so to speak, and I am not a princess.

HILTON KRAMER: The art world was getting bigger, the art public was getting bigger. There were more and more courses, more and more galleries. The museum public was expanding, museums were expanding.

HOWARD KISSEL: When I first saw the Guggenheim on a high school trip to New York in 1959, I had a great sense of discovery of the building and the abstract art.

GILLES LARRAÍN: The space of the Guggenheim is a great work of art, the most beautiful sculpture. And it was so unique at the time it came up, when everything else was straight and perpendicular. But it doesn't respect the art. Walking up the spirals, it is difficult to balance yourself and look at the art.

WALDO RASMUSSEN: The Guggenheim was an architectural experience and very shocking in the first days, such a nutty, fascinating building. The combination of a sloping floor and my fear of heights made me have a very hard time with it.

HILTON KRAMER: Frank Lloyd Wright had always been vocal in his denunciation of painting; he hated easel painting. He was determined to build a building where he was the most important artist, and he did. In the Guggenheim, nothing could compete with Frank Lloyd Wright.

JOAN WASHBURN: We all watched the Whitney Museum go up and the art world move uptown around 78th and 79th Streets. There was a lot of activity because of the proximity to the Whitney and the Met. Abstract expressionism was ascending to meteoric heights, while the beginning of pop art started up at Leo Castelli's in the 1960s.

The Guggenheim Museum—"such a nutty, fascinating building."

HILTON KRAMER: One of the most important consequences of the pop art movement was that it brought a whole new kind of art public into the art world. The public that responded to abstract expressionism was interested in the interior life of art, in art as a kind of expression of the interior life. It was complex; it had certain metaphysical implications, and it had a certain element of mystery.

Pop art was a kind of release for people who had never been able to connect with abstract expressionism. Here it was: familiar images from the supermarket, the Hollywood screen, the comics. It was cheerful, easy, accessible. There were no metaphysical implications, no psychological twists. And the public came running. Pop art was the first movement that was an instant success in the media, universities, the art market, the museums. It had taken two decades for abstract expressionism to acquire a mainstream public; it took pop art about two years.

Andy Warhol did the drawings for I. Miller Shoes and was a very gifted illustrator. But his real genius, I think, was in public relations, not art. He created the artist as celebrity.

When I lived on 12th Street, the Whitney was still in the old studio building at 8 West 8th Street. They closed after that and moved to West 54th Street in a building that opened to the back of the Museum of Modern Art. Once they were there, they realized they would never be anything but the tail on the back of MoMA. Later they built the building on 75th and Madison, which looks like a fascist bunker although the exhibition space is better than the Guggenheim's.

MARCIA TUCKER: In late 1968, the Whitney hired me and James Monte as curators. They took a chance, a big chance. We were two young people. I was an art historian and a writer; Jim was a painter. In those days there were no curatorial schools. In addition, I was the first woman curator at the Whitney. Up till then, women were the donors and secretaries.

The first show I did was a small exhibition of the work of Nancy Graves, the life-sized camels she was making at the time. It was totally controversial, which I never expected. Now they are icons of art history. My second show was done together with Jim. It focused on how the process itself would dictate the final form of the object. That was an opposite tack to Greenberg's formalism, to Greenberg's painting reduced to nothing but itself. It was the first museum show Eva Hesse was ever in. It had Richard Serra's splashes, the work of Joel Shapiro and Bruce Nauman. Rafael Ferrer did a wonderful piece where he filled a moat with ice and hay. The ice melted over time.

The show was controversial, the crowd was mistrustful, and there was a lot of hostility. A lot of people said, "This isn't art." Hilton Kramer, who was writing for the *Times*, was vituperative. I tore the reviews into small squares and hung them on a hook in the bathroom like the French do. I've had a really good career based on bad reviews.

The Whitney was run by the most amazing person—Jack Baur, a person of such honor. He was completely supportive. But when Tom Armstrong came into the Whitney in '76, I knew my time there would be at an end. By then, however, I had plans for a new museum.

The New Museum was characterized by experimentation, openness, risk taking, and rooted in the understanding that art is a vital social force, and that art and life are connected in inextricable and totally critical ways. It was also really democratic and collaborative internally.

Andy Warhol—pop icon—created "the artist as celebrity."

While I was at the Whitney, I had never thought too much about the audience. Then one day I saw a couple look at Lichtenstein's painting of Picasso's woman in a flowered hat. And the guy says, "So, Ethel, you see that upside-down donkey?"

She says, "Oh, yes, amazing, that's what it is."

Then they move over to Lichtenstein's *Golf Ball,* and she says, "You know I think that's a golf ball."

And the husband says, "You're right. It's a golf ball."

That totally changed my head around. I realized we had done nothing, nothing to help people see what was up there. And I couldn't do much about that until I was at the New Museum.

Somebody described me as antiauthoritarian. "Authority" is a bad word for me. In my role as a director, it was not about authority but responsibility. I'm sure a lot of those ideas come from the sixties.

HILTON KRAMER: When I got the offer to be art critic for the *New York Times,* my wife, who was an editor at *Art News* then, was slightly upset. "Are you considering it?" she asked. The *Times* art coverage had such a bad reputation in the art world that I think my wife worried whether anybody would speak to us again if I worked there.

I came in to meet Clifton Daniel, who was managing editor, and Turner Catledge, who was executive editor. They asked me what I thought of the paper's art criticism. I said I thought it was very superficial. Daniel said, "Well, that's why we're offering you this job."

The chief art critic of the *Times* then was John Canaday. He was hostile to the work that was going on. He hated Pollock, he hated Frankenthaler, he basically hated abstract art, and he was an avowed enemy of the New York School. John Canaday had many good qualities; his real interest was writing detective stories under the name of Matthew Head. But if John had to spend more than an hour writing a column, he'd just wind it up. He was very fast, dismissive of anything he didn't already know.

Turner Catledge said, "The way we used to hire critics on the *Times* was when their other jobs had become too strenuous, we'd give them a job as a critic. But our readers are too smart for that now."

The very first week I was on the *Times,* when I knew absolutely nobody, Clifton Daniel's secretary came to see me in the newsroom and asked if I could stop by Mr. Daniel's office at the end of the day to have a drink with him. He invited Craig Claiborne, the food editor, and Drew Middleton, the military editor, in to meet the new person. I can tell you that meant a lot. Both men became good friends of mine.

In the men's room soon after, I ran into one of the old-time editors who worked on the news desk. "Oh, you're the new arts guy," he said.

I said, "Yeah."

"Well, there's only one thing you have to know to survive on this paper."

"What's that?"

"It comes out every goddamned day."

That turned out to be very good advice.

I never discovered who it was who recommended me to the *Times*. My first year at the paper, more than fifty individual people on the *Times* and in the art world took me aside at various social events to confide to me that he was the person or she was the person who had gotten me my job.

Shortly after I was hired, the *New Yorker* hired Harold Rosenberg as their art critic. Bob Coates, who had been there for many years, was a perfectly good writer, but his reviews were thin. Soon after that, *Time* magazine hired Robert Hughes for the same reason and because they had been against everything modern. You couldn't really conduct that kind of journalism anymore. Art had become a part of mainstream cultural life, and journalism had fallen behind its readership. It was a very big change.

The *Times* tried to upgrade their coverage of the arts. They had never had an architecture critic, but now they hired Ada Louise Huxtable. Then they hired Clive Barnes, who had been the ballet critic of the London *Times* and the *Spectator*. I had read Clive in the *London Spectator* for years, so I was delighted. When the chief movie critic, Bosley Crowther, who had been at the *Times* for as long as anyone could remember, panned *Bonnie and Clyde*, it was a great embarrassment. That's when Vincent Canby was hired as his backup, and then Crowther was eased out. They offered the theater critic's job to Kenneth Tynan, who had made a great reputation on the *London Observer*. When he turned them down because he wanted to write for the *New Yorker,* they hired Stanley Kaufman—very briefly. Stanley didn't make a very impressive showing; he was very condescending to his readers. As soon as the *Trib* folded and Walter Kerr was available, they dropped Stanley and hired Kerr.

In the spring of 1972, I was sort of dragooned into temporarily giving up writing about art to work as the cultural news editor on the daily paper. The guy who preceded me was an old-time reporter. He had no interest in the arts, regarded it as a demotion that he had been made cultural news editor, and took it out on us. We complained bitterly to the management. The last straw for me came when the Museum of Modern Art was putting on the first de Kooning retrospective in New York, and I told him I needed extra space.

"Who the hell is de Kooning?" asked the cultural editor of the *New York Times*.

When I became cultural editor, I discovered Clive Barnes was manipulating the schedule every day to accommodate his conflicts. Clive wrote wonderfully in those days. He had been writing for a very knowledgeable ballet public in London, and he brought that same attitude to New York. But as soon as he came to the *Times*, he understood that in New York, the theater critic is top banana. Clive had his eye on the job.

When Walter Kerr left, Clifton Daniel offered the job of theater critic to Clive. But Clive didn't want to give up writing about dance; he wanted both jobs. At first they said no. Then Clive wrote a piece about the first Harold Pinter play done in New York in his Sunday dance column as if it were a dance subject. His pal at *Time* magazine called Clifton Daniel and said, "You only have to read what Clive wrote about Pinter to know that he's your theater critic."

So finally Daniel gave in and created this absurd situation where Clive was the first-string theater critic and first-string ballet critic. And it was a mess. Sometimes he would persuade producers to postpone the opening of a play to accommodate his crazy schedule. Sometimes he wouldn't review things until they were just about to close. It was a totally unworkable arrangement.

MICKEY ALPERT: As I heard it, the story goes that when Clive had difficulty with the *Times*, the Shuberts, who felt he was sympathetic to them, went to Rupert Murdoch and guaranteed a page of advertising once a week if they hired Clive. No one knows whether the story is true, but the Shuberts did take out a lot more ad space in the *Post* right around the time Clive Barnes became its dance and theater critic.

I met Clive in 1967 when he wrote his first theatrical review as chief drama critic of the *New York Times*. It was for *Scuba Duba,* a play I was handling written by Bruce Jay Friedman. Clive was the image of Broadway criticism, the most accommodating and most influential of critics. He worked seven days a week—he was really indefatigable.

HILTON KRAMER: It was too bad; Clive pissed away real gifts. Once we happened to converge in Paris and happened to see one of the Soviet dance companies that was doing something of Prokofiev's in Paris. His conversation about it was brilliant; he had such an encyclopedic knowledge about the whole history of ballet.

I began going to the New York City Ballet when it was still at City Center on 55th Street. Sometimes I would go three or four nights a week. That's when George Balanchine was doing some of his greatest ballets and had some of his greatest dancers. It was very cheap, but there was never a full house. For years, I would run into people on the street who didn't know my name and whose names I didn't know, but we would nod to each other because of all those evenings we saw each other during intermissions.

STANLEY DRUCKER: You had a definite core audience that would come to Carnegie Hall week after week. Tickets were handed down from father to son, mother to daughter. A special event would draw the core plus others. And then, of course, as we were in New York, there were always a lot of visitors.

Carnegie Hall had a wonderful sound. But Lincoln Center was a new concept, a great opportunity to have the arts in one place. I remember the groundbreaking for Philharmonic Hall at Lincoln Center, which opened in 1962. Eisenhower dug the first shovel. A temporary stage was set up on the site. Various dignitaries spoke. The Philharmonic played under the direction of Leonard Bernstein.

JOHN TAURANAC: I've frankly never been a fan of Lincoln Center. I never liked the idea of sequestering culture. One of the joys of passing by Carnegie Hall is hearing a hint of music from the crack in the window. To take culture with a "K," as it were, and say this is where we are going to have it, in this sacred place, doesn't work as far as I'm concerned.

CAROLE RIFKIND: Lincoln Center was a totality that they believed time wouldn't touch. It didn't want to recognize the messy vitality of the city. It was something that was controlled and symbolic, isolated, high culture.

HOWARD KISSEL: Lincoln Center transformed the West Side; it was a catalyst for an unbelievable transformation. That huge chunk of real estate that had been brownstones, tenements, *West Side Story*, was now devoted to culture. The tax roles increased beyond one's ability to imagine. The Met was the last of the buildings to open in '66.

ROBERT MERRILL: Together with a few other artists, I went to the new opera house at Lincoln Center to try it out before it opened officially. Some said it was too large. I did not think so. If you sing correctly and project, you'll sing well in every house. I did not miss the old Met. It had become difficult to create new productions there, to store scenery. Between productions, sets had to be moved to a warehouse. The old Met had had its day.

STANLEY DRUCKER: Once there was a Philharmonic Hall at Lincoln Center, that was the end of the Lewisohn Stadium summer concerts. An air-conditioned venue was preferable to an outdoor theater, and

Robert Merrill at the old Met.

Lincoln Center with the scaffolding still up at the Metropolitan Opera House

City College did other things with the site. But what a marvelous thing it used to be to play out in the open air on a summer night. You couldn't beat it.

Under the name of Stadium Symphony, the New York Philharmonic Orchestra would play a six- or eight-week season at Lewisohn Stadium, the athletic field of City College. It was a Greek-style colonnaded arena of concrete benches with some tables and chairs down below that held twenty-five thousand or more. Tickets cost from twenty-five cents to $1.20. We played six nights a week, had only one rehearsal per concert, and performed a different program every night. We covered so much music, all the Beethoven, all the Tchaikovsky.

KEN LIBO: There could be a symphony, a singer, a concert pianist, all top-notch acts. I may very well have seen Leonard Bernstein conduct, I may have seen the Pittsburgh Symphony, I may have heard Lily Pons sing. Graduations were held there.

Lewisohn Stadium, where the New York Philharmonic played every summer

Minnie Guggenheimer's mother was friendly with Adolph Lewisohn, which is how Minnie got the job of organizing the concerts and introducing the performers. She always made intermission speeches, prefacing her remarks with "Hello, everybody," and the audience would answer back, "Hello, Minnie." Once a member of the royal family in England was in attendance, and he got lost somehow. Minnie grabbed the microphone and called out, "Here, Prince. Here, Prince."

Now it's quite dreadful, really horrible. If you want to see a prison, why go to Danamora up the river? Save yourself the trouble. Go to Amsterdam Avenue and 136th Street to see this prison-like structure that is used for science—what else?—where Lewisohn Stadium used to be.

STANLEY DRUCKER: When I joined the Philharmonic in 1948, Bruno Walter was the chief conductor. The other conductors were Leopold Stokowski, Dimitri Mitropoulos, Charles Munch, Leonard Bernstein—a couple of good names. They were all top level. In New York you got the best the world had to offer. Some I loved less than others, but I respected and learned from each one. You collaborate with a conductor. It's like playing a duet. It's communication by a gesture, a look.

When Bruno Walter came out on stage, you thought you were in a cathedral. He walked slowly, his expression was serious. But his approach was quite emotional. I remember him conducting *Song of the Earth* by Mahler, and during the final movement, he had tears in his eyes. Terribly moving. He was a protégé of Mahler's in Europe; there was that link.

"When Bruno Walter came out on stage, you thought you were in a cathedral." Here the maestro conducts at Carnegie Hall in 1947.

Dimitri Mitropoulos had a great impact on me. He was Greek, a lean and lanky man who conducted without a baton. He was all over the place, more off the podium than on. Once there was a magazine photograph of Mitropoulos off the podium with the caption "Airborne Maestro."

Mitropoulos was passionate, wild. He could conduct anything, but he championed twentieth-century music, the harder the better. He was able to absorb very complex and complicated scores; he memorized complete scores. Often he'd rehearse without the score in front of him. And I would also say if there's such a thing as saintly, Mitropoulos would qualify. He performed many good deeds, helping musicians, buying instruments, paying for schooling, helping people's children. But his own lifestyle was very simple. He lived in one room in the Great Northern Hotel on 56th Street not far from the stage door at Carnegie Hall. He was a modest man in a way, but on stage he was tremendous.

Stokowski also conducted without a baton, but he was very different from Mitropoulos. Stokowski was the man in the ivory tower; you could not easily approach him. But he had a wonderful sense of balance and tonal quality, an interesting way of working. His way of rehearsing was to play. If he had to stop, and everybody has to stop occasionally, he would start again in the very place he left off. If in the time allotted he could get through a piece three times, he would do it.

In those early years, Lenny was one of the guest conductors. Whenever he conducted, it was an event. Of course, I didn't call him Lenny then; I called him Maestro, even though he was only in his thirties. Lenny was the kind of person who drew out what you had to offer. He approached conducting with love; it was a sharing of something. He was passionate; he had something to say, and he was burning with talent.

At that time, we didn't see all sides of his talent. But later on when he became musical director, all of the different facets of his brilliance came together. Conducting was only one of the things he could do. I don't know when he practiced the piano, but he was a soloist conducting from the piano any number of times. And of course he was a composer. Over the years we played many of his works.

When Leonard Bernstein became musical director in 1958, it was a major forward leap. We went from a twenty-eight-week season and six- or eight-week summer season to year-round employment because of the force of his talent and image. That summer we had a seven-week tour of South America—every single country, even Paraguay. The next year, there was a ten-week tour of nearly every country in Europe, including Russia and Poland—new territory in those days. Pasternak and Shostakovich came to the concert in Russia; Charlie Chaplin came in Switzerland. There hasn't been a tour of such length since.

RABBI JUDAH NADICH: Leonard Bernstein used to come to the Park Avenue Synagogue for Kol Nidre and during the day on Yom Kippur. I didn't speak to him, as I was busy, as can be imagined. He wasn't a member and I don't know whose seat he occupied, but he was always sitting there, to the right of the pulpit.

STANLEY DRUCKER: It was a no-no in concert history to socialize with the maestro. But Lenny was very approachable, and I got to know him quite well. The first time I was the soloist with him conducting was in 1961 when I played the Debussey *Clarinet Rhapsody* in a bunch of performances at Carnegie Hall. The next time was in the Carl Neilson *Clarinet Concerto*. He was a champion of Neilson's music. Lenny was instrumental in having the John Corleano Concerto written and conducting the work for me. Playing the world premier of that concerto was one of the high points of my life.

Lenny was very New York; he could speak jive talk, rock 'n' roll talk, 52nd Street jazz talk to percussion players about using different sticks. He spoke

Leonard Bernstein expanded the audience for classical music with the introduction of his Young People's Concerts.

multiple foreign languages and had an incredible command of English. He could communicate, and communication in the arts is the thing; collaboration and communication.

The orchestra loved him. He was flamboyant and powerful. Everything about him was bigger than life. Mitropoulos had a lot of that quality, too. When you're dealing with an institution like the Philharmonic, which is the oldest orchestra in the United States and one of the oldest in the world, you have this whole panorama, this whole sense of movement from one conductor to the next.

Chapter Seven

Making Music

Tin Pan Alley was the fountainhead of songs for singers like Bing Crosby (pictured here with Ed Sullivan).

JOE DARION: The Tin Pan Alley that I was a part of was in the late 1950s and early 1960s, just before rock came in. Once rock came in, that Tin Pan Alley disappeared completely. The lyricists and music men were replaced by performers who wrote their own songs because who needed any talent for that junk?

The heart of Tin Pan Alley was the Brill Building on the west side of Broadway between 49th and 50th Streets. On either side was a restaurant: Jack Dempsey's on the uptown side, and the Turf on the downtown side. Jack Dempsey's was the fancier restaurant where the publishers ate; the songwriters never ate there. It was a long narrow place with a dogleg in the back where the publisher and the secretary he was having an affair with sat—so nobody would know. The Turf restaurant had terrible food, just right for the songwriter who had just sold a song or had a royalty check. Most of the time, though, the songwriters made do with a frankfurter from the little stand on 50th and Broadway. That's all they could afford.

Although the food was terrible, the Turf had the greatest cheesecake in the history of the world. The basement was filled with cheesecakes stacked from the floor to the ceiling, ready to be shipped everywhere. The owner of the Turf raced horses. One year he ran one of his horses, Count Turf, in the Kentucky Derby. Every songwriter bet his bejeezus on it, and Count Turf won. Boy was that a week for the songwriters!

In the time of Tin Pan Alley, the whole Brill Building was filled with music publishers. The front door to every publisher was open, and you could hear a piano pounding from the inside somewhere. Standing in the hallway, you could go crazy—the cacophony was overwhelming! Every publishing house had an outside office where the secretary sat. She was called the "dragon lady" because you couldn't get past her. It also had an inside office that was a small room with a piano, and in that room sat the guys who were pounding out these immortal songs. It was very hard to get to the inside office.

America's popular music went from the Brill Building to the *Lucky Strike Hit Parade.*

On the sidewalk outside of the Brill Building, there would be a crowd of guys, all looking pretty down at the heels, each one holding a dirty manila envelope in his hands with his latest creations. These were the songwriters. They were all upward strivers; the really top songwriters didn't have to stand in front of the Brill Building. But every once in a while, one of us would have a bestseller. I remember one called "My One and Only Love," a lovely song that I still hear on the radio.

Out of maybe twenty songwriters milling around, maybe one or two of them would be women. There weren't many blacks at the time. They had their own labels and their own companies. Still, I never saw a sign of anti-black feeling. If you had a good thing, you could get on. And if they took your song, it didn't mean they wouldn't take mine.

On any given day, it got to be so crowded on the sidewalk outside the Brill Building that the police would come along and shoo us into the building. Then the building superintendent would shoo us out again. The cacophony outside was as bad as the cacophony inside. But it was out on that sidewalk where you made your contacts and partnerships, where you gossiped, where you found out who was up for a date, who was coming up to record, what music publisher was in with what record company, and when they were going to record. You ran your life according to that information. There were always arguments, bickering on the street, shifting partnerships of lyricists and music men. We never called the guy who wrote the music a composer; he was the music man. If you wanted to insult him, you'd say, "Oh, the composer!"—ironically. A few pairs actually stayed together, but most people shifted around.

An interesting phenomenon in Tin Pan Alley was the existence of the luftmensch, the third writer of a song. He'd come to you and say, "Hey, let's do a song like this because I know thus and so." So you'd do the lyric. Then he'd turn around and go to a music man and say, "I got these lyrics; you do the music." He claims he can do words and music, but he can't do either.

I would come down to the Brill Building with my dirty manila envelope and my two lyrics in it wondering where I would get a piano so I could sit down and work out a song with a composer. We were always fighting to get a piano for a few hours. One time we happened to walk down the block to Radio City Music Hall on Sixth Avenue, and behind it was the NBC Building, where there were uniformed guards who kept people from going in.

After we had been there for a while, we noticed that guys who came in with fancy briefcases and nice clothes walked right by the guards, and nobody said anything. We were so desperate for a piano, we said, "Hey, maybe we can get a place to work." So we went home and got briefcases and we put on suits, and we marched by these guys and wandered into the halls of the NBC Building. It had terrific studios, and half of them were empty. We would sit in the studios and work by the hour. It was heaven.

Once we got a song together, we had to get past one of the dragon ladies in the Brill Building to the inner office so we could demonstrate it. The composer would bang out the song on the piano (God help us). If the publisher liked it, the question became who would record it. They didn't have any judgment, although sometimes they had a feel for the market.

Goldy Goldmark was one of the more memorable publishers. He was about six feet two, and when he got excited, he'd get on top of his desk and jump up and down while he talked to you. I remember the time when one of our songs was being recorded and one of the musicians was tapping time with his foot. For some reason, Goldy Goldmark could not stand it when anybody did that. When they took a break, the musician took off his shoes. Somehow or other Goldy found a nail and a hammer, and he nailed that man's shoe to the floor.

Once I was sitting in one of the outer offices waiting to see this publisher with whom I had an appointment. After an hour, the dragon lady said, "Well, he had to go out." That happened a second time and then again. The last time, I was in the outer office, and I could hear the man speaking in the inner office. When the dragon lady said, "He's not in," I got so angry that I pounded on the desk and said, "Give me a piece of paper." I took a pencil off her desk, and I held it in my fist, and I wrote a big "DARION" on it and yelled, "Take that in to him!"

Songs were set into little scenarios on the *Hit Parade,* a favorite TV show of the 1950s.

She got so scared, she brought it in. I stormed out to the elevator, and the son of a bitch came running after me with the piece of paper. "What's this?" he said.

And I said, "You just remember that name because you're not going to have anything to do with it."

"Come back in the office," he said. I hated his guts, but I went back.

Another publisher once told me, "Never come in my office again."

I said, "That's bullshit, because if you can make two cents off me, I'll be back in your office and you'll have the red carpet rolled out for me."

The humiliations were very basic. If you're a shoe salesman and you don't make a sale, you can say the shoes aren't very nice. But if you're a creative person and they turn you down, it's a big humiliation inside, and it happens time and time and time again.

It was a very, very hard way to make a living. If you got a record, God help you, you got two cents: One cent went to the publisher, one cent went to the writer. If there were two writers, you got a half a penny for a record. The guy who threw the record across the counter in a store got twenty-five cents. What really saved our lives was the sheet music.

Today there is no such thing as sheet music, but at that time everybody had a piano, and people used to stand around the piano and sing. So sheet music was important, and you could really make some money on it if the publisher was willing to give you an honest count—which none of them were. That is until we finally got tired of it and formed the Songwriters' Protective Association for record and sheet music sales. Before we got our lawyers and accountants to examine the books, we were suddenly showered with checks.

I got into Tin Pan Alley and the whole business of writing pop songs by kind of backing into it. I was doing special material, work for nightclub comics, vaudeville comics, little songs, jokes. It was a miserable living. If my wife, Helen, hadn't been working, we would have starved to death. I didn't want to go near Tin Pan Alley for two reasons: I was scared of its reputation, and for God knows what reason, I was a bit of a snob.

One day I was sitting in my lawyer's outer office—I've sat in a lot of outer offices in my day. Why he took me, I don't know, because I sure as hell wasn't giving him a lot. Now he came out to me and he said, "Listen, I have Red Buttons in my office, and he's going to have a television program on prime time every week. If you could write him a song for playing him on and playing him off, you could do very well with it in ASCAP for the performance money. Talk to him."

So I went and I talked to Red, and considering who I was, he was very nice to me. We made a deal. It was understood that whatever I wrote, he would be on the song as one of the writers. "Show me something," he said.

Red has always had this little thing he does to space his laughs. He hopped on one foot, held his ear, and said, "Ha-ha, ho-ho, hoo-hoo, strange things are happening." My partner and I took this whole thing with the hopping on one foot, and the "Ha-ha, ho-ho, hoo-hoo, strange things are happening," and we wrote a song. Red liked it fine. He decided to use it.

Red had his first show. It was live television, and he did the song and the whole "Ha-ha, ho-ho, hoo-hoo, strange things are happening." Then, as the program was ending, he said to the audience, "Listen, I am going down to the studio to record this song. Why don't you all come along with me, and when I say 'ha-ha,' you say 'ha-ha,' and when I say 'ho-ho,' you say 'ho-ho.'"

So that's what happened. After the program, he marched out, and the whole bloody audience marched out with him down Broadway to a recording studio, and he recorded that song. He sang "ho-ho," and the whole audience sang "ho-ho," and he sang "hoo-hoo," and the whole audience sang "hoo-hoo." And all of a sudden lightning struck. For some goddamned reason I could never figure out, the song took hold.

But we couldn't get a publisher because they all thought, What other artist would sing "Ha-ha, ho-ho, hoo-hoo"? And who would buy a piece of sheet music called "Ha-ha, Ho-ho, Hoo-hoo"? And that's when the miracle happened. We made our publishing company: RB Music. We not only sold a bloody million records or whatever it was, but we got the publishers' share and the writers' share. Of course there were three of us counting Red, who got the lion's share, which I was happy enough to give him. Then, and I don't understand it to this day, we said, "Let's do the sheet music." What's sheet music? It's pieces of paper that you print on, you make a hundred thousand, two hundred thousand, three hundred thousand—it doesn't matter. And all of a sudden that song began to sell as sheet music. I think sheet music sold at that time for fifty or seventy-five cents, but it was all profit, you kept it all. We sold three quarters of a million sheets.

This is around the time that I began going down to the Brill Building. I was a very strange duck—a new guy who had had a smash hit! Nobody could figure out where the hell I'd come from, nor could I. I didn't have a clue about how to write a pop song. The publishers were in a very strange position with me. The stuff I brought in and started showing them was nonsense, but they were scared to let me out. I had had a hit, and that was the magic thing. That let me live long enough to learn my business, and I did learn it in a very interesting way.

At that time they were putting out little mimeographed pamphlets with the lyrics of the top fifty songs of the week. I brought one home, took the staples out, and laid the sheets of paper out on the living room floor in long lines. Then I laid my lyrics down side by side with them, and I went up and down the lines trying to figure out the difference between my songs and those that were successful. And I discovered the few simple but ironclad rules of writing a pop song at that time: (1) use concrete images; (2) write plots like you see in the movies, with a beginning and a middle and an end.

Red Buttons doing his famous number, "Ha-ha, Ho-ho, Hoo-hoo, Strange Things Are Happening."

"I found the note you left for me / The wording was so cruel and plain / 'I'm through with you,' it said / 'Our love is cold and dead / I'm leaving on the midnight train.'" The guy comes home; he calls for his wife; she's not there. It's a concrete set of images. "I rush to the station [concrete image] / Push through the crowd [image] / Fighting to reach the gate [image] / The headlight was gleaming / The whistle was screaming / 'Too late, too late, too late' [image]." Everything became an image. A plot, a movie plot. That was "Midnight Train," and it was a big hit.

One of my hit songs was "Ricochet Romance," recorded by Theresa Brewer. Don't ask me how my partners and I came up with it. It was one of those novelty songs, crazy songs like "Mairzy Doats"—they make no sense at all, but they have sounds that come into the ear and won't come out.

Crazy things happened. The phrase "Ricochet Romance" became part of the lexicon. A senator made a speech where he said something to the effect of he's not going to have a "ricochet romance" with something or other, and it got into the *Congressional Record* and made the headlines. Some girl in Canada was singing in a nightclub, and a drunk kept insisting, "Sing 'Ricochet Romance.'" She didn't sing it so he picked up a chair and brained her with it. She landed in the hospital, and that made the headlines.

It got to the top ten. Then it hesitated. The publisher got word from his spy in the record company (every publisher had paid spies in the record companies) that they were ready to put out Brewer's next record. I was in the publisher's outer office when I saw him go into the money man's office. He was an enormous man, and he came out of the money man's office with a roll of bills so big that his hand couldn't get around. He shook the roll at me and said, "You see this? This is three more weeks with the Brewer record." And he ran out. The Brewer record of "Ricochet Romance" stayed on the top ten for three weeks, and then it climbed to number one, where it stayed for months.

The publishers had song pluggers whose job was to see that their songs got played on the radio. They'd be blared out of every candy store on loud speakers; you'd hear them as you walked down the block. Payola was the paying of the disc jockeys on the radio to play a song. It got nastier and nastier as time passed because it got involved with the "crooked noses." It went from money to drugs and women. Everybody knew about it.

In those days you gave your copyright to one publisher. They'd sell it to another one and before you knew it, the name of the company changed, and they bought each other's catalogue and the result was you had no control over who had your material. This went on all the time, and it drove us crazy. But as a result of my having a publishing company with Red Buttons, I knew that if you were a songwriter and you had a hit, you had a nice year. But if you were a publisher and you had a hit, then you made real, real money. The difference between the two was not believable. And I knew in my heart that as soon as I had the muscle, no one would have my copyright.

One week three of the top five songs on the *Billboard* charts were my songs: "Changing Partners," "Ricochet Romance," and the "Ho-Ho Song." The result was that publishers were afraid to let me out of the office even if they hated what I brought in. Because I had these hits, I was able to make deals where I owned the copyright. Some of the composers I worked with sold their part to the publisher, but I never gave in. As a result, I own publishing rights to songs that composers I worked with don't have, and I make three, four, five times what the composer makes.

Once I had all these hits, the publishers were stuffing money down my throat. I couldn't go into the Brill Building without getting dragged into a publisher's office. And it was then that Helen and I looked at each other and said, "Yes, but where do we go from here?"

I knew that I had more to say than I was saying in these pop songs. It wasn't that I got tired of pop music; it was that I wanted to go beyond it if I could. I wanted to stretch myself.

Anyway, Tin Pan Alley was finished. I could see very plainly the handwriting on the wall. You'd go into a publisher and he wouldn't ask, "What's the lyric about?" He wouldn't ask, "What's the tune?" He'd ask, "What's the sound?" That was the death knell of what we were doing.

When Elvis came along, when rock 'n' roll came in, the Tin Pan Alley that I knew died. There were guys there who were so talented. They walked around like ghosts saying, "What happened? What happened?" It was so quick, overnight.

Joe Darion's
"Ricochet Romance"
was recorded by
Theresa Brewer

"When rock 'n' roll came in, the Tin Pan Alley that I knew died."

To me, it was a question of the writing. Take one of the rock lyrics and lay it down cold on the table, and see if you can read it. People who have three-hundred-word vocabularies or less are writers. There were singers like Theresa Brewer, Patti Paige, Rosemary Clooney—they sang like angels. Today's singers, today's songs are not for me.

JOEL DORN: When something is kind of defining itself like the record business was when it was still a cottage industry, there were opportunities. People who might have been furriers or dentists or clerks gravitated to this thing, got in on the ground floor. That was the music business in the fifties. In the sixties it matured. In the seventies it became a major American industry, generating billions and billions of dollars and spinning off other industries: concerts and promotions and T-shirts and endorsements. Nothing now is better or worse; it's just not what I grew up in.

I grew up in Yeadon, a very small town outside of Philadelphia, a Sinclair Lewis kind of town with a very conservative, prewar American sensibility. My father was in the *shmatta* business; he made women's dresses and blouses. Sometimes he would take me with him when he went to New York to do business with the manufacturers in the garment center. Coming out of the tunnel into the old Penn Station was like coming into a movie. The romance, the excitement of New York was just astounding. I would see the guys in the street pushing the racks. And all the taxicabs. And all the tall buildings. It was never a question in my mind if I was going to get to New York or that I was going to be in the music business.

I listened to pop radio, but then I started listening to the black stations at the end of the radio dial. They played swing in the forties, rhythm and blues—which was the root of rock 'n' roll—in the late forties and early fifties, and then rock 'n' roll and the new rhythm and blues in the mid fifties. I was born in 1942 so I was in a phenomenal position; I caught the whole run.

Three or four times a year, my parents would go to New York to see a show and eat at Sardi's. They stayed at the St. Moritz and had Nesselrode pudding at the old Rumplemeyer's. One weekend in 1956 when they went to New York and my brother and I were staying over at my grandmother's house, I was listening to Georgie Woods, a disc jockey on one of the black stations. It was Friday night, 9:15, when he played a record called "Ain't That Love?" by Ray Charles. And it was like the planet put its brakes on.

I had never heard Ray Charles before. I went nuts, but I couldn't find the record in the record stores. Then I learned Ray Charles recorded for Atlantic Records, an R & B label that had some jazz. I found an Atlantic record, and on the back it said "Supervised by Nesuhi Ertegun." It was an odd name. I wrote to him at his office in Manhattan and told him I was having trouble locating certain records. In addition, I sent him some of my ideas for records.

A year later, he wrote me back. That's how I started a correspondence with this man. Nesuhi Ertegun was a great jazz record producer. He and his brother Ahmet Ertegun, the ranking elder statesman of the record business, and another guy, Jerry Wexler, were the owners of Atlantic

After hearing Ray Charles for the first time, "it was like the planet put its brakes on."

Ahmet Ertegun, co-owner of Atlantic Records, signing Hall & Oates.

Records. It was a phenomenal independent label. Nesuhi and Ahmet's father had been the Turkish ambassador to the United States during the war, and was one of those who orchestrated Ataturk's takeover of Turkey in the thirties. The brothers were Sorbonne educated, multilingual, and spent their teenage years in the Turkish embassy in Washington. They were also big jazz and blues fans, and in 1948, they started Atlantic Records. In the late forties, the fifties, and into the sixties, there was no other label like it. It had the best rhythm and blues, the best pop, the best jazz.

From the time I was fourteen, I knew that I was going to produce records, whatever that meant, and that I was going to do it for Atlantic. I kept up the correspondence I had begun with Nesuhi. He wrote back to me and sent me records. I enrolled in the communications school at Temple University and got my education as best I could in Philadelphia, but always with the goal of getting to New York.

When I was nineteen, I got a job as a disc jockey on one of the pioneer twenty-four-hour FM jazz stations in the country. I knew as a disc jockey I could establish relationships with the record companies and the artists who came to town and played the jazz clubs in Philly, and I could begin to get some kind of a national reputation. In those years, a good disc jockey would "break records"—that is, pick a cut on an album and play it. If it sold, they'd say, "Well, Joel Dorn broke it in Philly."

Nesuhi let me come to his sessions. I saw him record Herbie Mann, the Modern Jazz Quartet, Betty Carter, people like that. I remember the first time I walked into the studio at 11 West 60th Street. It was like going to the movies for the first time. It's dark. The board has all the dials: red, cobalt, amber, little baby pin-spots. And the sound—I never heard sound like that in my life. I had had no sense at all of what happens at a recording session. I never knew they sometimes cut the music first and put the singer on later, that things were put on separate tracks, that stuff was added.

Today you can learn record production and engineering at all the major music schools. Then you learned it like you learn a trade. I was lucky; I apprenticed to Nesuhi Ertegun, this gentleman record producer with exquisite taste. I was like a de facto producer-in-training. I started making records for Atlantic on an independent basis in the mid 1960s while I was still a disc jockey in Philadelphia, coming into Manhattan whenever I could. Then one day in May 1967, I got a call from Nesuhi. "Come to New York." He offered me the job I had been begging for for years.

I became a talent scout, record promoter, and record producer. That's what you did then. Today the A&R (artists and repertoire) man has evolved to become the one who works with artists inside the company. But in the beginning the A&R man was the producer. That was my job. I had to find the artist, sign the artist to the label, help the artist find material, produce the record, get the liner notes done, work with the cover artist, call retailers, and go on the road to promote the record on radio. Everything I wished for I had. I was the jazz producer at Atlantic.

In those years, the record business was a cottage industry. There were studios all over midtown, the independents like Atlantic, Bell Sound, A&R. The majors were Columbia, Capital and RCA. There was a neighborhood aspect to the music business in New York City, although the district was loose, not like the garment district. When I walked past the Brill Building, I thought it was the Taj Mahal. You would go there if you needed a song. But most of the time, they would cut demos and send them to you.

> "From the time I was fourteen, I knew that I was going to produce records."

Talk about New York: Everything was bigger, better, shinier. In the Village they had all these jazz shops; there were gospel shops in Harlem. The first time I came to New York, I went to Sam Goody. It had so many records you could spend a day going through them. You'd see a thousand, two thousand jazz albums; five hundred different blues records; thousands of pop records. If I could have pitched a tent, I would have stayed there.

It was a different time. The publishers had relationships with the record companies; the songwriters had relationships with the publishers. It was a chain of people who interacted with each other. Musicians worked their material out on the road. You'd make a year's worth of singles in two days and release them separately every three months. If the singles did well, you combined them to make an album.

The record companies stayed with artists longer; they developed artists. If it didn't work, the record company would say, "Ah, we didn't do it right; let's do another one." If you didn't make it in three albums, it was, "Ok, we tried." It was much cheaper to get in the game because radio broke records. Then you could make a record for a few thousand dollars, take a shot.

The company was more family-like in those days. If you had an artist who was successful and he wanted something, you'd give it to him. I had a very successful record with a jazz artist named Les McCann. He found a young singer in Washington and insisted we record her. As a consequence of Les's insistence, I signed Roberta Flack and produced her first five albums.

When Roberta came to the label, she was just another club singer. She had worked in a DC club for years, where she had a loyal crowd that filled the club every weekend. I recorded maybe thirty songs and picked eight, including "The First Time Ever I Saw Your Face," a long slow ballad written by a Scottish folk singer. She'd been singing it for years.

One day I came into the office and someone said, "Clint Eastwood's on the phone for you." I thought it was a friend of mine. I picked up the phone, and I said, "Listen, Clint, I can't really talk to you now. I'm on the other line with Winston Churchill."

But when he said, "This is Clint Eastwood," I recognized his voice.

"I heard this record by Roberta Flack you produced. I just directed my first movie, *Play Misty for Me*. And I want to use a song in a key scene, a love scene in a forest."

I said, "It's fine with me."

He said, "I ran out of money. I can only pay you a thousand dollars."

That's not much to pay for a song in a film. So I went to Nesuhi and I said, "We can get this Roberta Flack song in this Clint Eastwood film, but he doesn't have any money."

Nesuhi said, "A thousand dollars is not enough. Tell him you need more."

I called him up. He said, "I'm not bargaining; I don't have any money." I think the thousand dollars was from his own pocket. He had no budget left.

So I went back, and I finally convinced Nesuhi, "All he's got is a grand." Clint Eastwood put the song in the movie.

Now here's an interesting story that shows you just how random success is. The next thing I know we're getting hundreds of calls a week at Atlantic about the Roberta Flack song from the movie. The song was five minutes and four seconds, too long for a single. They wouldn't play a single over 3:00, 3:10 maybe. But all the radio stations were getting calls: "Play this song from the Clint Eastwood movie."

Bobby Mitchell, the program director of a pop station in New Orleans, calls Atlantic Records. "We're getting phone calls by the minute for this Roberta Flack song, but it's too long to play. Edit a single down."

So I went to the studio and edited a single. In those days we put it on acetates, metal records that would take a few plays. We sent it by special delivery to the radio station. We get a phone call from Bobby Mitchell's secretary. "Listen, we just got this edited version of the Roberta Flack song. You edited it all wrong."

"What should I do?"

"Edit it like this."

So for the hell of it, I did what she said. It was perfect. It sold four million records; it launched Roberta's career. It was the number-one record of the year for *Billboard*; it won the Grammy Award for Record of the Year.

"When Roberta [Flack] came to the [Atlantic] label, she was just another club singer."

By now Roberta's next two albums had come out, and I'm working on the fourth. She calls me at home from the airport in LA. "I just heard the most incredible song on the headphones in the plane." There was a young singer named Lori Leiberman, and she did a song called "Killing Me Softly" by two songwriters named Norman Gimbel and Charlie Fox. Roberta sings it to me over the phone. She says, "Listen to the song. Pick out a rhythm section. I'll come back, and we'll record this."

I hear it once; I pick out the players I think would be good for this song. She comes back. We record it in a half hour. Then for the next two days, we put all the vocals on—that was tricky. And for a couple of weeks, my engineer Gene Paul and I mix it. He wanted to make a record where the bass drum was a lead instrument. We spent a lot of time working on that. It had never been done before.

"She looked like a Jewish parrot, all colors and that nose."

I've only made two records in my life that I knew would be hits while I was recording them. The first one was "Killing Me Softly"; it went to number one in two weeks. The other one was in the early seventies. A friend of mine, Doc Pomus, who'd written a lot of great songs like "Save the Last Dance for Me," called me up and said, "I got your next star."

I said, "Who's that?"

"This lunatic from Hawaii. Sign her up."

Bette Midler had grown up in a Samoan neighborhood in Hawaii. Her father was a housepainter for the navy. I met her in a joint on 56th between Fifth and Sixth called Upstairs at the Downstairs. She looked like a Jewish parrot, all colors and that nose. A bizarre but original look. Before she sang a note, I had the feeling if she was good, she'd be good like Jolson.

The stage was tiny. She had a piano player, a drummer, a guitar player, and a bass player. She goes up on stage. Because I make records, I shut my eyes to see what she sounded like. I figured if she was a dynamic performer, I could get tricked.

She's in the middle of her second song, I've got my eyes closed, she stops and she says, "Hey, you, big shot; what's the matter? You going to sleep?"

I said, "No. I'm here from the record company. I'm trying to listen to you."

Atlantic was a little reluctant to sign her because the word was that she was a terrific visual act that wouldn't translate to records. But I knew she could.

We got two hits from her: "Do You Want to Dance?" and "Boogie Woogie Bugle Boy." She was like Sophie Tucker; she just nailed them.

With the rock revolution and the Beatles, the recording industry exploded. People who didn't listen to music before started listening. Conglomerates started buying up the record companies. Atlantic was bought up by Kinney Parking Lots, which was then bought by Warner Seven Arts. By the mid 1970s, the record business I dreamed about and grew up in was over. Music had become big business.

Today a record company owns a distribution company. So you don't have dozens of distributors all over the country fighting to distribute the different labels. But I can remember when a guy named Murray or Harry or Sol was on the phone with a distributor from St. Louis. I can remember when the business was filled with wildcatters and con artists and gangsters. There had always been a mob element in show business; the mob had a piece of a club, a piece of this, a piece of that. That's just the way it went.

There were places where all these characters hung out. A bar called Jim and Andy's on the West Side in the 50s where all the musicians went between their recording sessions. A steakhouse called Al and Dick's, also in the 50s. All the record guys would come there. Everybody was hustling, everybody was conning, everybody was scheming, everybody was bobbing and weaving. You'd get one story after another. "I got a record in Detroit." "I just heard a girl—she's the best ever." "I cut a session last night. You never heard anything like it." "We're gonna ship three hundred thousand." "I'm on the air." They were peddling dreams.

DAVE HART: After the war when my father became a copywriter, we became more affluent and moved from Queens to New Rochelle. My mother was a pianist, and it was a very rich cultural life; there were a lot of books, art, and of course music.

We had a black maid who would come in, and after my mom would leave for work, she'd go over to our record machine and put on records. I was about nine then and a rebellious little kid, so I loved it. She'd play the B side of a Ritchie

Valens record called "Hey Señorita," which was a Latin-flavored rock tune, high powered. And she'd sweep me off my feet, and we'd dance to "Hey Señorita, please let me take you home." I loved it; I loved the rhythms of rock 'n' roll.

I was bored stiff in New Rochelle and wanted to get into New York City. Starting when I was twelve, I'd get on a train with my friend and go to Carnegie Hall to see Ray Charles and the Raylettes. His music was the R & B basis of rock 'n' roll.

In 1965, I went off to the University of Miami, and when I came back the next summer, my hair was very long and my musical tastes had changed. I was into the much heavier English-based rock 'n' roll, like Jeff Beck and Eric Clapton and the Yardbirds and the Beatles and the Rolling Stones.

That September, I began film school at NYU. Martin Scorcese was the professor. This was before anybody knew he was going to be great. He was like a little *Il Duce*; he would wave his arms around and wax poetic about films. But even though it was wonderful to have this exciting guy as a teacher, I was bored stiff because it took so long to make a film happen. I was young and impetuous, excited about life.

NYU was on Washington Square, but some of our classes were over on Second Avenue between 6th and 7th Streets. It was a mixed neighborhood, Polish, Irish, and Ukrainian. Young people were living there too, including a friend of mine who had an apartment on Avenue B. It was a drug-infested slum, a great place to be when you're eighteen years old.

I saw Cream at a theater on Second Avenue, a big place that held about twenty-five hundred people and did some wonderful rock 'n' roll shows. It was Bill Graham who rented this theater, which was now renamed the Fillmore East. Bill was a promoter, but he also had the idea of selling chunky cookies and granola bars at rock concerts. He took this San Francisco vibe and brought it to New York.

A friend of mine worked there as an usher. One day he called me up. "Why don't you come and work on my crew?"

Normally the Fillmore East schedule was two shows on Friday and two shows on Saturday, with the ushers getting paid fifteen dollars a night. Then we got a string of shows with Crosby, Stills, and Nash for only one show a night. The word comes down through the house manager that the ushers would be paid $7.50 for the night. The ushers complained. "Dave, why don't you say something about this?" they said to me. I was something of a mouthpiece.

Crosby, Stills, and
Nash frequently
appeared at the
Fillmore East.

I mentioned it to the house manager, and he said, "No problem. Bill will talk to you after the show tonight."

After the show, we go up to talk to him, all twenty of us. Bill was a tough, forthright guy, willing to put his position out front. "Okay, what's the problem?" he says.

I stand up. "Normally we get paid for two shows. Now we got a string of Crosby, Stills, and Nash, and we're only getting paid for one show. Our pay is cut in half, we still have the same expense of getting here, being here. We think we should get more." I sit down. I must have had a little snort of coke. I was energetic that night.

"Okay," Bill says, "I'll think about it."

I come back the next day, and he calls me into his office. "You know you're a smart kid."

"Thank you."

"First thing," he says, "you're gonna get your raise. Everybody's getting ten bucks for the Crosby, Stills, and Nash show."

"Fine."

"Second thing," he says, "you want a job?"

"Sure, I'd love to have a job."

"Want to go to San Francisco?"

"Well," I say, "I just met this girl, and I got this great apartment over in the West Village."

He says, "Don't worry about it. How about working upstairs? Go up to the third floor and see Herb Spar. You'll be an agent."

"Really?"

"Yeah, go ahead."

That was Saturday. Monday, I go up to the third floor. I walk in and I meet Herb Spar, who has just left William Morris to come and run the Millard Agency for Bill Graham. I introduce myself. Herb interviews me. I know a lot about English rock 'n' roll because it's my love. I tell him about a group called Yes, for instance. He freaks out; he just heard about it. I had hit the right chord. He offers me $125 a week, which back then was a lot of money.

I'm an agent. I represent It's a Beautiful Day, Santana, Janis Joplin, Sea Train—some pretty spectacular groups. I have a territory. I get on the phone and call colleges and local promoters and try to sell them these groups. This little agency isn't your standard agency. It's fresh and exciting. It has the power of Bill Graham.

At the same time, all the new cutting-edge acts were coming into the Fillmore, setting the tone for a new kind of rock 'n' roll. If you played the Fillmore and were successful, you would explode across the country. It was like playing the Palace in the days of vaudeville.

I saw all this because I had also become a security specialist, the front-door operator, and a roamer, who roams around to solve problems, because I was always a good talker, able to use my mouth to negotiate people out of situations.

The first night the Allman Brothers came to the Fillmore East, they were the opening act. I'm not sure exactly when this was; you know what they say about the sixties—if you remember it, you weren't there. But I do remember they showed up in a converted schoolbus that broke down on 6th Street. They came out and did a fifty-five-minute set and just blew the sold-out house away, completely plastering everybody who was there up against the wall.

The first time the Chicago Transit Authority performed, the first time Elton

John performed—as the opening act to Leon Russell—were amazing nights. There were so many of them at the Fillmore East. It was such a powerful time in terms of music taking a quantum jump in its ability to push into your brain. It was incredibly exciting to see these bands come on stage and blow people away with volume, with talent, with new sounds, with the blues-based gutsy, nasty music that came out of the blues of the black man. Bill was great at seeing that his shows were racially mixed. He loved the Chambers Brothers, would bring them in all the time.

"The hardness, the gutsiness of the rock 'n' roll I was into was about power and strength."

The crowd was your typical long-haired, late sixties–early seventies youthful audience. There was a light show; the psychedelia would flow. Drugs were always there. It was easy to obtain just about anything, and it was okay to take a drug any way you wanted to—intravenously, rectally, nasally.

As for sex—it was a wide-open situation. There was a lot of experimentation; you could do just about whatever you wanted. It was part of the culture—free sex, free drugs. There were none of the fears then that there are now except for the fear of getting arrested. But the police were very understanding and knowledgeable about the crowd; if there was a problem, they would solve it. There were frequent fights, but we had a real good security staff to handle them.

We were a nice bunch of friends who worked at the Fillmore East who did lots of different drugs and had lots of different sex. We had a magical life. One of my friends was Michael Emerald. He came from Massachusetts and lived in a car until he got a little apartment on the Lower East Side. He had long black hair, was incredibly strong, a well-built character, and a wonderful sculptor. At the Fillmore, he was the sweep. Someone throws up, call Michael. After the shows, Michael sweeps up. That's what he did.

When the Grateful Dead came to the Fillmore East, we would make special arrangements for people who took LSD. There was an artists' office off the stairs to the second balcony where we put kids who were freaking out. We had a doctor on call who was real good at dealing with freak-outs.

Once, near the end of a Grateful Dead show, when the crowd was crazy, I see this kid come running down from the upper balcony. He was just going *va-va-va-voom*! He runs past the break between the upper balcony and the mezzanine, hits the mezzanine stairs, goes right past me and another security guy, dashes up to the rail, and jumps over the rail. We try to grab him; we miss him. I'm thinking there will be a couple of dead kids down there in the orchestra. But luckily right in front of the balcony was kind of a light stanchion, a box that held equipment. He hit that, and we were able to get ahold of him and pull him up. It was one of those moments when your heart is in your throat.

Occasionally you'd go into the men's bathroom and look in one of the stalls and there'd be two guys sixty-nining each other. Or there'd be a couple up in the balcony who were naked and getting it on, and you'd have to break it up. But those kinds of things didn't happen very frequently. If people were drugged, it was normal; experimentation was par for the course.

I never went to see *Hair*. Who had to see it? I lived it. *Hair* was for suburbanites; it tried to explain to them what we were doing. Besides, the music sucked. The hardness, the gutsiness of the rock 'n' roll I was into was about power and strength. It was the basest, nastiest part of the blues amplified to 110 db with guitars and bass and drums pounding. This was not about the Age of Aquarius; this was about the power of the Age of Sex and Drugs and Rock 'n' Roll.

Around '71, Bill closed the Fillmore, and the Millard Agency moved uptown to East 52nd Street. The rent was radically increasing, and his profit margins were decreasing. If a tenant makes a whole lot of money, the landlord's going to want it. That's what happened here. But during its time, the Fillmore East was truly a magnet in Manhattan. Kids from all over flocked there.

Today I tell people I worked at the Fillmore.

"You did? I used to go there."

"Yeah, I was the one who told you to put your cigarette out."

("But it's a joint!" "Sorry, you gotta put it out.")

"Ah," they'll say, "you were the guy at the end of the aisle."

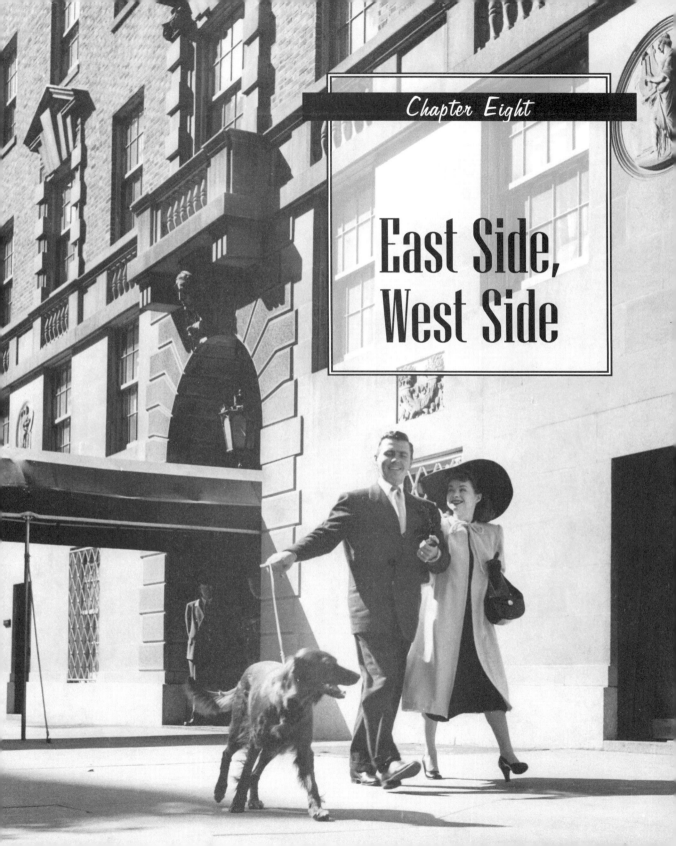

Chapter Eight

East Side, West Side

FATHER PETER COLAPIETRO: As a kid, I always saw Sixth Avenue as the dividing line between the East Side and West Side. The East Side was Rock Center and St. Patrick's Cathedral; the West Side was the stuff on 42nd Street. It was like you needed a passport to go from one to another.

HOWARD KISSEL: Central Park divides the city in two. I was on the bus going up Third and as we approached 79th Street, a woman got up to get off. There was a tone of hysteria in her voice as she ran to the back and cried, "Back door!" I knew this woman was getting off to take the crosstown bus; she was running back to her side of town.

Street scenes on the Upper West Side

The East Side has always been more settled, certainly from Fifth to Lexington. I've always thought of it as the adult side of town. Someone once explained to me that in the really exclusive buildings on Fifth and Park, you knew whether they admitted Jews if there was a thirteenth floor. If it went from 12 to 12A, it was a gentile building and Jews should not apply for a co-op there.

When I arrived in New York in the fall of 1960 to begin college at Columbia, I was deposited on a Sunday morning at the Greyhound bus depot and took a taxi up Amsterdam Avenue to Columbia. It was pretty frightening. I saw a crowd of people outside a bar; a fight was going on. I

remembered how my parents were afraid to send me to New York, and seeing this fight, I had the thought that this is a tough city.

In 1961, my parents wanted to visit me so my mother gave me the names of hotels to inspect. I thought they all were great and selected a place called the Coliseum House on 71st between Amsterdam and West End. I had not noticed this was around the corner from what was then called Needle Park, that there was a motorcycle gang on the corner. My mother was just terrified. I didn't understand. As far as I was concerned, I was in the Emerald City.

A week before I arrived at Columbia, a murder took place in Morningside Park. I read about it in a Milwaukee paper; the headline was *The Savage and the Savant*. It was about how difficult it was for Columbia to maintain itself in the presence of this hostile, dangerous community.

ANDREW BUSHKO: Columbia is a campus in the city, unlike NYU, whose campus *is* the city. I came back to Columbia after having been dean of students at Park College in Kansas City from 1968 to 1970. That was a tough couple of years to be dean of students. All you kept on saying was, "I hope it doesn't happen here."

I knew about the riot at Columbia in 1969. Still, instead of being scared, I was happy to be going back to New York, where the only responsibility I'd have would be to go to school. But I found that the great Ivy League institution was frayed around the edges. People were living in the aftermath of the huge campus conflict; there were still what was known as "trashings" going on. You'd be sitting someplace on campus and all of a sudden some people would run by with lead pipes and buckets of red paint. They'd storm into Putin Hall, where allegedly defense research was going on, smash things in the laboratories, throw red paint all over the place as if it were blood, and say they were demonstrating against the war.

The overall neighborhood was pretty gritty. The part where I lived on 121st Street, between Broadway and Amsterdam, was okay, though, because almost all the buildings were university housing. There was a real sense of neighborhood. Mrs. Zersass was an elderly woman who lived in the apartment house, and if you didn't see her for a couple of days, you would go by and check to see how she was. It was that kind of a community.

George Carlin grew up in that building, and his mother still lived there. She was a middle-class Irish woman who even in 1970 would not go out without white gloves and a hat. I'd see her going down the block to Corpus Christi Church, where she and the nuns would say prayers for George. You'd come home at night and there would be a message stuck to the elevator wall saying, "See George Carlin on the Johnny Carson Show tonight. He'll be wonderful," signed "Mary Carlin."

HOWARD KISSEL: The neighborhood around Columbia was very cosmopolitan, but working-class cosmopolitan rather than sophisticated cosmopolitan. There were all kinds of little restaurants. There was a Hungarian restaurant on Amsterdam, there were Italian restaurants, and there were those chains like Bickford's and Riker's, advertising "no better food at any price"—the big lie technique because the food was awful. Bickford's was a cafeteria and it struck me that the most forlorn people in the neighborhood went there. Chock Full o' Nuts was around. All those chains that were uniquely New York and which are all gone now.

There were still dairy restaurants on the Upper West Side. A friend of mine ordered herring, and on the menu it said, "With all fish dishes you get cole slaw." When my friend asked for his cole slaw, the waiter said, "You consider herring a fish?"

The West Side was supposed to be the intellectual side of town. So you had artists, teachers. And though in the fifties and sixties the area was economically depressed, it was still one of the last refuges for middle-class people.

JOE DARION: Our lawyer was also the lawyer for Jackie Gleason, and when Gleason moved his whole setup down to Florida, we were able to get Gleason's producer's apartment on Riverside Drive. The living room had an enormous bar that ran from one end of the room to the other. It had been a gift from Gleason.

One day we got on the elevator going down, and this very tall woman with three enormous men were there talking about a baseball game. "As soon as the center fielder began to move to his left, I knew the pitcher was losing his stuff," the woman said.

"That dame must sure know something about baseball," I said to my wife as we walked out of the building.

The doorman overheard me. "Don't you know who that is?" he asked. "She's Babe Ruth's widow." It turned out, as every taxi driver who ever drove us home confirmed, Babe Ruth had lived in our building.

But for a long while the Upper West Side was run down. The brownstones on the side streets had been turned into SROs (Single Room Occupancy dwellings). The landlords were looking to get out, and they weren't taking care of the buildings.

MAURICE RAPF: My son came home one day and told me, "I saw someone lying on the sidewalk with blood running out of him." I went down and sure enough there was a dead body around the corner. Once my daughter was in the elevator and someone tried to rape her. She got off at the twelfth floor and ran up the steps to the roof to get away from the guy. All my kids had experiences seeing people stabbed and so forth. If I encountered anyone who seemed like he was going to try to intimidate me, I would turn around and growl.

My wife and I and our three young children had moved to New York from California in 1951. We sublet an apartment at 325 West 86th Street. In California, I only knew movie people. But here all these different kinds of people lived in my apartment building—doctors, lawyers, engineers. They became my friends.

The reason I came to New York was that I was a member of the Communist Party and therefore blacklisted as a screenwriter. Before I left California, I burned my twenty-four-volume set of Lenin, published by the International Publishing House. I was afraid to leave it behind and afraid to take it with me.

There was a whole community on the Upper West Side of people who were escaping the Hollywood blacklist. The building at 344 Central Park West housed so many of them it was called the Kremlin of the West Side. The most famous of the left-wingers were on the top, and they got less famous as you moved to the bottom floor. Who lived there? I won't tell. The bulk of them worked in the Broadway theater, which did not have a blacklist.

Every day I would meet my friends at the Tip Toe Inn on 86th and Broadway. All the left-wingers gathered there. It was like a Hollywood studio commissary except that the waiters were insulting. That was something new for me coming from California, but the lunches for $1.25 were wonderful, the Nova Scotia salmon, the chopped chicken liver. If you had lunch at two in the afternoon, that would do you for the day. One block east was Lichtmann's, the bakery on the corner of 86th and Amsterdam. It was owned by Jewish people from Vienna. They must have had a smell machine—you couldn't walk by there without being sucked in by the smell.

I knew Zero Mostel from California, where he used to entertain at left-wing parties. He was so overpowering, he drove you crazy. When I met him again in New York, he had lost a lot of money because of the blacklist. I bought a picture that he painted when he was broke. But my wife hated that picture so much that to this day I don't know where it is.

I joined a poker game that had started in Zero Mostel's place on 28th Street. Then Zero and the poker game moved to the Belnord, an expensive apartment house that occupies the entire block from 86th to 87th Streets, Amsterdam to Broadway. We would order our midnight snacks from the Carnegie Deli, which delivered to us all the way uptown, or from Barney Greengrass.

SAUL ZABAR: In the 1960s, I knew the Upper West Side was considered a dangerous place, that people were moving out to Westchester and Long Island. From my standpoint, however, it was never dangerous. West End Avenue and Riverside Drive retained their integrity. The Irish had moved from Amsterdam and Columbus, and that part of the neighborhood became Hispanic. But to me it still seemed like the same West Side I had always known, the same customers going about their lives and buying things.

Isaac Bashevis Singer was a customer at Zabar's. He lived in the Belnord. He frequented the Senator Cafeteria on 96th and centered his stories on the literary crowd that hung around there. They could sit there all day long, speak in Yiddish, read the Yiddish newspapers, shmooze with each other, write their stories.

HOWARD KISSEL: In 1972, we paid an agency five hundred dollars for a rent-stabilized apartment on 88th and Central Park West. They were delighted to have a middle-class couple. As we were moving from 90th and West End, we schlepped a lot of stuff over ourselves. We were a little nervous. You were either west of Broadway or east of Columbus. In between was a no-man's-land that was thought to be dangerous. Only a few years earlier, it was not safe to walk on the side streets, where there were rooming houses filled with druggies and prostitutes. Turned out that had already changed. Due to the urban renewal project, people had bought brownstones on those blocks between Columbus and Amsterdam for thirty, forty, fifty thousand dollars. By the mid seventies, the West Side was turning around.

Soon after we moved to Central Park West, I took a walk down Columbus, which was sort of brave. I thought I had entered a time warp. All the storefronts I saw had probably been there in '42, '52, and '62. Old hardware stores, groceries, mom and pops. But one of the things I noticed was a restaurant called Ruskay's with a hand-painted menu in which it not only told you the dishes of the day but the chef of the day. It was the beginning of the culinary revolution. In a few years Ruskay's was so hot you couldn't walk down that side of the street.

KEN LIBO: When I first moved to Chelsea in the early sixties, there were three of us living in three rooms on the top floor of the old Victor Herbert mansion at 424 West 22nd Street. Then I moved in with three army intelligence officers in the London Terrace between 23rd and 24th and Ninth and Tenth. It was built in the late twenties, and I heard from many sources that in its day it was the largest apartment complex in the world; it takes up an entire block.

The Irish landladies were very conspicuous in Chelsea at that time. They owned the SROs, town houses that had been built in the middle of the nineteenth century for merchants and their families by Clement Clark Moore, who wrote "The Night Before Christmas." The tenants were mostly single or widowed men who worked on the wharves, and retired stevedores who'd sit on the steps outside the houses smoking their pipes. The Irish landladies sat on the steps too, although there was very little mixing. But as you came down the block, you felt very safe because these landladies on the stoops were like policemen. After all, their children were policemen, and so they knew how to manage. They were there all the time, watching.

Because there were so many people living in a compact area, you saw the life cycle played out in front of your eyes. Here is Mrs. O'Leary. Mrs. O'Leary has a son. Maybe he's old enough to live on his own, but Mrs. O'Leary is a protective Irish mother who wants one of her children to be with

her in her old age. She selected this son, and they live on the ground floor of this town house that they bought for fifteen thousand dollars. When you see Mrs. O'Leary, she smiles. She treats you very much as if you were living in a small town. "How are you?" she asks. "Did you have a nice day?"

I didn't get to know the stevedores or Irish landladies personally, but I did get to know Louise Bourgeois, whom many consider America's foremost sculptress. There she is, Louise, part of the neighborhood. She's from France. "You know, I was married to a Jew," she'd tell me, "but when our son Jean-Louis was born in Paris, I did not have him circumcised even though his father was Jewish."

"Oh, Louise, why is that?"

"I love Paris so much. If Hitler had won the war, I would want to go back with Jean-Louis, and if he were circumcised it would be very dangerous."

I also got to know Ben Zion, a very famous artist in the fifties and sixties.

London Terrace, one of the first large-scale housing developments in New York, is in Chelsea.

His widow, Lillian, has made a museum of her house, which gives you a wonderful sense of his career. Here were two artists, stevedores, Irish landladies.

And the Chelsea Hotel, which made a big impression on me at the time. Dylan Thomas and Brendan Behan had lived there.

HILTON KRAMER: In 1957, I rented an apartment in Hoboken. The fire station was only four doors away from my building. Nevertheless, not long after I moved in, I returned from a weekend away to discover there'd been a fire. Fortunately I hadn't unpacked my books yet. So I moved into a small furnished apartment on the sixth floor of the Chelsea Hotel, where I lived for the next three years.

The people who ran the Chelsea were Hungarian Jews. I found you had to sort of qualify to rent a place there. The manager said to me, "What do you do?"

I said, "I'm an art critic."

"A kind of writer?"

"Yes."

"Ah," he said, "we like writers here. We've buried some of the best of them."

While living at the Chelsea I had a very dramatic experience. The poet Delmore Schwartz was married to a writer, a beautiful blonde woman named Elizabeth Pollet.

The summer of 1957, they were at the Yaddo Colony in Saratoga, New York. When Delmore left for a few days to give a poetry reading, Elizabeth availed herself of his absence to leave him. He had been very abusive to her, and she just disappeared. It turned out afterwards she had gone to a friend in California.

By sheer coincidence, some weeks earlier Elizabeth had asked me if she could try out as a reviewer for *Arts Magazine*. I said sure and wrote her a letter telling her what the deadlines were for the fall issues.

When Delmore came back to Yaddo and found his wife had left him, he also found this letter from me. Convinced Elizabeth was living with me, he moved into the Chelsea Hotel and began calling me at odd times, threatening to kill me. Once he called just after I returned from a difficult weekend in Massachusetts, where I learned my mother had a fatal illness. "I can't

They liked writers at the Chelsea Hotel. "We've buried some of the best of them," a newcomer was told.

really deal with your situation right now. I have a lot of family problems," I said, and hung up.

The next day he called again. "I know what your family problems are. You're divorcing your wife to marry Elizabeth." I'd never had a wife.

Labor Day weekend, I stayed in New York hoping to finish a writing project. Delmore called Saturday night. "I know Elizabeth is up there with you, and I'm going to come up and shoot you," he said. Sure enough, a few minutes later, he's banging on my door. I put the chain on and opened it just enough to see him standing there with a gun. I slammed the door shut. Fortunately the Chelsea was built like a fortress.

I called down to the desk. Delmore had been at the Chelsea for weeks by this time so I didn't have to tell them how crazy he was. The night manager came up. "Now Mr. Schwartz," he said, "if I go in and search Mr. Kramer's apartment and I don't find Mrs. Schwartz there, will you believe me?"

When Delmore said, "I won't," I said I would call the police. Hearing that, Delmore went back to his room.

I put a few things in a bag and went over to Hoboken to spend the night with a friend, who came back to Manhattan with me the next morning. We went to the local precinct station to file a complaint. Since I hadn't suffered any injury, they didn't want to have anything to do with the situation. But I made such an issue of it that just to get rid of me they assigned an officer to come back to the Chelsea.

We're in the lobby. We call to Delmore's room, and he isn't there. Just as we're losing hope, into the lobby walks Delmore. The policeman starts questioning him. He says I'm making it all up.

I had told the police that Delmore had been in and out of psychiatric care. The policeman asks Delmore for the name of his psychiatrist. Delmore says the name and telephone number are in his room. So my friend, Delmore, the policeman, and I take the elevator up to his third-floor room. Now he somehow manages to unlock the door, push his way in, and close the door behind him. "You can't come into my room without a warrant," he says. Meanwhile we get a little glimpse into the room, which is total chaos.

Now the policeman becomes interested and calls the precinct to send a detective over. The detective tells Delmore he has to come down to the station for questioning. Delmore tries to talk his way out of it but can't. They call a psychiatrist from Bellevue down to the station. Delmore is shrieking so much he more or less convicts himself. He admits he did have fantasies of his wife sleeping with other people, one of them being Nelson Rockefeller. They lock him up in Bellevue.

When they heard about it, Leslie Katz, Saul Bellow, and some other people put together a sum of money to get Delmore out of Bellevue and into Paine Whitney, a private clinic. It was a very beneficent thing to do, but Paine Whitney couldn't keep him there unless someone in his family took responsibility for signing him in. No one knew where Elizabeth was, and Delmore's brother couldn't be located. So the upshot was Delmore signed himself out and then demanded Katz and Bellow hand over to him the money they had put together for his incarceration.

The first thing he did was go to see a former student of his who was now a lawyer. He brought a lawsuit against me on charges of false arrest and alienation of affections. I didn't have any money in those days and had to borrow from one of my brothers to hire a lawyer. My brother always thought I led an irregular life. This confirmed all his misgivings.

The lawsuit was still on the books when Delmore died several years later, because whenever it was time for depositions, his lawyer, who was devoted to him and wasn't making a penny out of this, was smart enough to know the case would be lost if Delmore ever had to go before a judge and give a deposition. So he kept postponing, hoping I'd make some settlement out of court. All the while, Delmore was on the loose.

That Sunday morning before I went to the police, I called a few people I knew were close to Delmore to ask their advice and see whether they could get him off my back. One was Saul Bellow, who advised me to call the police. Later he wrote a novel about Delmore called *Humboldt's Gift*. There's a very minor character in that novel who is on the make. The narrator, the Saul Bellow character in the novel, says, "Afterwards, this young man put it about that I advised him to go to the police." That character was supposed to be me. In those days in the literary world, the idea of turning a poet into the police was unacceptable.

So the Chelsea Hotel turned out to be an interesting place in which to live. Virgil Thomson had had an apartment there for many years. The painter Sam Francis had a big studio on the top floor that John Sloan had occupied at the beginning of the century. You always knew when Sam Hunter was in residence because on Sundays, limousines would pull up and these couples, the women in full-length mink coats, would arrive for brunch. Arthur Miller lived there for about six months. The artist David Smith used to stay at the Chelsea while I lived there, although when he started making money, he switched to the Plaza. It was not until after I moved out that the hotel became a scene for rock music and drugs.

The neighborhood itself, however, was very undistinguished. Usually I ate in the Village or uptown. There was an Automat nearby, and if somebody I knew was coming to New York, we'd often go there. The food was remarkably good; they had the best baked beans in New York.

KEN LIBO: At six or seven in the morning, the Automat was open already; it was always open. What a great pleasure it was on a spring morning to be able to go into the Automat and have a good cup of coffee from a shiny ornate urn with a spout that looked like the mouth of a lion. You'd get your nickels from the man in the center, on a surface made of marble with a little indentation. He was so quick; you gave him two dollars, you got forty nickels. And then you had the great joy, the real joy of New York: a hard roll. Good hard rolls are hard to come by. If you have the misfortune of walking around at 8 o'clock in the morning in St. Louis, Missouri, or Montgomery, Alabama, believe me—you'll have to walk far and wide before you find a New York hard roll.

I remember the wonderful people that you'd see in the Automat, people who lived in SROs, people on the fringe of society, barely getting by, individuals growing old, finding it hard to walk. The Automat was a place for them to go. They could sit down at a table and be a mensch.

One of the great tragedies of modern civilization is the disappearance of the five-and-tens. I go into CVS and say, "What's going on? Where is the five-and-ten of yesteryear?" The five-and-ten on 23rd and Eighth was the center of the village of Chelsea. All the goods were behind counters, which are so much more pleasant than shelves, and there were so many kinds of different things. There was a lunch counter where you got coffee and decent apple pie, cokes in the actual little coke glasses. The waitresses were kind and hardworking, a little long in the tooth, probably with drunken husbands at home.

But Eighth Avenue seemed the most depressing avenue in the universe. There were no lights from stores, only dim streetlights on the corners. It was like a scene out of Charles Dickens, only worse because it was devoid of atmosphere.

For whatever reason, in the 1970s gay life began moving north from the West Village into Chelsea. There were a few bars on the periphery of Chelsea, like the Spike and the Eagle on Eleventh Avenue near the warehouses; there were dangerous bars located in what was appropriately called the meatpacking area, which catered to people who were into self-mutilation. One known as the Mine Shaft was perhaps the most nefarious of all, although I happened to have known the owner, and he was a very nice person. There was no AIDS fear then, lots of pot, lots of amyl nitrate, which when sniffed from a bottle would intensify your erotic sensitivities for twenty or thirty seconds, but would also make your heart beat faster.

"At six or seven in the morning, the Automat was open already; it was always open."

The Irish landladies, as I remember, would take an interest in the gays. After all, New York has always had an enormous ethnic, religious, racial and cultural mix. In 1654 when the first Jews came to New Amsterdam, there were twenty different languages spoken amongst a group of fifteen hundred people. And it was the very same thing among these Irish landladies in Chelsea. They were used to having people radically different from themselves. The gays didn't live in the rooming houses at this time. But they would walk by, and the landladies would be quite friendly to them.

I had dinner with W. H. Auden because I got to know his assistant, a six-feet-five strapping youth from Arkansas named Orlon Fox who lived in Chelsea. What Orlon assisted with, I don't know. It was their business.

The dinner took place in Orlon's apartment on 22nd just off Eighth Avenue. Auden had told Orlon, "Invite three or four of your friends, and I will join you for dinner." And there was the great man himself wearing a pullover that looked as though it hadn't been brushed for many months and trousers that hadn't seen a crease in a long time.

When I came to New York in the 1960s, gays were very much undercover. I remember hanging around in a gay bar, and who should be standing there but the man who hired me for my job. "Oh, my God, my whole life is going to fall apart because the man who hired me knows I'm gay," I thought. Of course I was so stupid because obviously he was gay as well.

I had become very friendly with the head of a major New York publisher. We used to go to a bar that would be packed with gay people, and every so often, the police cars would drive by with their lights on and flash them inside. We would get frightened by it, and yet we sort of grooved on the fear that any moment they were going to throw us into jail. That was part of gay life at that time. We felt perfectly happy and relaxed going to our little gay parties where people were gay or gay-tolerant. But outside of that circle, and the mothers of gays who were very open about it, you wouldn't discuss the fact of your being gay.

ELAINE MARKSON: I remember sitting next to a young man on the bus. We began chatting. When he told me he liked the color lipstick I was wearing, I said, okay, this is the signal that he's gay. He didn't know where to go. "Get off the bus with me," I said. "I'll walk you down 8th Street and show you." There were gay bars in Greenwich Village in the 1950s, but they were gentler.

The Village was a bohemian neighborhood then. All these writers and artists were around. A guy who looked like Eugene O'Neill would walk down the streets, and if you bought him a cup of coffee and a Danish he'd tell you what he was writing and whom he knew.

The *Village Voice* was the real center of Village life. You got your apartment through the *Voice*, you read all the articles. It was our Bible.

HILTON KRAMER: Greenwich Village was still Greenwich Village in those days, not expensive shoe shops. It was full of marvelous bookstores. The Eighth Street Bookshop was a great literary center. It had the best inventory of literary classics, including modern literature. Anatole Broyard, whom I was instrumental in having the *Times* hire many years later, had a bookshop on Cornelia Street. It was a very literary secondhand bookstore. Anatole wasn't buying junk. If he didn't like it, he wouldn't stock it.

Together with a friend, Anatole Broyard taught a course at the New School. The whole point of it seemed to be to meet pretty young girls, whom they both had a keen interest in. The New School was an intellectually lively place in those days, with a much more bohemian atmosphere than Columbia. Most of the professors were adjuncts, and I think for most of that period they were paid according to the number of people who signed up for their courses. Meyer Schapiro, who was a professor of fine arts at Columbia, gave lectures on the history of modern art at the New School. It was always standing room only. He was almost a matinee idol—charming, handsome, eloquent and learned. About two-thirds of the audience were female of every age, and they would come back year after year to hear the same lecture. Although I have great respect for Meyer, I sat through quite a few of those lectures, and I must say at some point I found all of that eloquence fatiguing.

ELAINE MARKSON: In the fifties and sixties, people who didn't have a lot of money were able to live in the Village. We had a big beautiful one-bedroom apartment on 11th Street and Seventh Avenue that cost us a hundred dollars a month. I had two children there.

It was hard to find an expensive meal in the area, and there were many wonderful Italian restaurants. Foreign films began coming into the small art theaters; some of them served coffee. The Limelight was a coffee shop on Seventh Avenue South that was always packed. I don't remember people drinking coffee though; I remember them drinking booze. Then they'd go to one of the local diners to sober up.

There was a lot of drinking going on in the literary milieu. MacDougal and Bleecker Streets had all these bars; the White Horse and the Lion's Head were on Hudson and 11th, and each one had different crowds of noisy people who hung around all night. But in the 1950s, the scene in these bars was sweeter, more intense and writerly, even though being a drinker was part of being in the group. People wanted to drink the way Dylan Thomas or Malcolm Lowry drank.

Fred Exley would come for dinner and afterward he'd say, "Let's all go to the bar now," and my husband, David, would say, "Fred, Elaine can't—she has two children to take care of." That was the routine. The men did not have parental responsibilities.

We got to know Jack Kerouac through his friend who lived next door to us. After he had written *On the Road* and had become famous, Kerouac stayed with us for a while. He'd write these copious notes for his novel, pages and pages and pages. I thought he was funny, quite charming and very handsome. But he drank an awful lot, and looking back, I think he was on marijuana as well. He was very much of the time, the Beats, the late 1950s.

ANDY BALDUCCI: The Village had a lot of beautiful people. Not much money, but rich in culture and talent. Boris Karloff was one of our regular middle-of-the-night customers. Regardless of the weather, in the snow, rain, he'd come by two, three o'clock in the morning for a couple of tomatoes, a couple of peppers, a cauliflower, some leftovers. "Tell Andy I'll stop in tomorrow to pay," he'd tell the night man.

A few days later, he'd come by. "Andy, I was in the other night, I took so and so. Would fifty cents be all right?"

"Okay, Mr. Karloff, it's all right."

I didn't know how famous the man was.

Judy Holliday was a regular, a very simple young lady, a little bit shy.

NINA BALDUCCI: She would come in with her mother and her three-year-old boy in a stroller. I only knew her as Mrs. Oppenheimer, the doctor's wife. James Beard lived on 12th Street. Once he discovered us, he came in almost every day or he'd ask for produce to be delivered. He loved raspberries.

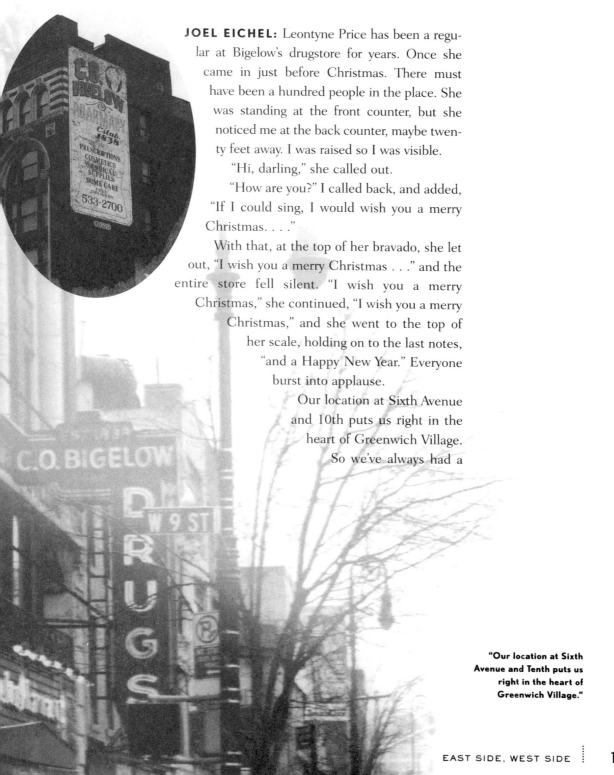

JOEL EICHEL: Leontyne Price has been a regular at Bigelow's drugstore for years. Once she came in just before Christmas. There must have been a hundred people in the place. She was standing at the front counter, but she noticed me at the back counter, maybe twenty feet away. I was raised so I was visible.

"Hi, darling," she called out.

"How are you?" I called back, and added, "If I could sing, I would wish you a merry Christmas. . . ."

With that, at the top of her bravado, she let out, "I wish you a merry Christmas . . ." and the entire store fell silent. "I wish you a merry Christmas," she continued, "I wish you a merry Christmas," and she went to the top of her scale, holding on to the last notes, "and a Happy New Year." Everyone burst into applause.

Our location at Sixth Avenue and 10th puts us right in the heart of Greenwich Village. So we've always had a

"Our location at Sixth Avenue and Tenth puts us right in the heart of Greenwich Village."

million and one actors as customers, some famous and some journeymen, a tremendous amount of models. When I first started, this lady was banging on the door one night after we had closed. She opened up such a big mouth that she scared me, and I let her in. It was Bella Abzug.

Ed Koch's been a longtime customer. He used to come behind the counter even though we wouldn't allow it and tell us how to organize our displays. His father owned a shoe store, he said, and he knows.

Our customers have been the cream of the crop of the whole country, like the guy from Nebraska who's going to write the great American novel. He doesn't, but he ends up being a professor at NYU, lives in the Village, and shops at Bigelow's.

In the early 1960s, I was a student at the Brooklyn College of Pharmacy looking for a job. I didn't know anything about the store or the area. But as soon as I walked in the door, my heart started pumping, ba-boom, ba-boom, ba-boom. I felt like I was a cartoon character, that everyone could see the beating of my heart through my shirt. I saw the high ceilings, the elaborate gas chandeliers, the nineteenth-century oak fixtures, the bronze plaque on the wall from the late 1920s that marked the 85th anniversary of the store. I had never seen anything like it. And it was hopping.

The going wage was $100 a week. I asked for $125 because I had been working in neighborhood drugstores in Brooklyn and Queens since I was about eight years old. I was hired, and my adventure at Bigelow's began.

IAN GINSBERG: My grandfather, Willie Ginsberg, was a little Jewish guy, an immigrant from Austria, who became a pharmacist. He owned a lot of little drugstores with other guys, made a living. Then in 1939, he bought Bigelow's from Mr. Bigelow, who was an anti-Semite by the way, and that became his main store. It had been kind of trashed during the Depression, and my grandfather got it for real cheap.

Pharmacy became the family profession; my father, my uncles and cousins worked at Bigelow's. When I began, we still had eight or nine pharmacists sitting behind the second barrier, each one in his own space, with his own typewriter to type out the labels and a long stick with a spatula on the end to reach the pharmacy books on the higher shelves.

JOEL EICHEL: By the time I came on board, Ian's grandfather was semi-retired. But Uncle Willie, as they called him, taught me a lot of compounding tricks, gave me insights into the way things are done. A few years after I was hired, Ian's uncle retired, and I became partners with Ian's father.

IAN GINSBERG: I used to deliver to the Electric Lady Land Recording studio that Jimmy Hendrix had built in the 1960s. Since I was a musician, I was absolutely enamored. I also delivered to the Women's House of Detention across the street; the women would scream at me out the window. On Sundays, when the husbands and kids used to visit the women, they'd come into the store with various papers they needed to have notarized. A notary public who'd been working for us for fifty years, would take out the old *pharmacopoeia*, which has all the data and requirements of pharmacy, have them put their hand on it like it was the Bible, and raise their right hand. He'd say, "Repeat after me . . . ," and they'd say, "I do, I do." It was a whole ritual.

JOEL EICHEL: My most memorable experiences were the two blackouts, one in the late sixties and the other in the early seventies. People didn't want to go to sleep, or they couldn't get to their apartments with the elevators not working. Everybody was on the streets. Gay guys came out from the West Village on roller skates. They rolled onto the intersection of 8th Street and Sixth Avenue and began directing traffic very flamboyantly with elaborate arm gestures. They were beautiful to watch. It was like a ballet.

We stayed open all night using the old gaslights to illuminate the store; women were buying cosmetics by gaslight. We still had the soda fountain then, and people were having sandwiches until we ran out of food. At about six in the morning, the bread truck came in. The driver didn't know what was going on. All the restaurants and stores were closed, and he had a whole truckload of bread. He said, "I'll dump it all here. Whatever you don't use, I'll take back tomorrow." The egg man came in from Jersey. Same thing. He loaded us with eggs from the floor to the ceiling.

Then people began coming in for breakfast. The grill worked on gas so we were able to make eggs and toast the bread. We were able to make coffee because it was on gas. We were in business.

I always used to say if anyone in this world gets to heaven, it's going to be the man who made lamps on 14th Street. He was a true Village character and one of our best customers, a guy about sixty years old, married with two or three kids. He was completely unkempt, a free spirit with hair like Einstein's going its own way. Except in the coldest weather, he walked around barefoot.

But what he did was take in runaway children. You know the kind, a fifteen-year-old girl who gets off the bus at the Port Authority, gets grabbed by some sleazeball who makes her into a junkie and a prostitute. He would find kids like this, take them in, teach them the craft of making lamps, keep them going until they could get on their feet. He had a charge account, and it was a big account because he took care of so many people. At any given time, he'd have his regular family and a couple of kids he'd taken in, some who had just had babies and needed diapers, baby formula, and baby creams. All these people would be charging to him.

One day not long ago, a young man came into the store holding the hand of a little boy. "Hi," he said, "do you remember me?" I didn't.

"I'm Joel. This is my son."

I looked at him; I couldn't believe it. He was one of the runaways, a junkie.

"I live in California now with my wife and son. We came back to visit."

"What are you doing?" I asked.

"I got a lamp shop."

ANDREW BUSHKO: I arrived at NYU the summer of '62, having gotten into a master's program at the School of Education. NYU was vastly different from Cornell, where I had been an undergraduate. It was not much of a residential college at that time. The new library was not yet there. When you finished an evening class, you had the feeling that things were closed down. The West Village was always hopping, but toward the east, it was still light industry. Factories closed at five, and the storefronts were covered with metal doors. It was not a hospitable feeling.

On the other hand, Washington Square Park was filled with people, especially on weekends, when long-haired troubadours, who probably came from Long Island, descended on the square. What a great way to spend a Sunday afternoon, sitting around the circular fountain or staking out a little space on the back of a park bench and serenading people with songs of protest or English-Irish ballads about women with broken hearts. This was the time of the Civil Rights Movement, the freedom rides and sit-ins in the South—the early Kennedy years when we had the feeling things were changing. There was such an optimism.

South of the square were wonderful places like the Bitter End and Gerde's Folk City, where people like Bob Dylan and Phil Ochs entertained. People were very respectful of each other and the performers. You'd sit there with a cup of coffee and talk politics and music. I saw Simon and Garfunkel in one of those clubs; they were just becoming famous then. Art with his long hair and Paul with his short hair looked just the way they were supposed to look: cool.

Every so often, you'd see mimeographed flyers announcing there was going to be a "happening," say on Sunday at one o'clock. The word would get around, and on that day, everyone would gather, some wearing outlandish things like you'd see at Mardi Gras. There would be street performers, singers and dancers, mimes, people on unicycles, jugglers. There was a feeling of brotherhood, of being one with one another, of being where it was happening. There was a great emphasis on the love-in kind of feeling.

NYU had an extensive program of tours for people who were visiting the university, and during the summer of 1963, I had the job of taking these groups around to the museums, Rockefeller Center, the Federal Reserve Bank, behind the scenes at Macy's. There were about fifteen people in the group, most of them here for the first time. A good number were nuns studying at

"What a great way to spend a Sunday afternoon, sitting around the circular fountain."

NYU, and most of them were still wearing habits. There I'd be with five or six nuns going over to the A train, going four blocks this way or that way, saying, "Sister Marie Louise, be sure you get on the train, Sister Mary Jean, we're getting off at the next stop." I was always counting heads, fearful I would lose this nun from Indiana someplace on the A train. Eternal damnation.

November 22, 1963, seems to mark the beginning of the long, dark period that culminated in 1968 when it all fell apart with the assassinations of Martin Luther King and Robert Kennedy and the chaos of the Democratic Convention. The day President Kennedy was killed, I had just returned from lunch and walked into the Loeb Student Center toward the front desk. There was a radio on, and someone said there's a report that the President had been shot. We got as close to the radio as possible. Events unfolded. Everyone was walking around in a daze, kind of dopey.

When I left NYU for Fargo, North Dakota, in the summer of 1964, Greenwich Village was already not as nice a place as it had been when I arrived. Drugs were coming in, protests were no longer peaceful, and the atmosphere had become more mean-spirited. When I was an undergraduate

"Washington Square Park was filled with people, especially on weekends, when long-haired troubadours descended on the square."

at Cornell, the big fight was to allow Gus Hall, secretary of the American Communist Party, to speak on campus. The whole notion was that you were supposed to have a world where anyone could speak their piece and let their words either redeem or condemn them. But things were now moving to where people were starting to shout other people down. This was still early in the protest against the war, but already it was not possible to question anybody's antiwar position.

ELAINE MARKSON: From 1958 to 1961, we lived in Mexico and sublet our apartment in the city. A lot of people did that. When we came back, you could tell the money was moving into Greenwich Village. Washington Square Village had been built, which was kind of amazing. There were all these white luxury buildings that hadn't been there three years before. But it was still a beatnik scene.

Then in 1966 we went to Europe, and when we returned in 1968, the changes were astonishing. It was the time of Vietnam, of political activism, and the Village was at the center of it all with candlelight vigils and protest marches. I returned in time for the Oceanhill Brownsville school strike with two small children who were entering public school. A group of parents who were liberal and interested in education broke into the school to conduct classes during the strike. As a result, we got the Board of Education to allow us to start a new school, P.S. 3 on Barrow Street.

The Village was a hotbed of political activity. There were political positions on every issue you could imagine. Some argued there should be restrictions to keep people from peeing in the sandbox while others said that that would be restricting what people should be allowed to do. It was quite hilarious.

But the drug situation was hardly funny. Washington Square had become a little drug scene. We were living in a brownstone on West 4th and MacDougal by then, and Dan Rather did the first segment of *48 Hours* from my living room, calling it "48 Hours on Crack Street." You could look out the window and watch all the exchanges taking place. My children learned how to open the door, looking around to be sure they were not going to be threatened before taking the keys out, how to negotiate the streets.

When they went to Intermediate School 70 on 17th Street between Eighth and Ninth Avenues, the kids were not allowed to go out the back door because the High School of Humanities, which was around the corner, had too many bad kids. But with all of this we never felt the Village was unsafe. In fact, I felt it was the safest place one would possibly want to live. There was always street traffic. You were never alone day or night.

In 1970, I began working for a literary agent in the basement of my brownstone. After two years, I went out on my own, first in my apartment and then at 44 Greenwich Avenue, which was the headquarters of Vietnam Veterans Against the War when I took it over. It was a mess.

It was the emergent feminist movement that motivated me to start my own agency. There were a lot of women agents in the business, but not many who owned agencies, so I was part of a new breed. I had two small children and a husband, but husbands didn't cooperate much in those days, so it wasn't easy.

The publishing world wasn't a collection of huge conglomerates then. They were small companies, all centered in New York, run by people you would actually get to talk to. I got to know all the editors and publishers. It was much easier in that respect. Being a woman in the Village had a lot to do with my getting so many female writers. But also, I knew many people from the political scene, like Victor Navasky, who sent me a lot of my clients. I met Grace Paley through the activism. She told me, "When my agent dies, I'll come to you," and she did.

LACONIA SMEDLEY: I came to New York from Detroit, Michigan, the summer of 1956. I got off the train at Grand Central Station and took a taxi uptown along Fifth Avenue, which was still two-way. And as soon as we

Greenwich Village in the late 1960s— "There were all these white luxury buildings that hadn't been there three years before. But it was still a beatnik scene."

reached 110th Street, I sensed a change. Downtown it was bum-bum, bum-bum, bum-bum—very regular, everybody marching with their little briefcases. But at 110th Street, it became da-dum, da-dum, da-dum; the swift repetitive beats had become a relaxed kind of syncopation. Without hearing it, I felt a different rhythm.

Then I noticed the radical change of people from mostly white folk to mostly black folk. The suits and ties had come off; I saw people walking with no shirts, I saw a guy walking with a mattress on his head. It was a high-powered energy that I felt when I came into Harlem that first time. It made me relaxed but at the same time apprehensive because it was a vibration I had never felt before.

Coming from Detroit, which had a communal sense, and a family sense, and a respectful sense, I was in culture shock. In Detroit, you had your black sections. We lived on one side of Warren Avenue, and on the other side were Polish people. But Harlem seemed an enclave by itself. In Detroit, the fathers had factory jobs at Ford, Chrysler. The family unit was intact. Here everyone was out on the street in the middle of the day; I saw people nodding on the streets. In Detroit, people didn't use profanity. If you cursed, the neighbors would say, "Now there, watch your mouth." But what I heard immediately on the streets of New York was raw talk, vulgar talk, disrespectful talk that made me think everybody was getting ready to fight, and I was afraid.

There was such a mixture: the churchgoers, the street people, the people who hung out in the bars. Not that you didn't have a rowdy section in Detroit, but it was just a couple of strips on the east side. We were cordoned off from it, protected from it. It wasn't the whole area. Harlem was a bigger canvas, a multiplicity of classes, different kinds of people all together.

But once I got settled in, I knew if someone called someone else an "MF," it didn't mean that they were going to fight. It was a product of stifled anger, not a matter of imminent violence, a way to express rage. Harlem was one place where you could express yourself, where you could say, "This is me. I don't give a damn what anybody else thinks."

I had come to New York following my uncle, Professor Edward Boatner. He wasn't my uncle genetically, but in the black family you adopt people. He was a larger-than-life type of person, very dynamic and direct, a big, bug-eyed, powerful black man who scared his choirs into singing. Like many of the black professionals of that time, he always wore a vest and a tie. And he was a very good cook, especially of Creole food.

I became an assistant teacher to Professor Boatner. My students were people from the neighborhood. Some went on to make a name for themselves, got into Broadway shows, became well known. Others were people seventy, eighty years old who wanted to take piano or voice, wanted to do the things they weren't able to do before because they had to work so hard to raise their children. I marveled at the little black fingers of these elderly people learning to play for the first time.

Once a year, Mrs. Thornwall, one of the women who sang in Professor Boatner's choir, would invite all thirty-five people in the choir to a big dinner in her apartment. She lived in Graham Court, the building on Seventh Avenue between West 116th and 117th that had been commissioned by William Waldorf Astor. When it opened in 1901, Harlem was like the suburbs to Manhattan. It's the most luxurious apartment house in Harlem, with eight elevators and a two-story arched entry that leads into a gardened court.

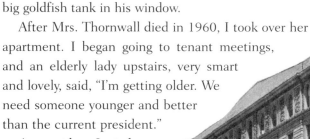

When Graham Court on Seventh Avenue between 116th and 117th Streets opened in 1901, "Harlem was like the suburbs to Manhattan."

After Astor, a man they called Daddy Brown owned it. He was going with a young lady named Peaches. It was the talk of the town. Then a series of managers took over the building who were not very good. By my time, the people in Graham Court were middle-aged to elderly. I had the impression that some of them worked for wealthy people who had turned the apartments over to them. But there was a mixture of people in the building, a dentist, a doctor, some teachers. There was a Dr. Anderson who had a big goldfish tank in his window.

After Mrs. Thornwall died in 1960, I took over her apartment. I began going to tenant meetings, and an elderly lady upstairs, very smart and lovely, said, "I'm getting older. We need someone younger and better than the current president."

As president I tried to get landmark status for the exterior and interior. They had cut up some of

"At first I worked in the Thirty-first, Thirty-second Precincts in Harlem."

the apartments in the 1950s so we couldn't get interior landmark status, but we did get exterior.

Harlem has always been unique because you have the combination of so many different kinds of people. You had the Harlem Renaissance with all the great writers in the twenties and thirties, and the street people were right there, maybe next door. The writers and artists fed off what was happening around them. Sometimes in the struggle and isolation, you create a lot of beauty. It's like a beautiful flower growing from manure; it's the coming out of something that makes you rise up above it.

ALVIN REED: In 1965, I took the police test and was disqualified because I was missing seven teeth. The impression that I got was you failed the medical, and that's it. On the train going home, I saw one of the other guys who was disqualified. I sat down next to him. "What was your problem?" he asked. "You got a heart murmur, too?"

"No," I said. "I got too many teeth missing."

"They disqualify you for that?"

"Yeah."

He said, "You know what to do? You go to a dentist, tell them to make up a cheap bridge and then you call up and get a reexamination."

It seemed he had been through the process; he knew a little more than me. So I did exactly what he told me.

The dentist charged me a hundred and twenty dollars. "Don't wear it now," he told me. "When you go up for reexamination, wait till you're on the elevator going upstairs, and then you put it in."

It killed my mouth, but I passed with honors. Then white kids were asking me to help them out; it was a whole new awakening for me.

At first I worked in the Thirty-first, Thirty-second Precincts in Harlem. I saw instances where someone said, "Let's see who can knock him out."

"Go ahead, take a shot."

"Oh, man, you can't hit hard."

Meanwhile, the poor guy's—you know. I've seen where they handcuffed a guy to the chair and everybody came by and took a shot. A couple of times the black officers just walked out. I didn't get along with people who beat on people, who hit people.

TOM SLATTERY: When I was twenty-one, I became a police officer assigned to the Thirty-second Precinct in central Harlem. The first few months I walked a beat, then I was in a radio car. I thought I was doing something important, and I got along very well with the people. That was from 1956 to 1963, when the uniform had a tremendous respect in the community, although if it was fear or respect, I don't really know. Many police officers kept complete neighborhoods under control and never, never had to use a gun. There was one fellow who used a rolled-up newspaper as he worked his beat. The police knew the people, and the people knew the police.

We had disturbances but no riots. One night my partner and I were on 147th and Eighth Avenue when we got a call to assist a patrolman on 125th and Seventh Avenue. Usually, by the time you would get down to, say, 141st Street, you'd get the message "No further assistance required." But not this time. We were the first car to get to the scene, where a mob had stopped traffic. The African Nationalists were on one corner, and the Muslims were on the other. Some of the Nationalists had rifles and shot into the other group. We never found out the story as to what the final outcome was. But as we came out of the car without a nightstick or anything, four men with rifles were marching toward Eighth Avenue. We shoved them into a hallway. More police arrived, and it was over. That went down in the papers as a minor disturbance.

On the other hand, we might respond to a noise complaint and join the party. We "divorced people"—sometimes the same people twice a month, common-law couples who'd had a spat. We would settle it with "You're divorced."

Nothing ever happened on the ground floor. It was always on the top floors or rooftops of walkups. We were always taking people to the hospitals, taking dead bodies out. I delivered babies in apartments, in basements, everywhere. I think I delivered well over forty babies in close to eight years. Some were named after me.

In the early years, I looked at the job as a big game, cops and robbers. Then it got very serious as I saw what things could happen. The biggest problem in Harlem was drug trafficking. Druggies were a nuisance to the average working family. They'd break into apartments, steal toasters and TVs. There were crimes of violence perpetrated between friends. And drug lords would shoot each other in the bars.

Still, I always looked around Harlem. I was very impressed with Strivers' Row, the area around 137th Street between Seventh and Eighth Avenues with beautiful town houses owned by mostly professional people. I noticed these beautiful stone pillars engraved with the inscription "Private road, walk your horses."

"I started following jazz to be cool. You take a young lady out, show her a sophisticated atmosphere."

DOROTHY WHEELOCK: As the features editor at *Harper's Bazaar*, I sometimes had six or ten pages to fill when there weren't enough new fashions. Once I did a nightclub piece, "Your Night to Howl," and my husband and I went to about three nightclubs a night for almost three weeks.

When James Mason's mother-in-law, who was from that big English movie family, came over, the only thing she wanted to see was Harlem. So we took her together with James and Pam to the Harlem Ballroom. Immediately the black guys asked the mother and Pam and me to dance. They had been sitting around at tables, having a drink, waiting for tourists to come in. But when James and my husband asked the black girls to dance, they wouldn't dance with them. They were so mad because we were having such a good time. Those guys were very fancy dancers.

ALVIN REED: I was an excellent dancer, excellent. We did the mambo, we did the slop, we did what we called walk-the-floor—it was like a two-step. All the dance halls had live music; the dj's didn't come in until later on.

Live music was better. You had a partner, you looked in her eyes, you asked her name, you made conversation. Then when the dance was over, you'd take the young lady back to the table where you got her from. A lot of times her parents were there to kind of watch the young lady, to make sure she met the right kind of man.

"Hi, young man," the father would say. "Have a seat. What's your name? Do you work?"

MONTE IRVIN: There was a group called the Savoy Sultans that played at the Savoy Ballroom over on Lenox Avenue between 140th and 141st Streets. That was the place to see great dancing, particularly the group that did the jitterbug, the lindy hop. Cootie Williams and Erskine Hawkins would always appear there and play great, great music.

We knew a lot about the Renaissance Casino because we used to play an annual college basketball game there. The Rens, a legendary basketball team, played at the Renaissance regularly: Tarzan Cooper, Eyre Saitch, Bill Yancey, who was a shortstop and a great basketball player. First there was a game, then there'd be a dance. Count Basie or Duke Ellington might be playing. We were very partial to Basie, Ellington, and Billy Eckstine. They were big baseball fans and stayed at the same hotels down South that we did when we were barnstorming.

I used to come to Harlem with Joe Williams, Don Newcombe, Roy Campanella—guys from the Negro Leagues I hung out with. We'd go to Smokey Joe Williams, a bar on Lexington and 126th. Smokey Joe was the bartender there. Campy and I used to stop by and talk to him. He'd name some of the old Negro players. When we really wanted to relax, we'd take our wives to Sugar Ray Robinson's bar on Seventh Avenue and 124th Street. Sugar Ray prided himself on the fact that he could sing a little; he was a pretty good dancer, too. There were jazz clubs all over the place, and that's where we would hang out.

ALVIN REED: Harlem had a club on every corner, two, three of them, and they were all packed. You couldn't wait to hit eighteen to get into the clubs. I actually joined the National Guard when I was seventeen—you were supposed to be eighteen—to get a photo ID so I could get into the clubs.

We went to Club Baron on Lenox and 132nd, Small's Paradise, Count Basie's, Well's, Jock's Place. A lot of those places, we'd go in, have a drink, and move on. The price was a little high for us. Sometimes we went to the Red Rooster at 138th and Seventh Avenue, which was mostly for professional people, politicians. Adam Clayton Powell—that was his hangout. Heavy conversations, political conversations—we didn't stay for that.

People would come to Small's Paradise (pictured below) for the chicken and waffles, and the great jazz.

MONTE IRVIN: The fellow who owned the Red Rooster was one of the greatest Giant fans who ever lived. After I became a Giant, I'd leave him tickets and he'd come particularly to the afternoon games.

ALVIN REED: I started following jazz to be cool. You take a young lady out, show her a sophisticated atmosphere. She thinks, "Oh, this guy's really heavy here." But then I began to like it, not so much over the radio, as live. Live jazz was totally different. You see the expression on the guy's face, you see the sweat.

MONTE IRVIN: The bars would usually close at four o'clock, but there were these after-hours clubs that would open up a minute after four. Nobody was ready to go home yet. We came along in a great era musically, a wonderful, wonderful era. Sinatra was just coming into his own; there was Harry James, and Ella Fitzgerald and all these wonderful, wonderful people would hang out in Harlem. There was Nat Cole—at that time he was playing the piano—he wasn't doing much singing, but he'd be there. Joe Louis was around; he was a big jazz fan.

LACONIA SMEDLEY: If you came to Small's Paradise late enough, and that's what people did, you would have chicken with waffles and hear some very good jazz.

White jazz musicians would come in the hopes of sitting in with some of the jazz greats. I went to see the saxophonist Sonny Stitt play at Baron's. A couple of white folks in the audience wanted to play, so Sonny's piano player invited them up. They played pretty good, but what Sonny would do—he was very devilish—was run the keys. These folks were obviously more than just beginners, they were pretty proficient, but to be able to play in all the keys and improvise in all the keys was something else.

"In the clubs of Harlem, people really let their spirits soar."

I was kind of conservative and focused on my teaching. I wasn't the person to drink and smoke and go to bars. But a friend of mine, very relaxed where I was kind of uptight, would say, "Come on, let's go out." So we'd visit the clubs. I found it all very exciting because the energy of the people was so high and the musicians were so fabulous.

ALVIN REED: The Rhythm Club on 133rd between Lenox and Seventh was a club for musicians. All of them were in there: Billie Holiday, Sarah Vaughan, Cab Calloway, Bojangles—it was like a kind of private club. I guess it started off because a lot of blacks couldn't always play downtown so they stayed there. They had really cheap meals. Down in the basement you could gamble. They had a little chalkboard for the musicians. You put your name on that board and what instrument you played, and when downtown needed a saxophone player they'd call up, and the guy on top of the list would go down. They'd cross his name off the top of the list, and everybody would move up. Meantime, they're playing a little cards, they're eating. That was how they got their gigs.

Every now and then the police used to come with the paddywagon and shoosh, all the people would come out in handcuffs into a lineup because of the gambling that was going on. Every now and then I saw my father come out in handcuffs. The next evening, they were all back there again.

LACONIA SMEDLEY: In the clubs of Harlem, people really let their spirits soar. If you are sensitive enough spiritually, you could actually feel the vibrations of those places when you walked in because the people who played there had left their essence behind.

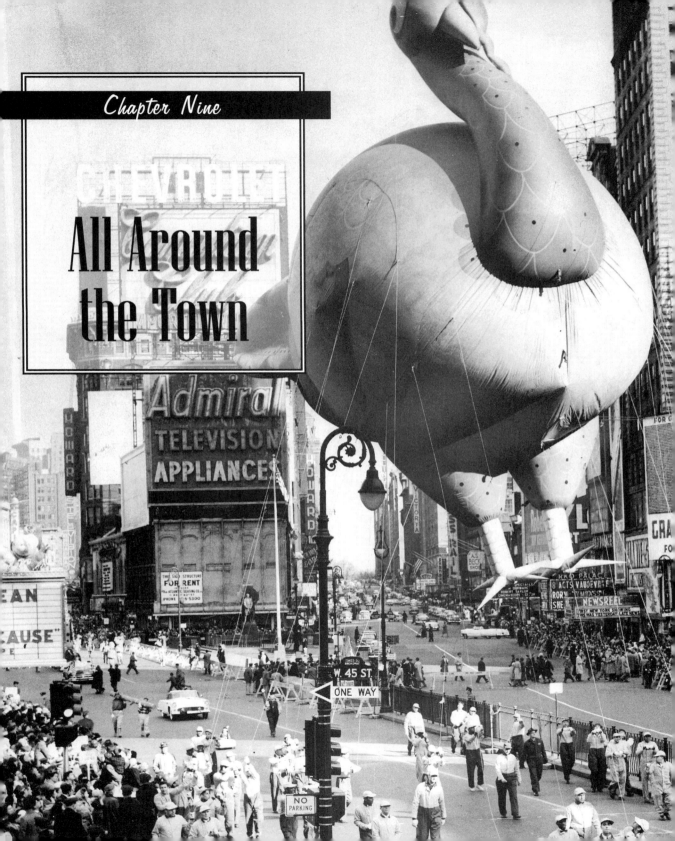

Chapter Nine

All Around the Town

There were twelve major dailies and each had its own character.

LEONARD KOPPETT: The way of life that made New York City what it was in the fifties and sixties was peculiar to that time. New York had become the most affluent and influential spot on the face of the planet. And the people making decisions were forming their concepts of what was going on from what they read in the New York newspapers. Television was still new. Radio was rudimentary, essentially bulletin news. The newspaper was the major source of current affairs and features. "I read it in the paper" meant it happened.

In 1948, the morning papers were the *Times*, *Herald Tribune*, *Daily News*, and *Mirror*. The *Times* and *Trib* were a nickel, the *News* and *Mirror* were two cents. The afternoon papers were the *Sun, Journal American*, *World Telegram* and *Post*. There were others: the *Compass*, *PM*; the Yiddish papers were also very strong.

BILL GALLO: Each newspaper had its own character. I envisioned the *Times* as an aristocrat smoking a cigarette with a cigarette holder. The *Trib* was a professor, not too concerned with money although well dressed, not pompous like the *Times*. The *Mirror* was a kid on the block running after things, while the *Post* was hard driving, intellectual, and liberal but with the tone of a loser. The *World Telegram* was a respectable sort of a guy who minded his own business.

He was steady, wanting to improve all the time, and had a little more class than the *Journal American,* which was the only one of the newspapers who didn't know who it was. It had a sort of schizophrenic personality, gossipy one day, trying to start a war the next. But the *Daily News* was a person with a great sense of humor who was very sure of himself.

LEONARD KOPPETT: There was a strong rivalry between the *Times* and the *Trib*. The *Trib* was clearly the better paper in terms of the quality of writing and how it handled its coverage. Walter Lippman was still there. It was frankly Republican while the *Times* was Democrat but not quite open about it. However, the *Tribune* was badly managed, and after the war it started to get into financial difficulties, while the *Times* was brilliantly managed all along.

BILL GALLO: There was this great rivalry between the *News* and the *Mirror*. The *Mirror* was a Hearst paper but they couldn't get the ads.

LEONARD KOPPETT: The *World Telegram*, which absorbed the *Sun* around 1950, was essentially wishy-washy, on the mainstream side, attracting straight, non-tabloid readers of an afternoon paper. The people who read the *Times* and the *Trib* in the morning would read the *World Telegram and Sun* in the afternoon. Most people read at least two papers a day.

JACK LANG: I liked the *Journal American*. It was a Hearst newspaper with columnists like Dorothy Kilgallen and Westbrook Pegler and loaded with information about what was going on in entertainment and sports.

JOHN CAMPI: The *Daily News* was size and power. When I started working there, it was still on 42nd Street and, like most newspapers of that time, written and printed in the same building. When those presses ran, you could actually feel the building shake.

Most people read two newspapers a day.

JACK LANG: Where they drop the ball on New Year's Eve, there used to be a newsstand that sold all of the out-of-town newspapers. Every once in a while I would get a call to cover something for the daily Oklahoma City newspaper. Two days later I would go over to that newsstand, pick up that paper, and see my story.

BILL GALLO: At the *News*, the reporters would go out and get the story. Then they would phone it into the office, where a staff of rewrite men turned it into great copy. It was always a double byline.

There were real stars in the newspaper business. Jimmy Powers was the sports editor of the *News*. Ed Sullivan, John Chapman, and Mark Hellinger had columns. The *Mirror* had Dan Parker, Walter Winchell.

MICKEY ALPERT: When my parents were out, my sister would turn on the radio to Walter Winchell. "Good evening, Mr. and Mrs. North and South America and all the ships at sea. Let's go to press . . . ," he would say with the noise of the teletype in the background. It would scare the hell out of me.

From what I heard, Winchell was a very vindictive guy. The movie *Sweet Smell of Success* was based on him. The late and legendary press agent Mike Hall tells the story of how Winchell forbade the press agents in New York to go see the screening of the movie at the Loews State. They sneaked in, pulling up the collars of their coats to hide their faces. When they came out, there was Winchell across the street, making notes.

BILL GALLO: Winchell was a great newspaperman but a nasty son of a gun. When he started becoming a big deal at the *Mirror*, Patterson, the owner of the *News*, started looking for someone to counter his popularity. He found Ed Sullivan, who was originally a sportswriter and then a Broadway columnist on the *Graphic*, a newspaper that had a fake page one with fake photographs of dead bodies. Everybody knew it was a fake but they bought the paper anyway.

Winchell may have been a better columnist than Sullivan, but Sullivan knew everybody in New York, and he knew a good story—that was his talent. What you saw on television: the deadpan expression, the bent posture—that's the way he was. He never improved, and he never got worse. But he was a very decent man.

Sullivan began his television show *Toast of the Town* on Channel 11, WPIX, which was owned by the *Daily News*. Later he moved to CBS. *The Ed Sullivan Show* ran for twenty-five years. At the start, all the acts came on for free in return for a line or two in his column. He made no bones about it. Dean Martin and Jerry Lewis made their first television appearance on that show. Nobody knew who they were then.

ROBERT MERRILL: Most of the people on the *Toast of the Town* sang songs from Broadway, movies, popular things. But when I appeared early on in the show, Ed felt I should do an aria. It worked out very well; I went on to do about ten or twelve more shows with him.

MICKEY ALPERT: I was working for Joe Levine, the movie producer, when he bought the movie of the ballet of *Romeo and Juliet* with Margot Fonteyn and Rudolf Nureyev. I called Sullivan's office and said, "How would you like the balcony scene with Fonteyn and Nureyev dancing for your program?"

He came to look at the picture at 1301 Sixth Avenue, a fabulous screening room in what was then the J.C. Penney Building. He said, "Thank you. I'll take it; I'll use it Sunday." It was great for us, great for him.

Sunday I'm watching the Giants football game in the afternoon. They announce, "Tonight on *The Ed Sullivan Show* . . ." and mention all the acts, but not Fonteyn and Nureyev. I watch the whole program; it's not on. I'm ready to have a heart attack. The next morning, I call him. "Something happened," he says. "I'm going to use it this Sunday."

The next Sunday, again I'm watching the Giants football game, and again they announce, "Tonight on *The Ed Sullivan Show* . . ." Only this time, they say Margot Fonteyn and Rudolf Nureyev. Thank God.

I watch the whole program; he doesn't run it. I call him the next morning. "Myron Cohen looked so great in the dress rehearsal that I used him instead," he tells me. The comic Myron Cohen bumped Nureyev and Fonteyn.

Who am I to argue? He'd have five singers, put them all on in a row. Then he'd have four comedians with a juggler in between. Whatever he did, it worked.

Once Federico Fellini was here for a picture called *Juliet of the Spirits*, and I made an arrangement with Sullivan for him to take a bow from the orchestra. Fellini was furious. He didn't want to go. He was invited some-place else. I said, "No, no, you have to come with me to *The Ed Sullivan Show*."

I take him to the show. He's sitting in the orchestra for the whole thing. Finally Sullivan says, "And out in the orchestra tonight we have the director Federico Fellini, who's here for his new picture, 8 ½." It's live, it's over, that's it. Fellini hardly spoke English. The only words he understood were "Fellini" and "8 ½." He wanted to kill me.

BILL GALLO: Ed Sullivan was this Irish guy who married a Jewish girl, Sylvia. They had a great marriage. Sylvia was crazy about Ezio Pinza, who played the lead in *South Pacific*. One Sunday morning the bell rang in their apartment at the Delmonico Hotel. Ed said, "Sylvia, you answer that." She opened the door, and there was Ezio Pinza singing "Some Enchanted Evening."

MARGARET WHITING: I was in Ed's apartment at the Delmonico many times. His daughter Betty and I were good friends. But it was always such a hurried environment. Secretaries would be booking people. Producers would come in. Phones would be ringing.

BILL GALLO: Ed Sullivan and Walter Winchell had a big rivalry, and our editors hated Winchell because of it. After the *Mirror* folded, Winchell came to our managing editor and offered to work for no salary. He was turned down. You would think that would be the end of it. But it wasn't. Every Saturday he would come up to the *Daily News* city room, sit on the bench and tell tales of his newspaper experience. The editors just ignored him.

Ed Sullivan at El Morocco with his wife, Sylvia, and daughter Betty.

MICKEY ALPERT: For a while he worked for the *Journal American*. Then they cut his column to one day a week. Then he worked for *Women's Wear Daily*. He was just trying to hang around.

BILL GALLO: Winchell was once one of the most powerful men in America, and now he was done.

MICKEY ALPERT: He was scraping until he died. And only a couple of people came to his funeral.

After the terrible newspaper strike around 1962, '63, the *Mirror* was the first to go. The *Journal*, *World Telegram and Sun*, and *Herald Tribune* closed around the same time. As the *Trib* folded, they put together a Sunday supplement called "New York," edited by Clay Felker. That was the start of *New York* magazine.

BILL GALLO: Dick Young was one of the most famous and widely read sportswriters of his day. A lot of people didn't like him because he was so outspoken. But he was a real New York sportswriter, a good man, and my best friend. To give you an idea, when Larsen pitched the perfect game in the World Series of 1956, Joe Trimble was covering the Yankees. He had a deadline to get the story in, but after the game, he suddenly started to sweat, got up and walked away from his typewriter. "Get Dick Young over here, please," he said to me.

In a second, Dick knocked out the line "Don Larsen, the imperfect man, pitched the perfect game." Period. As soon as Joe Trimble saw that, he no longer had writer's block. He was able to write a beautiful story that won awards. But it wouldn't have happened if Dick Young hadn't given him that impetus.

At Dick's retirement party upstairs at Gallagher's, about 150 newspapermen were present. A lot of people offered tributes and stories. Finally, Joe Trimble got up and told the Don Larsen story. "I never told this story," he said, "and what's more, and what makes me feel so good about it, Dick Young never told this story either."

At the *News*, we competed with all the other newspapers to get the story first, to get the scoop. That all changed with television. Once one of my

heroes, Tony Marino, got a tip that something was going to happen in a hotel barbershop. Tony went up there with a photographer and saw the mafioso Albert Anastasia shot. The *News* got the exclusive on that one.

But overall there wasn't that much crime in New York City in the postwar years. The *News* invented Willy Sutton. In reality, he was a dull kind of character with a pencil-thin mustache, a loser who spent most of his life in jail. He read a lot because he had a lot of time to read. He never killed or hurt anybody and only had a fake gun, which is what he used to escape from jail. But he had that one good line. When they asked him why he robbed banks, he said, "That's where the money is."

The big crime news in the 1950s was the Kefauver Senate Hearings into organized crime, which were televised. The star was the big mob boss Frank Costello, who took the Fifth more than anyone who had ever lived. It got so boring. But this TV director noticed that whenever Costello pleaded the Fifth, he made some nervous movement with his hands, and that's what he focused the camera on.

The old Madison Square Garden was the scene of sporting events, circuses, even political conventions.

One night at Madison Square Garden, Rocky Graziano came over to me. "Come on. I'd like you to meet Frank."

"Frank who?" I asked. "Frank Sinatra?"

"There's only one Frank—Costello, the godfather." Like many guys in those days, Rocky Graziano respected the gangsters. He had a diamond pinky ring that he was very proud of because Al Capone had given it to him.

Costello was there with his bodyguard. Rocky brings me over. I put out my hand, but Costello won't shake hands with me. I guess he looked at me as a wiseguy newspaperman. I don't know what got into me, but I said, "I don't recognize your face, Frank, but I know your hands very well."

He snapped, "Get this son of a bitch out of here."

You couldn't be in the newspaper business and not know these guys. They were all around.

JACK LANG: Frankie Carbo was a mafioso from Philadelphia who owned the contract on several fighters. You always saw him at the fights.

This was the time when boxing was king. Every Friday night you had eight or nine boxing bouts at the old Madison Square Garden on 50th and Eighth. They televised them on the Gillette Cavalcade of Sports. Celebrities, show business, theater people, you name it, loved to be seen at the fights.

BILL GALLO: The gangsters and celebrities usually sat in the first row behind the working press. They would glitzy up. Usually an older guy would be with a young girl, sometimes two girls all draped in fur stoles. But the lobby of the Garden belonged to the newspapermen. We'd meet there before a fight, have a frank and orange drink at Nedick's, and bandy around stories. Once in a while, a fight trainer would walk by, and we would get some items from him.

"Celebrities, show business, theater people, you name it, loved to be seen at the fights." Sugar Ray Robinson (standing) about to be declared winner over reeling Randy Turpin.

The newspapermen also hung out at Costello's on 44th between Second and Third. Hemingway used to eat there. Many foreign correspondents came in. James Thurber drew on the walls. I did, too. There was a whole wall of art there.

I had wanted to be a newspaperman since I was a little kid. I applied to all the New York City dailies and got two job interviews scheduled on the same day, one with the *News*, the other with the *Mirror*. When I got off the subway, the *News* was closer.

All through the years, my romance has been with the newspaper business—the hanging out, the having fun, the meeting so many people. Even when you weren't working, you were out there working for your newspaper. If I went to the theater and something happened, I would call it in to the *News*. I didn't get paid extra; I got the satisfaction of being a good newspaperman. There were many of us like that.

Being a reporter made you a well-known figure around town, a Humphrey Bogart type with the fedora and trench coat. Doors opened for you. We of the printed word were kings of the media.

JACK LANG: Mama Leone's was right around the corner from the Garden. The basketball crowd lived in there. If you were covering basketball, you could go in and sign Madison Square Garden's name and eat all you wanted. They gave you good-sized portions of good food, and there was always a big hunk of cheese on the table.

Crowds were always standing outside waiting to get in, but if you came up to the front and mentioned Madison Square Garden, you got in right away.

LEONARD KOPPETT: When I joined the *Trib*, the Knicks became one of my assignments because they were the least important of the basketball hierarchy. They played most of their games in the 69th Street Armory, which held five thousand and didn't sell out very often. The few games they played at Madison Square Garden were sold out when George Mikan and the Minneapolis Lakers came to town. The marquee would say "Mikan versus the Knicks." But the crowd was passionate. Kids had grown up playing and betting on basketball in the settlement houses, in high school. Pro basketball was a glamorous version of what had always been their game.

The real rivalries were the local college teams, who played in college gyms that seated three thousand at most. When NYU played CCNY, they would rent one of the big armories, 168th Street and Broadway or 25th Street and Lexington Avenue, for one night, and they would fill it up.

JACK LANG: They packed in eighteen thousand every time they played a doubleheader in Madison Square Garden. It got all the college people, the gambling element.

LEONARD KOPPETT: In 1951, the big college basketball scandal broke. That made the NBA, which had not been touched by the scandal, more important. Their rise began from that moment in time.

JACK LANG: You had two or three football teams, a couple of hockey teams, three New York racetracks. Four hockey games on a Sunday was the rule at Madison Square Garden. And you had three great baseball teams. For an eleven-year period, except for 1948, a New York City baseball team was in the World Series. There was no city that had as much going on in sports at one time as New York City did back then.

The great sports columnists like Jimmy Powers, Bobby Considine, Red Smith, Bill Corum, Frank Graham, Arthur Daley—they worked every day, did all sports. With me, from about 1949 on, I did nothing but baseball.

LEONARD KOPPETT: The Polo Grounds and Yankee Stadium were one subway station apart, but people wanted to see the glamorous Yankees. In the 1950s, the Yankees are the lords of baseball. They win more than anybody. Everybody hates the Yankees except the diehard Yankee fans. They happen to be in the Bronx, but it is not a local Bronx thing since they are the aristocracy.

JACK LANG: Before the war, the Giants were the big favorites of the show people. The Wall Street crowd also flocked to the Giants. This continued after the war but not as much. The Giants started to fall on hard times as the neighborhood around the Polo Grounds started to deteriorate.

GIANTS CAPTURE N
5-4 IN 9TH ON T

An unforgettable moment in New York City baseball history when the Giants beat the Dodgers with "The Shot Heard Round the World."

Right after the war the games at Ebbets Field, Yankee Stadium, and the Polo Grounds started at 3:15 in the afternoon. They wanted to give the Wall Street crowd fifteen minutes after the market closed to grab a subway and get to the ballpark.

MONTE IRVIN: Hank Thompson and I were the first black players on the New York Giants. We reported the same day, the first week in July 1949. I remember thinking how the Polo Grounds was more like a polo field than a baseball field. But I was very grateful that I had cracked the color line on the team that was in Manhattan, the capital of the world.

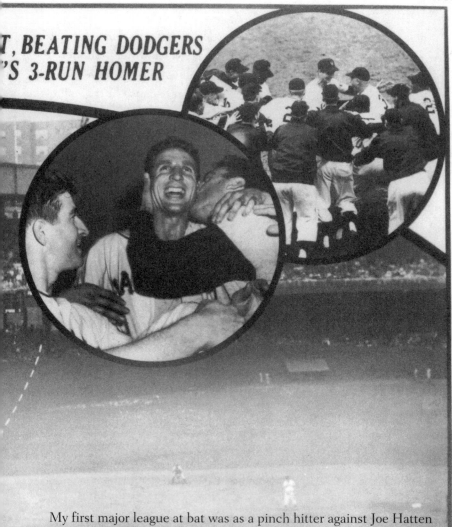

T, BEATING DODGERS
'S 3-RUN HOMER

My first major league at bat was as a pinch hitter against Joe Hatten of the Brooklyn Dodgers. Leo Durocher had said, "Monte, get a bat. You're gonna pinch-hit regardless of what the next batter does." On deck, my knees started to tremble a little bit. I couldn't believe this was happening to me. I was thirty-one years old, and I had been a star in the Negro Leagues for ten years. I ended up walking, but I was just glad to get on base.

Leo would invite Tony Martin, Stewart Granger, Frank Sinatra, Dean Martin and Jerry Lewis, people like that, into the clubhouse. Some of them would work out with us. They didn't ask for our autographs, and we didn't ask for theirs.

In the years after the war, there were certain restaurants where you'd feel prejudice. If they weren't friendly, we wouldn't go back. Emlen Tunnell, the big defensive running back for the New York Giants, was one of the pioneers in terms of breaking down segregation in midtown because he'd go all over with Tom Landry, who played for the Giants then, too. Later on when we came into the majors, Emlen would take us to the places he liked, and we'd be treated very nice because we were with him.

As the year passed, I became more confident and started to go out a bit more. People would recognize me. I'd go to a restaurant or a jazz club and they'd ask me to stand up and take a bow. That rarely happened when I was on the Newark Eagles in the Negro Leagues. Maybe it did in some places up in Harlem, but now it would happen downtown. And then of course when Willie Mays came along in '51, he made things easier for us all over—uptown, downtown, everywhere because he was so popular.

JULIE ISAACSON: Every major league ballplayer as well as all the actors and actresses came to the Stage Deli. The sandwiches were named after celebrities, but Max and Hymie Asnas fed more poor people than anyone else. Max was on the floor. Somebody would walk in. "What do you want? Sit down," he'd say, and feed you like you were a millionaire. He knew the hang-around guys, the people who didn't have money.

When Roger Maris was going for the home run record in '61, he would eat only bologna and eggs for breakfast. Every morning we would have breakfast together at the Stage Deli. We had the same waitress, and I'd leave her the same five-dollar tip every time. After, I would drive Roger up to the stadium.

The Stage Barbershop was right next to the Stage Deli. Ten o'clock Friday mornings, I would go to get a haircut. One day I got there about ten minutes early and sat down. A guy walks in and talks to my

Monte Irvin

barber. Then he comes over to me and asks if I would give up my place so Joe DiMaggio can get a haircut.

"On one condition," I say, "provided I can get an autographed picture."

Although I saw him come into the Stage Deli and the Stage Barbershop many times, I never got to really know Joe DiMaggio. He was aloof. Rao's is a restaurant in Harlem that is world known. It has fourteen tables. If you call for a reservation, they tell you to call back next year. DiMaggio ate there for maybe thirty years when the old man and lady owned it. He never got a check.

Vincent and Anna Rao passed away; the place is now run by Ron Straci and Frank Pellegrino, their nephews. Joe comes in there with a couple of friends. Like his aunt and uncle, Frankie always makes room for Joe. This time a customer is there with his little boy. Frankie waits until Joe is having his coffee. Then he asks Joe to sign an autograph for the kid.

"You know, Frankie, I get paid for signing autographs," DiMaggio says.

As DiMaggio and his friends are leaving, Frankie says, "Joe, you are not welcome here anymore." DiMaggio never came back. This is a true story, the *emis*.

JACK LANG: DiMaggio always got a premier table at Toots Shor's, right in the front. He took Marilyn Monroe to dinner there several times. Toots Shor's was one of the great sports hangouts. On Friday nights, the place would be empty until the fights at Madison Square Garden were over. Then everybody would come crosstown, and Toots would be mobbed until two in the morning. On any Monday after a Giants' football game, the Madison Avenue types would be six deep around the circular bar. Monday-morning quarterbacking was in vogue. At the same time, Toots would be staging a Football Writers' Luncheon in the basement of his restaurant for a couple of hundred writers and star players. Visiting ballplayers like Stan Musial or Ralph Kiner always came in. Toots made sure they got preferential treatment.

Toots was a big New York Giants baseball fan and was very close with Horace Stoneham, owner of the Giants, and Leo Durocher. Both of them were in his restaurant all the time. The famous story about Horace is that he was out drinking all night. When he got home, it was raining. He phoned the Giant office. "Call the game off. It's raining." By one o'clock in the afternoon the sun was shining. I was at the game at Ebbets Field that day, and on the scoreboard it said, "Giant game canceled because of rain."

MONTE IRVIN: We didn't like to go to Toots Shor's because he was so rough. He was usually half loaded, and he could act terrible. We'd go in there quickly and not linger too long.

JULIE ISAACSON: One day Roger Maris and I went to Toots Shor's for lunch. Roger never dressed up; he always wore a sweater. Toots took a look at him and said, "You can't come in here. You're dressed no good." I cursed him out, and we never went back there because he insulted Roger. Toots was good friends with Jimmy Hoffa—the money for the second restaurant came from Hoffa.

JACK LANG: Toots could be surly if he didn't like you. He turned a lot of people off. But those he liked and those who liked him were treated royally. His given name was Bernard; he was a great big heavyset guy who'd been a bouncer in Philadelphia and came up to New York during Prohibition to be a bouncer in a famous speakeasy.

Toots originally opened a place on 50th Street after the war. When the building it was in was sold, he moved to 52nd Street between Fifth and Sixth Avenues, right next to the 21 Club where all the swells went, across the street from CBS, and right around the corner from NBC. TV, radio, and advertising people came in all the time. It was a celebrity place. I'd see Leonard Lyons there four, five times a week, writing things in his little notebook.

You entered Toots Shor's through a revolving door. There was hat check to the left and a huge oval-shaped bar to the right. That was what Toots wanted—a place where people could see each other. On any given night you could go in there and run into anyone and everyone. But not Walter Winchell. He was a regular at the Stork Club and friendly with Sherman Billingsley, who did not get along with Toots.

People used to say that you don't go to Toots Shor's to eat, but he did have very good steaks. And his lunches were great, especially the roast beef hash made from the ground-up roast beef of the night before. By one o'clock, they were out of it.

There was always a lot of table hopping. One night I was sitting at a table with Leonard Koppett of the *Times* when Howard Cosell came in. We invited him to join us. "I have to catch a train," he said. "But I'll stay for a minute. He ordered a shrimp cocktail. The next thing you know he went over to somebody else's table and had a bowl of soup. And before we left, we saw him having dessert with someone else. It was that type of restaurant.

When Jackie Gleason was starting out as a comedian, he and Toots became friends. Toots let him eat in his restaurant for nothing. One night Jackie asked Toots for a hundred dollars. "What do you mean a hundred dollars? I'm letting you eat here for nothing. What do you want the money for?"

"To tip the waiters."

Toots and Jackie were drinking late at night, as the story goes, and got into an argument over who could outrun the other. They decided to race around the block, and whoever came back first would win a hundred dollars. Jackie said, "You go that way toward Fifth Avenue. I'll go this way toward Sixth Avenue." Jackie walked down to the corner of Sixth Avenue, hailed a cab and was waiting in front of the restaurant when Toots finally made it around the block.

Walter Winchell was a regular at the Stork Club, one of the famous night spots of the era.

"How did you get here before me?" Toots said, huffing and puffing. Then suddenly he realized that he never passed Jackie on the way around.

Toots was friendly with members of the Kennedy family, particularly Steve Smith, who was married to one of the sisters. Around the time that Bobby Kennedy was running for senator from New York, I told him, "Toots, we would love to get Bobby Kennedy to speak at the New York Baseball Writers' Dinner."

Toots said, "I can't stand the little prick, Jack, but if you want him, I'll try and get him." So he picked up the phone and called Steve Smith's office in Manhattan. The word was that Smith was on one of the Caribbean islands. Toots told the secretary to try to reach him.

I went back home, and about seven o'clock that night, my phone rang. It was Toots. Steve had called him from the Caribbean and gotten in touch with Bobby Kennedy.

"Jack," he said, "you got the little son of a bitch."

Governor Carey was in Toots Shor's a lot, but not Rockefeller, who was more the 21 type. Mayor Wagner was in there a lot, as was Frank Hogan, the Manhattan district attorney who wound up prosecuting all the college basketball players who fixed games in the fifties.

One time, I was there with Toots. The place was basically empty. All of a sudden Joey Rivera, one of the waiters, came over and whispered something in Toots's ear. "Okay," Toots said, "set up the table."

About forty-five minutes later, Frank Sinatra came in with about twenty people. They were coming back from the cemetery where they had buried Frank Sinatra's father. They sat down, with Sinatra at the head of the table, had one round of drinks, got up, and left.

That day, every waiter and every captain got tipped one hundred dollars. Joey Rivera used to say, "When Mr. Frank comes in, he pays the rent."

JULIE ISAACSON: Sinatra was a New York man. All his friends were here: mob guys, restaurant guys, nightclub people, entertainers. He was a real New York character.

JACK LANG: In those days they had what they called house accounts. You got a bill at the end of the month. The Baseball Writers had an account at Toots Shor's. At the end of the year, we got a bill for fifteen hundred dollars. Toots wanted the sportswriters to come in there because we mentioned the name of the restaurant in the papers all the time. I don't recall ever spending a nickel of my own money there.

After a while a lot of people didn't pay their house tabs, and Toots finally lost the place. He opened another one that didn't do so well. Finally he went out of business altogether and sold his name to Restaurant Associates, which opened up a series of bars around Manhattan with his name.

I was one of the honorary pallbearers at his funeral at Temple Emanuel on Fifth Avenue. The place was packed with celebrities who came from all over. It was a sad thing to see him go.

ELAINE KAUFMAN: Years ago I was at P. J. Clark's late one night. Some people told me Toots Shor was there and that he wanted to meet me. I said, "Okay, fine, I'll go over to him." He was an older man by that time.

They said, "No, no, he'll come over to you." They brought him over and he said, "I just want to see the broad that's going to take my place."

I used to have this restaurant called Portofino's on Thompson and Bleecker Streets in Greenwich Village together with Alfredo Viazzi, the man I was living with at the time. The business suited me just fine. I met the most interesting people. Then in the early sixties, Alfredo and I separated. At first I thought to take over the restaurant, but then I said to him, "No, you take it."

I had decided to open up my own place, but I couldn't afford the Village. Some people I knew who lived uptown suggested I look around Yorkville. A realtor showed me an Austro-Hungarian mom and pop operation called Gambrino's on Second Avenue with long kitchen tables. It had a big fan, no air conditioning, but it was a good-looking place. I thought, I'll take a chance and start a Village-type place like Portofino's here.

Elaine's became a kind of network, a way people met and found out about jobs.

When I opened in April 1963, there was nothing much in the neighborhood. Park Avenue and East End Avenue were posh, but in between it was working class, where the chefs, the cooks, the nannies, the people who ran the fancy households lived. If Greenwich Village was the creative heart of the city, this area was nowhere.

But I knew a lot of people from working in the Village, and one by one they started to come in. One of the first was the journalist Dorothy Kilgallen. She lived a little farther downtown and would go to the Stork Club and those kinds of places, but she had no place to meet people and hang around uptown. The theater people from the Village came in: Jose Quintero, Jason Robards, the people who were doing the Beckett plays in the Cherry Lane Theater. Liz Smith came. I knew her from downtown. We were a destination restaurant from the start.

It jelled pretty fast. Writers and cartoonists from the *New Yorker* started to come in. George Plimpton and Arthur Kopit, Norman Mailer and Irwin Shaw—they'd work all day and all night and then they'd remember, "Oh, I forgot to eat," and they'd come over, meet their friends, sit down and have dinner. Pete Hamill, Frank Conroy, Joe Heller, Dan Jenkins, Mike Lupica, William Styron—they all came here. Many of them weren't famous yet. Some knew each other, a lot of them I introduced. It wasn't just sitting down for dinner. Elaine's became a kind of network, a way people met.

A table up front was called the "writers' table." The waiters would put tops on, it would get bigger and bigger. Early on when many of these writers didn't have money, one guy would take all the checks, and it would be his chit. He'd pay me when he could.

After a few years I needed extra room so I bought out the TV repair store next door. I needed an air conditioner, better stoves, better refrigeration. I had to make improvements, change the lights, replace the chairs. But everything had to come out of the cash register because as a woman, I couldn't get money from a bank.

But it was always like a big reunion, a big party. Jackie Gleason came in when he was doing a picture with Art Carney. "This is my place," he said. "There's nothing left like it." Frank Sinatra would walk in the door and start yelling, "Where's Mama?"

Elaine Kaufman, proprietor of Elaine's: "I guess we've come pretty far. 'It's a bit of all right,' as they say."

Early one morning, about one a.m., a bunch of us were sitting around and talking, the bartender was wiping down the bar when suddenly he stopped and said, "Elaine, Jackie Kennedy is outside."

I said, "Come on, stop carrying on."

He said, "No, she's outside."

We got up and went to the door, and there she was like a princess in a gold boucle Chanel suit with a big emerald sunburst on it. Mike Nichols and Richard Avedon, Adolph Green and Susan Sontag and Lenny Bernstein were with her. This was after President Kennedy was killed; Jackie was still in mourning. They came in and we made big antipastos. We had the music going; everybody was working to cheer her up.

Some time ago, a woman came here for dinner. Afterwards her mother told her, "Oh, Grandpa had a place there." It turned out this woman's grandfather had owned a wine store on the site of Elaine's back in 1918. I guess we've come pretty far. "It's a bit of all right," as they say.

TOM SLATTERY: About ninety percent of the taverns in the City of New York used to be owned by Irish people; the Italians opened up restaurants. Before the el came down, there used to be neighborhood saloons all along Third Avenue: Clancy's, Blarney Stone, P. J. Clarke's. Music would play from the jukebox. People drank bottle beer and Scotch—usually J&B or Dewar's in a shot glass, three quarters of an ounce for forty, fifty cents. The Irish saloons in the postwar years were places where a person who wasn't an executive could afford to eat. A White Rose, a Kilarney Rose, McCann's, Martin's—they were all over town. They served roast beef, pastrami, corned beef, brisket of beef, boiled or mashed potatoes—French fries didn't come in until later on.

In 1963, after I retired from the police force, I went into business with some family members in a bar and restaurant called Donahue's on 31st and Third. It was a great opportunity because the el was gone by this time, and the area was gentrifying. It used to be like Hell's Kitchen on the East Side, blue-collar workers, some unemployed people, a rough crowd. Many good families but also some problem people who had gone to jail, who liked to

Eddie Condon with his guitar. His Greenwich Village club was a favorite night spot.

Glamour at the St. Regis (from left to right): Mary Martin, Tallulah Bankhead, Dorothy Rodgers

throw their weight around the neighborhood and get into fights at local bars.

But now, the neighborhood saloons, the "buckets of blood" were closing down, and new pubs and restaurants like Donahue's were coming up. We'd still have a fight every night and two on Friday. It was friends of this family against friends of that family. Four, five times a week, sometimes even the same night, I'd leap over the bar. "Outside," I would yell. "There'll be no fighting in here."

I can remember when it used to be a neighborhood crowd with thirty customers a night, and the fourth drink always being bought by the house. By the late 1960s, however, the East Side had become a singles scene, and the whole atmosphere had changed. Bartenders became snappier, speed became important, and the shot glass got in the way. The free-hand pour became in vogue. Then they came out with measured pourers that would stop and flow, stop and flow. Controlled beverage pouring became an industry in itself because with the crowd, the volume, you had to expedite more.

MICKEY ALPERT: You'd go into Sardi's at 11:15, the place would be jammed. The theater didn't start until 8:30, so the shows ended after 11:00. The jazz joints on 52nd between Sixth and Seventh would stay open until the bars closed about four in the morning. There were all these late-night places like Monte Proser's La Vie en Rose, the Blue Angel, Julius Monk's Upstairs at the Downstairs, the Astor Bar, Vincent Lopez and his band at the Taft Hotel. There was the Maisonette at the St. Regis where Mabel Mercer used to play. She was an old lady then and would sit in an easy chair and sing.

Hotels were known for their supper clubs. Jackie Onassis dancing with Peter Tufo at the St. Regis.

MARGARET WHITING: Hotels were known for their supper clubs. There was the Persian Room at the Plaza and the Starlight Room of the Waldorf, where you had dinner and saw a show. Audiences were more subdued there than in the nightclubs, which attracted racketeers and a more raucous, spirited crowd.

The Copacabana and the Latin Quarter were the two big ones. People came there to have a good time and dressed to the nines. They had the best entertainers. Everybody who was on the nightclub circuit would get booked there for two or three weeks. There was a twenty-two-piece band, dancing girls, one show about 8:30 and another about 11:00.

I appeared at the Copa with Joe E. Lewis, but I also went there to see others perform: Martin and Lewis, Phil Silvers. Sinatra played the Copa often, so did Tony Bennett. It had a Brazilian motif, a bunch of trees, tables all over the place.

A spirited crowd and
the famous floor
show at the
Copacabana

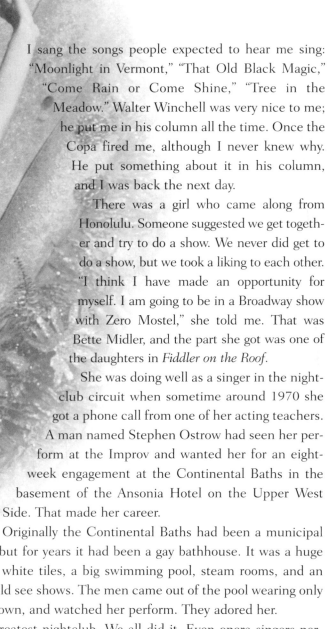

I sang the songs people expected to hear me sing: "Moonlight in Vermont," "That Old Black Magic," "Come Rain or Come Shine," "Tree in the Meadow." Walter Winchell was very nice to me; he put me in his column all the time. Once the Copa fired me, although I never knew why. He put something about it in his column, and I was back the next day.

There was a girl who came along from Honolulu. Someone suggested we get together and try to do a show. We never did get to do a show, but we took a liking to each other. "I think I have made an opportunity for myself. I am going to be in a Broadway show with Zero Mostel," she told me. That was Bette Midler, and the part she got was one of the daughters in *Fiddler on the Roof*.

She was doing well as a singer in the nightclub circuit when sometime around 1970 she got a phone call from one of her acting teachers. A man named Stephen Ostrow had seen her perform at the Improv and wanted her for an eight-week engagement at the Continental Baths in the basement of the Ansonia Hotel on the Upper West Side. That made her career.

Originally the Continental Baths had been a municipal bath, but for years it had been a gay bathhouse. It was a huge space with white tiles, a big swimming pool, steam rooms, and an area where you could see shows. The men came out of the pool wearing only white towels, sat down, and watched her perform. They adored her.

It became the greatest nightclub. We all did it. Even opera singers performed there. Straight couples, dressed in tuxedos and evening gowns, became part of the audience. But for me, the gay men were one of the great audiences of all time. They loved the music. They were artistic. They had feeling and heart.

RUSSELL BERG: In 1964, I went with my college roommate to his aunt and uncle's apartment in Lincoln Towers, which had recently opened. Two elderly men, or so it seemed to me, joined us for dinner. But then, in the middle of things, they got up and left, which I thought was kind of weird. The next day when my friend called his aunt to thank her, she said, "Did you know who our friends were?" It turned out they were Morris Carnovsky and another major star of the Yiddish theater, and they were in makeup. They had left so abruptly to make a curtain.

KEN LIBO: In the 1960s, the Yiddish Theater on Second Avenue was still barely subsisting. When you entered the Yiddish Anderson Theater, you felt like you entered an enormous old-age home because it looked like the actors were nurses and they wanted to be sure that the audience was comfortable, that the oxygen was flowing. They would improvise skits. One in particular I thought was very funny was when a leading lady fell flat on the floor, pre-arranged, and the actor turned to the audience and said in Yiddish, "Look what happened, my prima donna has fallen on the floor. Is there a doctor in the house?"

And then a woman who was a plant on the balcony yelled in an enormous voice, "Give her an enema."

The actor on the stage ignores her and turns away. Again she yells, "Give her an enema."

He yells back, "Lady, it wouldn't help."

And the lady yells back, "It wouldn't hurt."

Well I'd never been in a theater like this. I didn't know what to make of it. But the audience was very amused. This was the last gasp of the Yiddish theater. They were no longer doing Shakespeare in Yiddish.

ANNE BERG: In the mid 1960s when the Yiddish theater declined, some of the downtown theaters were transformed into rock 'n' roll concert halls. The Second Avenue Theater became the Village Theater. Then it closed down for renovation, although when it opened as the Fillmore East it didn't look very different to me.

I used all my baby-sitting money to buy tickets because through my high school years, I spent every weekend at the Fillmore East or at Café au Go-Go

Bette Midler entertained at the Continental Baths, a gay bathhouse. The men there adored her.

in Greenwich Village, a much smaller place. I lived in Croton-on-Hudson, but my dad worked for the railroad so I could travel back and forth for nothing. We saw everybody from B. B. King to Eric Clapton to the very first performance of Blood, Sweat & Tears and every other rock 'n' roll act that you can think of.

Here I was one night in my green vinyl skirt—I made all my own clothes in high school, one outfit more outrageous than the other—sitting in the front row with my feet up on the stage. Eric Clapton was on. I was wearing braces with orthodontic bands to move my jaw. I opened my mouth, and one of these rubber bands shot into his enormous Afro. "Oh, dear," I thought to myself, "I can't interrupt him in the middle of a song and pick it out."

MICKEY ALPERT: The Broadway chroniclers wanted to see what the young people were doing, and that was why Earl Wilson and Leonard Lyons made Arthur's—the first chic discotheque in New York—their next-to-the-last stop of the evening. It was where the original El Morocco with the zebra skins used to be and where the Citicorp Building is today. Peter Cook and Dudley Moore from the show *Beyond the Fringe* started it in the 1960s, and Sybil Burton, who had just broken up with Richard Burton, fronted it.

Arthur's was small and dark, no windows, and no live music. The musicians union was very angry; they said places like this would put musicians out of business. But it was something new, a different kind of dancing, a different kind of music. And Studio 54 was on the horizon.

Ian Schrager and Steve Rubell turned this old opera house on 54th between Broadway and Eighth into a discotheque in the mid 1970s. Ian Schrager was one of the most gifted men I ever met for his visual skills—every night was a visual experience, freaky, outlandish, beautiful. Maybe fifteen hundred to two thousand people would come in the course of a night, including celebrities like Mrs. Lillian Carter, the Shah of Iran and his wife, Elizabeth Taylor, Candace Bergen. The next day their pictures would be in the paper. It became an international institution.

This was a much different New York than the one I knew as a kid, when I would come in with my parents from Brooklyn to see a Broadway show like *Pajama Game* or *New Girl in Town*. There were so many of them.

At that time Broadway music was the popular music of the time. You turned on the radio and that was all you heard. Guys like Burton Lane,

Theater was the center of life and glamour in New York. Everyone could still afford a ticket to a Broadway play.

Richard Rodgers, Alan Jay Lerner, Jerry Herman, Frank Loesser, Yip Harburg, Cy Coleman—they made a career that lasted years and years.

LEONARD KOPPETT: Theater was the center of life and glamour in New York until the late fifties, early sixties. Everyone could still afford a ticket to a Broadway play.

MERLE DEBUSKEY: As a kid, I had heard Winchell on the radio and read his columns. It seeped into my consciousness so I knew there was such a thing as "The Great White Way," that there was great theater in this country. My image of Broadway was that it was a romantic place, a broken heart for every light.

After the war, I came to New York and took graduate courses at the New School, where I fell in with a crowd that was interested in creating a cooperative theater. We used to hang out in the Village, where for twenty cents you could kill a night over a couple of beers, arguing and talking and making yourself seem interesting, if not important. I had had some theater-related publicity jobs. So when these people fired their press agent and asked if I was interested, I decided to do it.

I did publicity, but I also painted scenery and was an extra when necessary. We decided to work in a studio, to affect a style something like the Group Theater. A schism developed among us, and the group split in two.

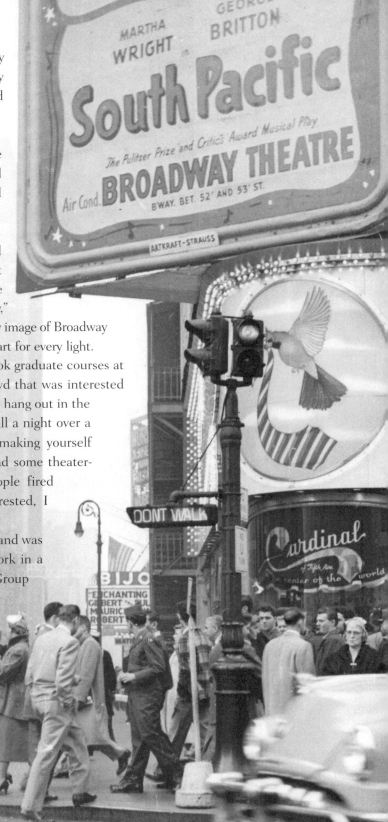

The one I went with included Kim Stanley, Gene Sachs, Bea Arthur. We formed a separate company.

The summer of 1949, there were five or more groups operating off-Broadway, although it did not yet have that designation. There was no union arrangement. We played in places like the Provincetown Playhouse, the Cherry Lane. Then we joined forces into a federation we called the League of Off-Broadway Theaters. If people came into your theater, you would give them information about everybody else's theater. If you wanted to borrow a drop, a prop, you could borrow it from another company.

At the Cherry Lane, we performed a play called *Yes Is for a Very Young Man* by Gertrude Stein. All the major critics came. It was the first time they came to an off-Broadway show after the war.

At Carnegie Recital Hall, the group we had left behind, the Interplayers Group, got raves with an O'Casey play. The others also did very well. But Equity came down and said that their players could not play in our houses. That killed the shows.

The League got together and decided to do something. The only one who knew anything about publicity was me. We went on the attack. We worked out a small theater formula with Equity that later evolved into the off-Broadway contract. And that was the beginnings of off-Broadway in the postwar years.

As a result, my name began to appear in the papers. I got a call from the press agent of Cheryl Crawford, a well-known producer in those days. They were going into rehearsal for *Regina*, a Broadway musical based on a Lillian Hellman play, written and composed by Mark Blitzstein.

I came to the Martin Beck Theater. Cheryl Crawford was there. The director Robert Lewis was there. And up on the stage was one light shining on a grand piano, and seated was Mark Blitzstein. He then proceeded to perform the whole score. He did all the vocals. It was absolutely fascinating; I swallowed it up.

Regina closed in four weeks. It was too much out of the norm to be popular as a Broadway musical. Crawford did a second play written by the great actor Alexander Knox, *The Closing Door*. Knox also starred. Lee Strasberg directed. It was a disaster. With all the method acting, no one could figure out what they were supposed to do.

That was my introduction to Broadway. I was unemployed after eight weeks. But then I got involved with Mike Todd's *Peep Show*, directed by Bobby Clark. No more of this serious shit. Instead the epitome of Broadway: beautiful women, expert comics, jugglers. Todd was a Runyonesque character, a guy with moxie, a mug. If you liked mugs, he was great.

I was called back to work with Cheryl Crawford. We did *The Rose Tattoo* and *Paint Your Wagon*—both were very successful, and now I knew what a hit musical was like.

I was an intimate of Joe Papp's from the very beginning, before he even decided to produce plays. We used to have great fun. We could sit for hours talking to each other. The idea of free Shakespeare in Central Park—the idea of going out there in this beautiful park, sitting on the grass while the sun goes down and the lights go up and the majestic words of Shakespeare are laid out for you—it was spectacular. Joe Papp had no money, no important education, no important family members, no support system. He had energy and ambition and street smarts. He had to fight for every inch, culminating with the big battle with Robert Moses, which he won.

Then Joe decided we needed a contemporary theater to go along with it, and we settled on what became the Public Theater, with no money at all. It had just been sold by the Hebrew Immigrant Aid Society to a real-estate developer. We had the Landmarks Commission landmark it. And that was how we got it.

LEONARD KOPPETT: By the middle of the 1960s, the nightlife scene was unraveling because the people who were part of that scene, for the most part, were no longer living in the city. You came out of the theater at 10:45, got in your car and drove home to the suburbs, or you competed against hundreds of people for a taxi. Also ticket prices were so much higher, and you had a television set at home. The nightlife on the streets began to dry up.

HOWARD KISSEL: My first year at *Women's Wear Daily*, I used to get something called the *Theater Information Bulletin*, which listed what was in the Broadway theaters and what would be opening. There were not more than a dozen shows. Most of the theaters were dark. Around that time, the curtain hour was moved to 7:30 because they were afraid people wouldn't want to stay in the city too late.

But then, in 1974, '75, things started to change. Maybe what prompted the turnaround was that the season before, *Pippin* had been a big hit, probably the first in a long time. Once you have a big hit, people with money are willing to put money in. Also they were bringing over a lot of things from England. That season began with the revival of *Gypsy* with Angela Lansbury, then you got *Equus* with a young Anthony Hopkins, a wonderful version of *Sherlock Holmes* with John Wood, Diana Rigg in *Pygmalion*, Rex Harrison in *Pirandello*. And at the end of the season you had *A Chorus Line,* which had opened downtown at the Public Theater in the spring of '75 and on Broadway that fall. It exploded; it primed the pump. And for the next few seasons, it was like everything opened up again.

It's interesting that *A Chorus Line* opened around the time when the city was on the verge of bankruptcy. At a certain point, the West Side Highway collapsed, and there was this feeling that things were falling apart around us. But what happened was that people who normally eyed one another with extreme hostility or distrust had no choice but to talk to one another. The city had all these public schools they could no longer keep going, so they started leasing them for peanuts to artists. There was a turning around of public spaces becoming used in a creative way.

In 1976, the tall ships of Op Sail coming up the harbor against the backdrop of lower Manhattan provided the first romantic image in maybe twenty years. By then it was a new skyline because you had the Twin Towers and all the glass boxes—I liked the older skyline of towers better—but nevertheless, juxtaposed with the tall ships, it was a very beautiful image. That was when people began to perceive New York differently.

Part Three

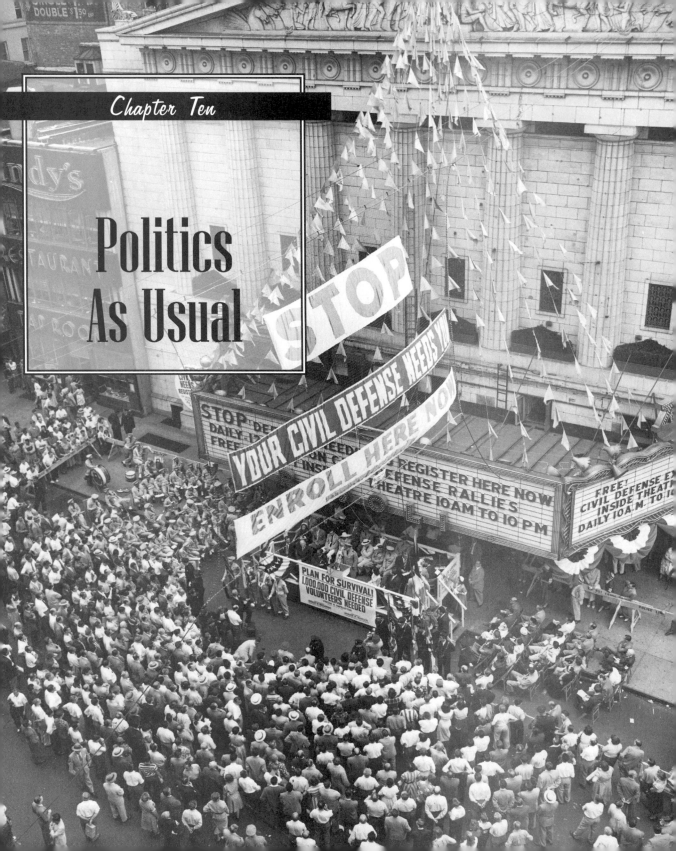

Chapter Ten

Politics As Usual

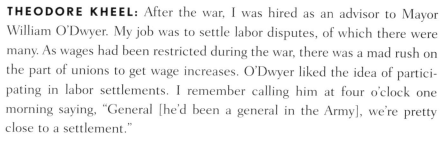

THEODORE KHEEL: After the war, I was hired as an advisor to Mayor William O'Dwyer. My job was to settle labor disputes, of which there were many. As wages had been restricted during the war, there was a mad rush on the part of unions to get wage increases. O'Dwyer liked the idea of participating in labor settlements. I remember calling him at four o'clock one morning saying, "General [he'd been a general in the Army], we're pretty close to a settlement."

He said, "Hold it. I'll be right down." And he came down to participate.

One of the big disputes was with the Transport Workers Union (TWU), which had lost membership after the war because it wasn't doing much for its members. Mike Quill, its fiery president, took a bold gamble and threatened the first citywide transit strike. His principal issue was exclusive recognition.

O'Dwyer called everybody to city hall. He appointed David Sarnoff, the head of RCA, as mediator. I became part of a four-member board that was to make recommendations.

We met in the Central Park South apartment of Samuel Rosenman. It was the summertime so we sat on the patio of his apartment and agreed on the general principles we would recommend. Arthur Meyer, who was chairman of the New York State Board of Mediation and chairman of our group, was to write it.

Arthur had never been to college, but he fancied himself a Shakespearean authority, and he loved to use three- and four-syllable words. He wrote a report and read it to us. We sat there. It was simply awful, not from a substance but from a style point of view. Finally, Anna Rosenberg said, "Arthur, that is the greatest report I have ever heard. There's only one thing wrong with it. Nobody will understand what you said."

Arthur took umbrage at that. "Well, you write it!" he said, and left.

I said, "We have the speechwriter for Franklin Roosevelt here. Why don't we ask him to rewrite it?"

Sam said he would if I assisted him. So we sat down and went over the report.

Sam told me that in 1936, when Roosevelt was running for reelection and was scheduled to speak in Pittsburgh, he remembered he had given a speech there in 1932 in which he promised to balance the budget. "Sam," the president said, "write me a speech that explains what happened." A couple of days later, the president asked, "Sam, have you figured out what to say about that speech in Pittsburgh?"

Sam said, "Yes, Mr. President. Deny you made it."

But we didn't deny the report Sam and I wrote. It made the TWU, as the largest of the transit workers' unions, the first among equals and set a pattern so that the others could not get more. It left open the question of strikes by municipal employees, but it led to the organization of many other municipal employees, like the teachers and sanitation workers.

I became assistant director and then director of the Division of Labor Relations. The transit workers were demanding a wage increase, but the money wasn't there. The fare was still the same five cents it had been when the first subway was built in 1904. Politically, the five-cent fare was sacrosanct.

The Executive Committee of the TWU, which was left-wing, voted to maintain the five-cent fare because it would help the American Labor Party candidate get elected mayor. At that point, Quill, who maintained the five-cent fare had to be increased, denounced the Communist Party. I called O'Dwyer, who was visiting his brother in California. "General, Mike Quill came out in favor of a fare increase."

And O'Dwyer said, "I'm coming right home."

At a meeting in the mayor's office, O'Dwyer said to Mike Quill, "How much of a wage increase do you need to beat the Commies?" He knew Quill was going to have a fight with them in his union.

Quill said, "Twenty-four cents an hour."

O'Dwyer said, "Will that beat the Commies?"

Quill said, "That will do it."

"Anything else?"

"The check-off [the deduction of union dues]."

"You got it."

The American Communist Party had been a power, but now it began to unfold.

The fare on the buses was raised a penny. Later, the fare on the buses and subways went to ten cents, then fifteen cents, then twenty cents, and on up to $1.50.

O'Dwyer was terrific when it came to handling these labor disputes. I'd brief him for maybe five minutes about what the union wanted and so forth, and he'd call in the press and speak for twenty minutes with complete

New York City Mayor Vincent Impellitteri with his wife—he ran his whole campaign against the bosses and won.

knowledge of all the subtleties. However, he became bored with the job of mayor, and after he was reelected in 1949, he resigned and became ambassador to Mexico.

In New York State, the gubernatorial election is one year after the mayoral election. But since O'Dwyer was retiring, there would be a second mayoral election. And then something interesting happened that hasn't happened again in New York. All four candidates for mayor were Italian.

The political practice was to have the position of the mayor, the comptroller, and the president of the city council filled by one person from the Bronx, one from Manhattan, and one from Brooklyn. One had to be Irish, one Jewish, and one Italian. Back in 1945, the party bosses selected O'Dwyer, an Irishman from Brooklyn, for mayor; a Jewish man from Manhattan for president of the city council; and an Italian man from the Bronx for comptroller. Then O'Dwyer announced he would not run with the other handpicked nominees of the bosses. So the party selected a Jewish man named Larry Joseph from the Bronx to run for comptroller. They still needed an Italian candidate from Manhattan for president of the city council.

The word went out. It was like the song from the show *Fiorello*—"What about so and so? / He's dead / What about so and so? / He's in jail."

They got out *The Green Book,* which lists every department and officer who works for the City and State of New York, and they went through it until finally they came to the name Vincent Impellitteri.

"Who's that?"

"A clerk to a Supreme Court justice."

"Where's he from?"

"Manhattan."

"Impellitteri—must be Italian."

And they grabbed him.

Impellitteri was a perfectly pleasant person, as mediocre as anybody in *The Green Book.* He ran with O'Dwyer in 1945 and got elected.

When O'Dwyer resigns, Impellitteri becomes mayor. Now there's a new mayoral election. Carmine De Sapio, the head of Tammany Hall, picks Ferdinand Pecora, an Italian and a justice of the state supreme court, to run for mayor. Impellitteri says as a loyal Democrat, he would step aside for any nominee of the party— except another Italian. If it's an Italian, he says, it has to be him.

So Pecora runs as a Democrat, and Impellitteri runs as an Independent. Edward Corsi is the Republican candidate, and the American Labor Party picks Vito Marcantonio as their nominee. There are four Italians running for mayor. They make wild charges against each other—Pecora is the candidate of the mobster Frank Costello; Impellitteri is dominated by Three-Finger Brown. But Impellitteri runs his whole campaign against the bosses, and he wins.

Impellitteri served out his term until 1953. Then Bob Wagner ran and won. Impellitteri was not prepared to be mayor, but Wagner was. He came from a family that knew New York

New York City Mayor Robert F. Wagner—he came from a family that knew New York government.

Chita Rivera, hostess for the 1965 World's Fair, pins Mayor Robert F. Wagner.

government. Wagner was a very nice man but a genius at postponing decisions. What Wagner liked best was not making decisions. Jim McFadden was the acting commissioner of a division related to labor matters, and a man Wagner didn't like at all. Wagner was reluctant to fire McFadden since he had the support of organized labor, but he would not appoint him as full-time commissioner either. The situation reminded me of the song from *Guys and Dolls* about "the oldest established permanent floating crap game in New York"—McFadden was the oldest established permanent floating commissioner in New York. He never got appointed.

In 1965, Wagner was succeeded by John Lindsay, who got elected because he was very attractive, spoke well, and had the support of the *New York Times*. But he did not have any understanding of the problem of labor-management relations. The first challenge he faced was the Transit Workers' strike. It started the first day of his administration—January 1, 1966—lasted eleven days, and shut the subways down.

The Transit Workers—the exclusive union for the subway workers and several of the bus lines by this time—was pushing for a cents-across-the-board increase. You would get twenty cents whether you're an electrician or a sweeper. In 1965, the sweeper was getting $2.56 an hour; the motorman was getting $3.46 an hour.

Mayor Robert F. Wagner and President Harry S Truman—two staunch Democrats.

New York City Mayor John V. Lindsay. He got elected "because he was very attractive, spoke well, and had the support of the *New York Times.*"

If each got a twenty-cent raise, the absolute differential of ninety cents was maintained, but the relative differential, or percentage, was changed.

The sweepers were increasingly blacks; the motormen were whites. There was an uprising of the whites, and Mike Quill realized he had to do something more for the whites than for the blacks because of the relative differential. Quill wanted to meet with Lindsay (he called him "Lindsley") but Lindsay—who was very partial to problems of minorities—was told by the *New York Times* not to make any deals with Quill.

All three commissioners of the Transit Authority and Quill were Irish. Quill said to the chairman, Joseph O'Grady, "Joe, I have an idea [he pronounced "idea" like "*idée*"]. Why don't I strike on Saturday morning, January first, and we'll settle this by midnight on Sunday."

Joe said, "Mike, if you do that, I'm going to get an injunction and put everybody in jail except you."

Quill said, "Joe, we've been friends for all these years. If anybody goes to jail, I have to go to jail."

Quill struck on Saturday morning, expecting to make a settlement by Sunday night. Joe got an injunction; he had to enforce the law, which prohibited the public employees from striking and imposed penalties on striking workers. Quill was put in jail. He had a heart attack and was rushed to Bellevue.

The strike was on, and it was devastating. The secretary of labor came to town, and the three mediators—of which I was one—were called to city hall. Deputy Mayor Bob Price said to me, "I'd like to talk to you privately."

We went down into the basement of the mayor's office. "We can do you a lot of good," he said. "This strike is killing us. Would you go to Bellevue and find out how much Quill will settle for?"

I said, "Bob, there's nothing you can do for me. I want this strike settled as much as you do. But I'm the wrong person to go."

"Why?"

"Because Quill's not going to negotiate with me. I'll tell you who should go."

"Who?"

"You. You can make a deal."

Price went to Bellevue and asked Quill what he'd settle for. Quill put up four fingers. Four bucks, a fifty-four-cent raise on the $3.46 motormen's hourly rate, or fifteen percent. That became the settlement. The fifteen-percent increase gave more on the motormen's $3.46 than on the sweepers' $2.56, so that stretched out the differential.

There followed a taxpayers' lawsuit that led to a court order canceling the increases and imposing fines on the striking workers. Quill died of his heart attack, and his successor appealed to Harry Van Arsdale, the head of New York City's Central Labor Council, who turned to Governor Nelson Rockefeller for assistance. The governor got a law passed repealing penalty provisions of the anti-strike law as it pertained to the transit workers and named a committee to write a new law regarding public-sector employment relations.

As I was a mediator in the transit strike, Lindsay and I started out disliking each other. But ultimately I came to like him. He was intelligent and able, but he was put into a position for which he was not fully prepared.

JIMMY BRESLIN: Lindsay was the best mayor we had on the topic of race. There were riots all over the country and none here because people trusted him.

HERMAN BADILLO: Mayor Lindsay was so terrified of riots that he allowed the City University to be destroyed in 1969 after a group of black and Latino students at City College demanded the admissions standards be changed so that there would be the same percentage of black and Latino students at CUNY as there were in the high schools. I was the only public official to come out against open admissions because I knew the value of the City University diploma would be destroyed if the colleges no longer had standards.

When I was a student at City College, we had a traditional curriculum and very tough courses. The students were the best in the city, the elite. When a professor would start to ask a question, twenty hands would go up: "We know the question, we know the answer."

KEN LIBO: I was swept in by open admissions in the early seventies; I rode the crest, becoming an assistant professor at City College. With few exceptions, the old guard could not adjust to having had Jonas Salk as a student in the 1930s and now having generally ill-prepared blacks, Hispanics, Chinese, Koreans. But I adored those kids.

HERMAN BADILLO: The change to open admissions came about during the time I was running for mayor. I was borough president of the Bronx then and had gotten a lot of good press. It looked very good for me. But there was the possibility that Mayor Wagner, who was then ambassador to Spain,

Herman Badillo, when he was running for borough president of the Bronx

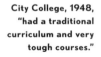

City College, 1948, "had a traditional curriculum and very tough courses."

Novelist Norman Mailer around the time he ran for mayor of the city of New York

might decide to run for mayor for a fourth term. I found that possibility strange because he had chosen not to run against Lindsay in 1965.

I met with Wagner and told him the Reform convention of the Democratic Party had voted to support me if I pledged to stay on as candidate, even if he were to announce his candidacy six weeks from now. "Tell me if you want to run for mayor, and I will be glad to support you," I said to him.

Wagner said, "I understand what you're talking about. I will not run."

I got the Reform endorsement, and six weeks later Wagner announced his candidacy. That was the first disaster.

The second was Norman Mailer. He had become close to Jose Torres, the light heavyweight champion of the world, who was a good friend of mine. Jose arranged a fund-raiser for me at Norman's Brooklyn Heights home. All of the intellectuals, Jack Neufield, Jimmy Breslin, and other such people who were writing for the New York press were there. I spoke and answered questions, and everybody was very impressed.

A week later Norman asked me to meet him for lunch at the Algonquin. "You know, you were very good," he said, "but I'm thinking I want to run for mayor myself. I talked to Jimmy Breslin and he agreed to run with me for city council president."

JIMMY BRESLIN: One night, Jack Neufield suggested Norman and I should run, and we called the Associated Press and said we're running. When I woke up in the morning, it was on the wire—too late.

HERMAN BADILLO: Mailer and Breslin went around drunk through the whole campaign talking about the fifty-first state. At one point Mailer was asked, "Assuming by some miracle you get to be elected, what are you going to do? You know nothing about running the city of New York."

He said, "That's okay. I'll appoint Badillo deputy mayor. He knows what to do." Even with Wagner in the race, I only lost by about thirty-nine thousand votes. But Mailer carried the Village and the West Side, getting around forty-three thousand votes that would otherwise have come to me. Because the liberal vote was split between Mailer and me, the most right-wing candidate, Mario Procaccino, won the Democratic primary. At that point, we in the black and Puerto Rican community decided to support Lindsay.

ELAINE MARKSON: I probably voted for Norman Mailer, I'm ashamed to say. He represented something very different. He was an intellectual; we thought he was going to do something for the city.

JIMMY BRESLIN: The trouble was the blind ignorance of the people around us. Norman and I thought we could learn something in the campaign that we could use in writing. But political stories are so hard to sustain because the election is over and everybody forgets about it the next morning.

HERMAN BADILLO: Mailer and Jimmy just wanted to have a good time. Mailer admitted it was a question of whether to run for mayor or write a book about the astronauts. It was all a joke. But it was a really serious thing, and I've never forgiven Mailer for that.

The next time around, in 1973, the state legislature—where I did not have the power—decided that they would have a runoff for the Democratic primary for mayor because they were worried I would come out first. This time the race was among Biaggi, Blumenthal, Beame and Badillo; the runoff was between Abe Beame and Herman Badillo.

During the campaign, a friend called me. "What are you doing in the Jewish community?"

"I'm just campaigning."

"No, no," he said. "There are flatbed trucks with Puerto Ricans and blacks going through the Jewish communities after ten o'clock at night, banging on bongo drums, shouting, 'Vote for Badillo so we can take over City Hall,' and distributing leaflets saying Badillo is endorsed by the Black Panthers and the Young Lords."

Jack Neufield called these the Stanleymobiles. Stanley Steingut was the county leader in Brooklyn. He had paid blacks and Puerto Ricans to go on these flatbed trucks through Jewish neighborhoods.

Abe Beame got elected because he was the city comptroller and supposedly understood money. But he died on that because once he got elected, the fiscal crisis came about. Beame was blamed for it, and properly so, because he knew what was going on. That cost him his legacy; he will be remembered as the mayor who presided over the city's fiscal crisis.

One of the things I had pointed out during the campaign was that normal day-to-day expenses were coming out of the capital budget. For years, the city

had spent more for day-to-day and year-to-year expenses than it collected in taxes, and that money was put into the capital budget. You can do that for a limited amount of time. Sooner or later, it catches up.

Because taxes don't come necessarily on schedule, the city borrows every day in advance of getting money from taxes. It borrows short-term for day-to-day expenses and long-term for the capital budget. Beame thought he would be able to talk the investment bankers into continuing to lend money to the city. But it had gotten to the point where there were billions of dollars in the capital budget. The financial markets came to the conclusion the city could not manage its budget. So they stopped the credit. The government couldn't meet its day-to-day expenses, and it came to a halt.

This problem was going on during Wagner's and Lindsay's terms, but they were able to get away with it. It was precipitated by the movement of the middle class out of the city after the Second World War.

THEODORE KHEEL: Back in 1945, New York City was largely white. The Highway Trust Fund, which opened up the highways from the central city to the suburbs, had a tremendous influence because the whites moved to the suburbs while the blacks and Hispanics came into the city. The city's problems were exacerbated because the minorities could not pay the taxes necessary to support the city's services.

JIMMY BRESLIN: They came into New York, these sad-faced women with their arms lagging from carrying babies. They arrived from Shreveport, Louisiana; Valdosta, Georgia; the Tidewater area of Virginia; North Carolina—driven off the cotton fields of the South by the invention of machinery that did the work of ninety field hands. They came to New York because of the hope that there would be more decent treatment here than any other place in the world. At the same time, there was a huge pouring in of people from Puerto Rico on flights into Idlewild Airport, which became Kennedy later on. They called them the flights of the chicken. These people would get out on a cold, windy night at the airport by Jamaica Bay, wearing summer dresses and short-sleeved shirts.

Everything stopped as large amounts of money were put into social services. A lot of people moved out—they didn't want their kids going to school with blacks and Puerto Rican kids. Financial stress and social problems resulted. Although the city of New York was hurt, it is something for which it shall forever be proud. We tried to feed too many people, to meet too many tremendous needs.

HERMAN BADILLO: One of the arguments I was making during the campaign is that we have to recognize the changing composition of the city, not just in terms of ethnic composition but in terms of poverty and class. Nobody wanted to face up to the fact that New York had become two cities.

When the city couldn't borrow money, it turned to the federal government to provide short-term assistance.

JOHN CAMPI: On October 30, 1975, the *Daily News* headline was FORD TO NEW YORK: DROP DEAD. It was a classic, and from what Ford said later on, it lost the election for him.

CAROLE RIFKIND: I do believe that headline galvanized people to feel proud about New York. The resilience, the ability of New Yorkers, of the city itself, to triumph over adversity was something many people on many levels felt.

HERMAN BADILLO: I was a congressman at that time, and I remember the struggle to get President Ford and Congress to support us. My colleagues in Washington didn't like New York. To them, it was a city of minorities: Irish, Italian, Jewish, black or Puerto Rican, not really part of America.

Fortunately Governor Hugh Carey came up with the idea of the Financial Control Board to guarantee that the state would oversee the operations of the city and make sure that it would have a truly balanced budget. He had been a congressman and had some credibility in Washington. On that basis, New York got federal aid.

The city was saved but it had to pay a heavy price. We had to fire tens of thousands of city employees and increase the subway fare. City services declined greatly. But the most tragic result of the crisis was the end of free tuition at the City University. Members of Congress hated the idea that the City University was the only free university in the nation. So they insisted that one of the requirements for providing federal aid would be that we impose tuition. It was a blow directed against the poor. Five generations of

New Yorkers had moved from poverty into the middle class through the City University. People like me and Abe Beame would not have been able to make it if not for the fact that we could go to a college that was free.

After graduating from City College, I went on to Brooklyn Law School, and then started a law practice. The judges found out I spoke Spanish, and they began assigning me to criminal cases, where I discovered a lot of young people were being unjustly held because they were poor and didn't have a lawyer. There was no legal aid in those days and hardly any lawyers who spoke Spanish. Finally I decided that I couldn't continue working on a case-by-case basis. I wanted to get involved with the problems in a larger forum. That was how I got into politics.

In 1962, I took over as housing commissioner as a result of the replacement of Robert Moses. He was capable but authoritarian. I opposed him on the Lower Manhattan Expressway. It was very close; he almost won. But Moses's day was over by that time.

I did not want to repeat the mistakes of the huge public housing projects like those in East Harlem. Say you're a Puerto Rican kid born on 112th and Madison. Wherever you go, you see a low-rent housing project. You grow up thinking the city is made up of nothing but blacks and Hispanics, and that all blacks and Hispanics are poor. Since it's low-rent housing, by definition anybody who works his way up has to move out, and new low-income people move in. And all the symbols of authority, the people who run the society, are white.

CAROLE RIFKIND: Previously, public-housing design was limited to the plain redbrick boxes, which are going to be recognized as better than we thought they were because they are nicely proportioned and simple. Unfortunately architects had to work within miserable limits, like urban renewal requirements stipulating no doors on the closets. But the architects did what they could, and the housing was built fairly well, with good ventilation. At first they were four stories, then six stories. But they grew with elevator technology up to twenty stories, and that's when you started to get a lot of social pathology.

ALVIN REED: At first, we in Harlem thought the projects were a blessing from heaven. My mother used to pray every night that it happen to us. When you are coming from rat-infested apartments, straight walk-through railroad flats where to get to the kitchen you got to walk through two bedrooms, the projects seem wonderful. They were just being built; they were brand-new, clean, modern.

By the time my mother finally did get into the projects, she was in her late sixties, and they had turned bad. "Ma, you don't want to move in there," we told her. But she still had that thing about getting into the projects.

LACONIA SMEDLEY: You had the city as the bad landlord. They started off okay. They screened people. Then they let anyone in.

ALVIN REED: It got to where everybody who was in there was on some kind of assistance, and if you had a job, they'd charge you so much more rent, and you were living next to people who were hardly paying anything.

LACONIA SMEDLEY: And there were those who were doing drugs, staying home all day, having babies, getting more welfare money, having more babies and not supervising the children.

HERMAN BADILLO: Between 1962 and 1965, I worked out a huge percentage of the urban renewal projects, including the West Side Urban Renewal Area, which involved a twenty-block neighborhood from 87th to 97th Streets and from Central Park West to Amsterdam Avenue. The original plan called for only four hundred units of low-rent housing, but when I and Judge Milton Mollen, coordinator of housing and development, got involved, we felt the number of low-income units should be raised to twenty-five hundred.

What we did, for the first time in history, was put low-income people in middle-income housing. Instead of having a building with one hundred percent middle-income people, we made it eighty percent middle-income and twenty percent low-income people. A new concept—eighty–twenty—was born.

Central Park West was perfect so we left it alone. But Amsterdam and Columbus Avenues were slums, and so were the brownstones between 87th and 97th Streets. We tore down the slum housing on Columbus and Amsterdam and scattered vest-pocket public housing throughout the area. Because the low-rent apartments were scattered in the buildings, nobody could tell who was who. At the same time, we rehabilitated the brownstones on the side streets and basically made them luxury housing. By doing that, we stabilized the neighborhood south of 87th Street and effectively saved the entire West Side.

CAROLE RIFKIND: What we don't talk about because of its absence is what was torn down for urban renewal. Lincoln Center is a period piece, and I've learned to respect period pieces. But to build it, they moved thousands of poor people out of that area, and when you uproot people, you create social problems. While people lived in their neighborhood, they had continuity; they lived with generations. If a kid misbehaved, the grandmother saw what he was doing. Once people were moved away from their connections, of course they acted out. And it was on such a massive scale.

Lincoln Towers was outrageous because they tore down poor people's houses and put in housing for upper-middle-class people. Some people said it was not urban renewal but Negro removal or Hispanic removal.

There were two phases of urban renewal: the Eisenhower-influenced years of the fifties and into the early sixties, and the Kennedy-influenced years starting in 1963, when there was massive federal assistance that had not been available before. High and good design was part of the mission of the second phase of urban renewal—a reflection of the influence of Jackie Kennedy, the association with culture, the spirit of innovation and rebelliousness that the

Urban renewal overlooks older tenement housing on Amsterdam Avenue from 120th to 129th Streets.

sixties brought with it. There was a new energy of planning in the city when
Lindsay, who loved high-design architecture, formed something called the
Urban Design Group. Later New York State formed the Urban Development
Corporation, and those two entities crisscrossed.

THEODORE LIEBMAN: Public housing in New York City is a miracle. All
over the United States, it is looked down upon and criticized. Not in New York.
Maybe that's because we accept the fact that not only do we live among poor
people and rich people, but we need people of every level to make the city work.

Right after the assassination of Martin Luther King, the New York State
Legislature, under very direct pressure from Governor Nelson Rockefeller,
passed the Urban Development Act of 1968, which created the New York
State Urban Development Corporation (UDC). As a result, over the next five
years, more than thirty thousand housing units and several new towns were
created throughout New York State. The UDC worked with every kind of
program and made use of the rather vigorous federal programs of that time to
get a mix of income in publicly assisted housing. Its president and CEO was
Edward J. Logue, whose previous great achievement had been the building of
the new Boston.

UDC was clearly the only public agency within the nation that was focusing not only on building numbers of units but in making them good architecture. I had worked for Ed in Boston, and so when in 1970 he asked me to become chief architect at UDC, I was eager to accept.

I admired Bill Chafee, the first chief architect at UDC, who had directed the program during its first two years. But the focus was on high-rise housing, while I was leaning toward low-rise housing solutions to problems of family housing. My instincts told me children were not suited to the elevator as their means of going out to play, nor was it good for parents to supervise their children from windows on the 19th floor.

I said I would accept the job if I could have the opportunity to see what public housing was like in Europe, where I knew there were better examples of low-rise buildings. And so for nearly a year, my wife and I and our very young children lived in eighty housing projects, in thirty-six different cities, in ten different countries.

"What we don't talk about because of its absence is what was torn down for urban renewal"—scenes of the neighborhood that was destroyed to create Lincoln Center.

People returned from the war and what did they build? The most modern thing: the tower in the park. At the same time, there was an intense need for housing coupled with improved technology that allowed you to build higher, and elevators that allowed you to go higher. But what I discovered, especially in England and Scandinavia, was the beginning of a social reaction to the policies of high-rise housing. And I came back with the idea that we develop a low-rise prototype for New York City blocks with the same or more density than high-rise housing. Ed Logue permitted this to happen.

At UDC, we were looking at some neighborhoods where four- or six-story buildings had been destroyed over the years. The choice was either to consolidate and replace with high-rise towers, or to create blocks identical to the ones that had existed. Our goal was to rebuild full neighborhoods and demonstrate that this type of housing fostered a greater sense of community and provided a more livable environment. We were able to build low-income housing of small units with twice the density of a tower. The spaces between buildings were smaller, but well defined, heavily used, and comfortable for people. We had seen too many examples of large undefined space that people were afraid to use. This was my focus for over five years at UDC.

CAROLE RIFKIND: If there is anything that represents the whole vision of that time, it is the development of Roosevelt Island. It had a lot of the idealism of the late sixties.

THEODORE LIEBMAN: When Ed Logue undertook developing Welfare Island, which became Roosevelt Island, even the economists at UDC were telling him: If you're going to build five thousand mixed-income units, start with the upper-middle and middle, and little by little add some low income. He refused a hundred percent. He insisted it be fifty-fifty. His dream was to demonstrate in a place where everybody could see it that all incomes could live together immediately.

Welfare Island was 147 acres in the East River across from the Upper East Side, a place of hospitals, ruins of an asylum, some outbuildings, and not one unit of housing. Many of the chronically ill patients I met when I first went there were in wheelchairs; they had not been off the island for years.

Ed envisioned turning this place into a car-free community for thousands of New Yorkers. "There should be a school system that's the best in the city so people should want to come here," Ed Logue said. "The poor kids and middle-income kids all going to school together in their youngest grades will learn to live together."

He brought many innovations to Roosevelt Island, like a Scandinavian vacuum system where garbage dropped in a chute was eventually processed at one end of the island, a thousand-car garage and free electric minibuses. The subway that was supposed to come in 1976 did not come until 1986, so as a way to bridge the gap, he bridged the East River with the tram—a gondola-type aerial cable car. We had two slogans: "Only four minutes to the island from Manhattan by tram" and "Four minutes by air to Bloomingdale's."

We challenged architects to think about a way to build housing that would work for everyone in a very dense situation where you could not have only low-rise housing. Philip Johnson did the master plan. The architects for the low- and middle-income aspects were Jose Luis Sert, who was dean of Harvard at the time, and Johansen and Bhavnani, who did upper-income housing as well.

Some of the people who created Roosevelt Island: Ed Logue (left) and Tony Pangaro

Roosevelt Island when it was Welfare Island, a place of hospitals

Views of Roosevelt Island—"It had a lot of the idealism of the late sixties."

UDC was the most powerful housing agency in the state, but it was run like a private company, with an enormous number of very bright lawyers and development-oriented kinds of people—young people who went on to become successful leaders in their fields. It brought a lot of minority architects to prominence. It created an awful lot of mixed-income housing. And Ed Logue was its guiding light.

It came to an end because federal aid was stopped on January 5, 1973, when President Nixon put a freeze on funds for public housing. We knew about this several weeks before and worked day and night to get projects in the pipeline funded.

But it also ended because of Ed Logue's personal boldness in confronting nine towns in Westchester County and attempting to force upon each of them a small increment of low- and moderate-income housing. It would not have meant a thing to any of those communities if the 100 or 150 units of one- or two-story housing were built. But it didn't happen. The winds had gone the other way. New York State pulled back its forces.

At a hearing in Bedford, one of the nine towns, Ed Logue had to have a bodyguard with him because of death threats, something he never faced in New York City. A woman in a long skirt got up and said, "You know it's not the families that live here now that are poor, but it's all of their friends from the Carolinas that they bring with them."

At the end, the atmosphere had become less pleasant. Questions of financial mismanagement were raised. Of course there was none. The truth was no one was willing to put money into housing, and therefore the agency that was geared up to produce it had to be retrenched. The office of the chief of architecture, the design arm that hired the architects and did the planning, was eliminated. Who needs to hire architects when no building is going on? When they stopped doing housing in 1975, the excuse was that the programs weren't there. The truth is the political will wasn't there. The day Ed Logue left UDC, the heart of UDC left with him.

As chief architect of UDC, my mission was to help create the best housing in neighborhoods that could be created, no limits. While it lasted, I had the best architectural job in the world.

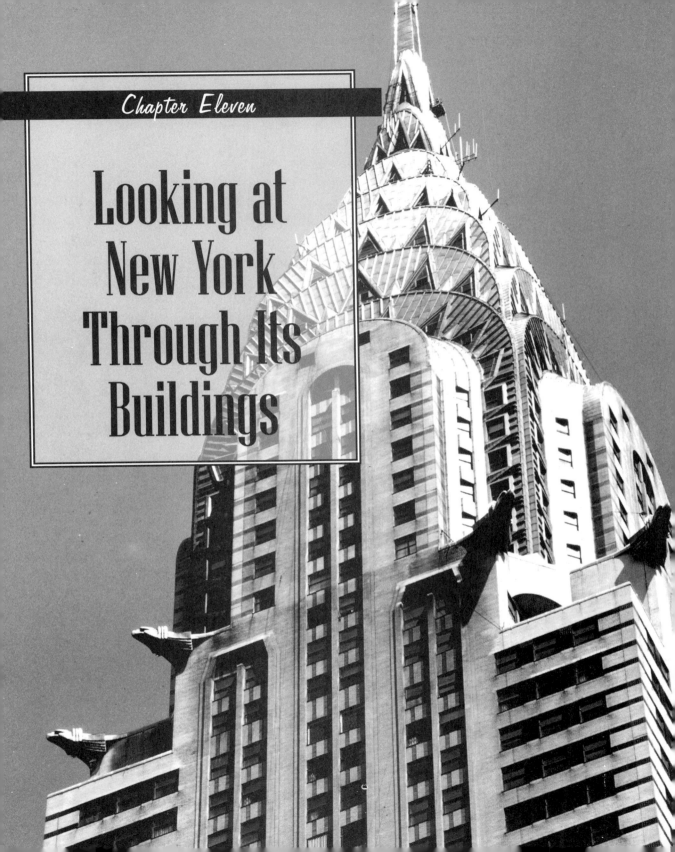

Chapter Eleven

Looking at New York Through Its Buildings

BILL GALLO: I always thought of buildings like heavyweight champions. The Empire State Building was the champion. Then the Twin Towers came up, and you felt sorry for the Empire State Building. That was still your champion.

MICHAEL GEORGE: A realtor once told me the mortgage on a new building in New York was twenty years. A building is built to last only twenty years because New York City changes so much that it pays to tear the thing down and build something fresh after that time.

The older guys built for forever. That's why when Penn Station was torn down, which I regret so much, guys came to knock this thing down, and it would not fall. It would not fall.

The Empire State
Building dominating
the New York City
skyline

Site of the future United Nations building: six riverfront blocks between 42nd and 48th Streets

I look at New York through its buildings. The city had grown up in the great classical age. The Public Library, which was built at the turn of the century, is an example of that kind of architecture. The sons of the people who did the Public Library continued to work in this style through the 1920s. Many of the architects who created the Greek classical buildings in Manhattan went to the Ecole des Beaux Arts in Paris or were influenced by it. When in the 1950s and '60s the international style became the aesthetic ideal, the calling card of architects in New York, that was the nail in the coffin of Beaux Arts architecture.

GILLES LARRAÍN: All the great architects came here after the war: Mies van der Rohe, who did Seagram's; Marcel Breuer, who did the Whitney. The Bauhaus idea was realized here. The power, the space was here. There are no ruins in America; you don't have to deal with the ancient times, to adapt to it, to transform it. You are free to invent your own idea.

CAROLE RIFKIND: The first modern postwar buildings of character and quality were the UN and Lever House in 1952 and the Seagram Building in 1958. The UN represented the tower in the park; it was Le Corbusier modern. Lever House has a low element that hugs the streetline. Compare that to the Seagram Building, which steps back in splendid isolation.

In the strong grid of Manhattan, it's really difficult to build a strongly modernist building. Lever was hesitating; Seagram was assertive. But Seagram was a building that could never be built by anyone else because it was built as a corporate logo and no cost was spared. It could afford to underbuild on the site, making for a confluence between economics and the ambition to state something assertively.

GILLES LARRAÍN: The Seagram Building, recessed in a plaza, nicely proportioned, has character. The metal beam that is the structure is very close to the

Greek column. The order, the repetition of that space creates a harmony.

CAROLE RIFKIND: The story of New York architecture is one of sacrificing to the expediency of real estate formulas, of the economic expectation one can get out of a site.

MICHAEL GEORGE: Park Avenue used to be a wonderful wall of apartment houses and hotels. They were part of the gigantic building boom of the 1920s, all uniform, of the same height and the same style that went down virtually to the New York Central Building and Grand Central Station and spilled down some of the side streets to Lexington Avenue.

In the 1950s and '60s, the neighborhood was remade. A series of junky buildings went up, the white-brick apartment houses and the glass office towers. They also extended from Park Avenue back to Lexington, Third and Second Avenue. To be effective, the modern building has to shock. The Lever House and Seagram Building were a big shock, the opposite of what had been there before. But once other buildings came up copying the green glass, the shock was gone.

Lever House on Park Avenue, built in 1952, was one of the first modern postwar buildings.

The Seagram Building on Park Avenue, Mies van der Rohe's masterpiece

The New York Central Building had dominated Park Avenue and brought it to its conclusion in the same way the Arc de Triomphe ends the Champs-Elysées in Paris. Coming south down Park Avenue, the view was perfect. But coming north up Park Avenue South and seeing the great Grand Central tower was wonderful as well. You'd come up this ramp, and it would slow you down even if you normally do not look at things.

In the early 1960s, the Pan Am Building (now Met Life) came up and destroyed that image. It was a direct attack on the kind of architecture that had been done in the 1920s. It's a much larger building than Lever House, twice as big as the Empire State Building, not in height but in size, probably half the size of the Pentagon.

Looking up Park Avenue to 42nd Street

Now there's nothing wrong with having a tall building on a street. There's nothing wrong with having a building behind another building. But there is something wrong with having a building neutralize perhaps one of the greatest views ever.

Here we are in the center of the world. In no other place would the center of town be a railroad yard. But here in Grand Central it is. The Grand Hyatt was originally the Commodore Hotel, which was done in the manner of Grand Central. But they stripped the thing down to its frame and put a glass wall on the outside. Behind the hotel is the smokestack, the power plant of Grand Central. You couldn't see it before when it was the Commodore, but with the glass wall, it just stands out.

Looking down Park Avenue to 42nd Street

GILLES LARRAÍN: Many of the uptown buildings that were built in the postwar period have no signature; they have no character. They are just efficient places for the purpose of functioning as offices or apartments or whatever. Space for the floor, ten-foot ceilings, because that is efficient. It's not designed with a vision; it's designed with a purpose.

CAROLE RIFKIND: The building of the 1950s and 1960s was very destructive of a highly designed college campus like Columbia. I had a personal association with a particular postwar building at Columbia, a mean ugly student center. Since this building came up just before I got to Barnard, I accepted it as given. But we would much rather go to the drugstore on the corner and have a coffee than go into that so-called student center.

This building was one of the first to actually break the scale at Columbia, to disrupt the pattern, the height. It was a pallid structure of about fifteen to twenty stories in a very weak, reduced kind of abstract Georgian style that picked up the mannerism of what the old architecture had been like but didn't really understand it at all. It came up around the time the college walk was enclosed. I suspect Columbia was having trouble attracting students to New York City with the social problems, the new immigrants that confronted prospective students. Maybe they were trying to isolate the students from the city. It was a time of pulling in, of the red scare, of xenophobia. The Columbia College campus kind of closed in on itself.

Buildings represent the culture of their time. Retrograde times, retrograde architecture. The serious Eisenhower years with all their qualities were represented by Lever House or Manufacturers Hanover Bank. Modernism? Yes. Progressivism? Yes. But kind of timid, fearful of Communism, reflective of corporate America, McCarthy years—kind of conservatism. Even Seagram's, great as it is, is not flaming modernism in terms of the ecological modernism of the Germans and the Bauhaus. It's an example of the conservative modernism of the fifties.

JOHN TAURANAC: Many great buildings had come up during the 1920s and early 1930s but those styles had ended. There wasn't any building to speak of during the Depression, and then the war came along when we were building bombers and not buildings. Building didn't really begin until the mid 1950s, just around the time the Third Avenue el was torn down.

MICHAEL GEORGE: The Third Avenue el was the last el in Manhattan. I can remember riding it when I was a child, and like any child, I ran to the front window and looked out. The next time I saw Third Avenue, the el was gone. Suddenly Third Avenue was bright. You could not believe how wide the street was. And it triggered an explosion of building.

JOHN TAURANAC: Third Avenue, which had been in shadow for so long, metamorphosed into a boulevard and developed in a rush. Manhattan House, between 65th and 66th and between Second and Third Avenues,

LOOKING AT NEW YORK THROUGH ITS BUILDINGS

was the first prestigious apartment house to go up. One of the early white-brick buildings, it was set back from the street, breaking the regular grid pattern. And it had terraces. A cartoon appeared around that time where a table on a terrace is set for two and the woman is crying, "Hurry, dear, your soup's getting dirty."

The white-brick buildings that arose overnight became emblematic of Third Avenue. You can find them elsewhere in Manhattan, even on Park Avenue. Still, the biggest concentration of white-brick buildings is on Third Avenue. They were all given names—York Towers, Buckingham—but they were carbon copies of each other, and the original was not a good standard. The white-brick buildings had no sense of place. Aesthetics were held to a minimum. It was just to make a buck.

MICHAEL GEORGE: Why did they use white brick in a city that has lots of soot? I don't know. But it became the material of choice along with the lower eight-foot ceiling.

There was tremendous change on the East Side. From First to Lexington had been a neighborhood of working people, with the exception of Beekman Place, Sutton Place, and Tudor City—which were along the river—and the area around Grand Central Station, which had lots of hotels. But the side streets and Third Avenue were lined with tenements. There weren't many restaurants because people didn't need restau-

rants; they cooked at home. You had grocery stores, fruit and vegetable stores, all the Main Street stuff. You could go two blocks and find it happening again. The idea was you never would have to walk more than two or three blocks to get whatever you needed. The people on Park Avenue had other people bring their food for them. Or they could go to the Waldorf or the Ambassador or one of the other hotels.

But once office buildings and apartment houses started to go up, they went up with tremendous speed. A building like the one on the northwest side of 54th and Lexington took a year and a half to build. Small stores and structures were cleared away and larger buildings taking up an entire block were put up.

JOAN WASHBURN: People still lived on 57th Street, but the property was becoming too commercial, and the landlords broke up the spaces, turning them into galleries or offices. Buildings were coming down and larger buildings were replacing them. There were a whole group of town houses on 57th and Madison taken down when the IBM Building came up.

MICHAEL GEORGE: The West Side changed too but not to the same degree. If you go along Broadway and Amsterdam Avenue, if you go north of the Museum of Natural History on Columbus Avenue, you can see wholesale changes where block after block has been wiped out. The way you can tell, if it's higher than six stories and there's no ornament on the outside of the building, it came after 1960.

The beginning of the movie *Breakfast at Tiffany's* shows Fifth Avenue as a two-way street. All the avenues were two-way streets. It was a big, big deal to convert them to one-way traffic. In the 1950s, a traffic commissioner by the name of T. T. Wylie—they called him "One-Way" Wylie—not only came up with the idea that traffic would move more smoothly with one-way streets, he also came up with the idea of synchronized traffic lights. To make more room for cars, the sidewalks were narrowed. It may only be a matter of three feet, but the space of green along the curb was taken away to make room for the cars. Nevertheless, Manhattan remains a walking city.

One of the postwar goals was to get rid of all the slums. Another was to make more parks. There was this movement to expand the kinds of things the wealthy enjoyed so that those who were not so wealthy could enjoy them as well. That was one of Robert Moses's visions. I don't think Moses was a villain. A lot of things he did were good, and a lot of the things he did had very bad results.

JANE JACOBS: Robert Moses was the monarch of the city in the postwar period and a terrible influence on New York. His emphasis was on automobile traffic while public transit was left to deteriorate. The Regional Plan Association, which I understand is very different today, was also a bad influence. Its scheme for crosstown expressways would have totally Los Angelized Manhattan.

Scenes of New York City's postwar building boom

But a loose federation of activists, residents of the city who didn't want to see what was being planned come to be, fought against such proposals. We weren't urban planners. We were part of a grassroots uprising of people who recognized things were being done that hurt the life of the city.

Edith Lyons, who lived on West 9th Street in Greenwich Village, was one of the activists. Together with another daring woman, Shirley Hayes, she came up with the idea of closing Washington Square Park to automobiles. Until 1958, a roadway that originally had been a carriage drive carried traffic through the park from its Fifth Avenue entrance to its south side. Robert Moses proposed to close this roadway but compensate for it by trimming down the sides of the park and widening the perimeter streets, encircling the park with a high-speed traffic artery. This scheme was fought and defeated.

Community activists fought and succeeded in closing Washington Square Park to vehicular traffic.

In the mid 1950s, Moses came up with a new plan: to build a major depressed highway through the center of the park that would carry high-speed traffic between midtown Manhattan and an expressway he wanted to develop south of the park.

This was the impetus for Edith Lyons's and Shirley Hayes's idea to close the park to traffic altogether. It became a popular cause in the community. Ultimately, through tough political pressure, the community won. The park road was closed, first on a trial basis, and then permanently, while the perimeter streets stayed as they were.

While the battle was being waged, I was down at a hearing at city hall in the Board of Estimates chambers when Robert Moses got up to speak. "They're nothing but a bunch of, a bunch of, a bunch of . . . mothers!" he said, characterizing his opponents.

They were a bunch of mothers who had gotten acquainted in the park as they watched their children play. But they, and other community activists, were the real leaders in New York, citizens who did stick their necks out and invested an awful lot of effort and time into what they thought was good for the city.

MARGOT GAYLE: In the early 1960s, the Jefferson Market Courthouse on Sixth Avenue and 10th Street, which was about half a block from where I lived, was put up for auction. They said they couldn't locate any agency that could find any use for that odd building. But I knew that with really strong community demands, things that were not considered worthy at that time could be saved.

"Why do you want to save that old pile?" people said to me.

"Well," I said, "I really like it. You probably don't, but let me remind you that your kids look up at the big clock in the tall brick tower when they go to P.S. 41, and you look at it when you take the Sixth Avenue subway. That clock is important in your life, and if you don't save the building under it, you won't have it." And so we founded this organization called the Village Neighborhood Committee for the Clock on the Jefferson Market Courthouse.

At that time, everything old was being torn down. People didn't think about conserving old buildings. Our committee, which included Lewis Mumford, Maurice Evans, and e. e. cummings, was in the forefront of something new. We met in my apartment. We had no money. But we did have an artist with us who designed Christmas cards of the Jefferson Market, and we sat on the steps of Jefferson Market and sold these Christmas cards. We got petitions signed. It was a heck of a fight that went on for about a year, but we succeeded.

Philip Wittenberg, a well-known lawyer, felt very strongly that the Village needed a new library. There was only a small library on Sheridan Square, and the Village was a highly literate part of town. He brought pressure that the Jefferson Market become a big central library. But here's a funny thing: When the mayor said he would restore it for the New York Public Library, the library said, "That's really nice. But we'd like to tear down the building and build a nice modern library."

"No way," said Mayor Wagner. He was a friend.

Giorgio Cavaglieri was the architect who transformed the Jefferson Market Courthouse into a library in 1967. One day I said to him, "I want to take you down to this area south of Houston Street and show it to you." We

The spire of the Jefferson Market Courthouse, top left, overlooks a Sixth Avenue that was still dominated by an el.

walked down there about eight o'clock on a summer evening. It was still light out. But there was no one in sight. "Let's get out of here," he said.

GILLES LARRAÍN: Although the buildings in the area were blackened with age and covered with dirt and decay from years of neglect, I was intrigued by their unique character, their majestic volume, their cast-iron Doric and Corinthian columns that architects of the 1800s had ordered from catalogues of manufacturing companies located in Pittsburgh. It was such an innovative idea at the time to construct these small buildings by ordering parts from a catalogue.

MARGOT GAYLE: The area had the greatest concentration of cast-iron architecture in New York. A lot of second-rate commercial and industrial activities on a small scale were going on. But here and there you saw a little box with geraniums on a fire escape—a dead giveaway that artists were living there. They were illegal occupants who paid rent for spaces not zoned for residential use, and so they had to be very furtive. The fire department called the section "Hell's Hundred Acres." If ever there was a fire, they wouldn't know where the people were.

Robert Moses wanted to build an elevated expressway along Broome Street from the Holland Tunnel to the Manhattan Bridge. Many of the cast-iron buildings are on both sides of Broome Street. The most famous is the Haughwout Building, which had been a furniture and china shop. Mrs. Abraham Lincoln owned a set of china from the Haughwout shop.

A street in SoHo when most of the businesses were second-rate commercial and industrial enterprises

Jane Jacobs led the fight against the expressway. At the hearing in 1968, Jane and her little coterie were seated in the room looking very innocuous. Then to the surprise of everyone, they walked up on the platform, and Jane grabbed the tape of the stenotypist, hauled it out, and tore it up. She announced since there were no records, there could not have been a hearing. The whole event was disrupted.

At the same time, people were pushing to have that area, which was a very amorphous section by the way, urban renewaled—in other words, turned into housing projects or an industrial park. But Jack Felt, the planning commissioner, and Mayor Wagner had the good sense to hold off. They commissioned Chester Rapkin of Princeton University to go through it and do a very thorough study and analysis.

Chester and his students went through the area building by building. They found the artists living in the lofts and concluded the neighborhood was worth saving. They put out an interesting report called "South of Houston," which was the basis for the acronym "SoHo"; it had never had anything to do with the British Soho.

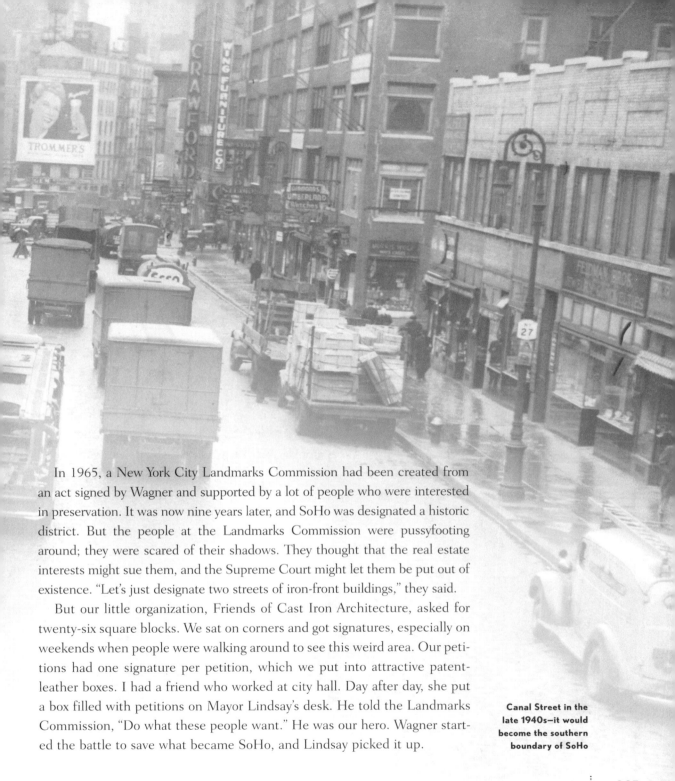

In 1965, a New York City Landmarks Commission had been created from an act signed by Wagner and supported by a lot of people who were interested in preservation. It was now nine years later, and SoHo was designated a historic district. But the people at the Landmarks Commission were pussyfooting around; they were scared of their shadows. They thought that the real estate interests might sue them, and the Supreme Court might let them be put out of existence. "Let's just designate two streets of iron-front buildings," they said.

But our little organization, Friends of Cast Iron Architecture, asked for twenty-six square blocks. We sat on corners and got signatures, especially on weekends when people were walking around to see this weird area. Our petitions had one signature per petition, which we put into attractive patent-leather boxes. I had a friend who worked at city hall. Day after day, she put a box filled with petitions on Mayor Lindsay's desk. He told the Landmarks Commission, "Do what these people want." He was our hero. Wagner started the battle to save what became SoHo, and Lindsay picked it up.

Canal Street in the late 1940s—it would become the southern boundary of SoHo

CAROLE RIFKIND: SoHo was drawn as a historic district from Canal to Houston Streets and from Broadway to West Broadway. But that was just a convenience. The area is remarkably cohesive, but if you start looking at it, there's also a lot of variety. You can also zigzag the line and see a beautiful cast-iron building on Lafayette and Crosby.

MARGOT GAYLE: Our opponents didn't see the value of the area. No one dreamed it would become what it became.

MARCIA TUCKER: I can remember the sculptor Richard Serra standing on the street corner of West Broadway and Spring Street back in the 1970s and saying to me, "One day all this will be boutiques!"

And I said, "Oh, Richard, you're such a pessimist."

There were people living in the neighborhood that became SoHo all through the sixties, but they were living in rough circumstances. Once you got below Houston Street into the warehouse district, it wasn't the Village anymore. It was dark; it was nothing.

GILLES LARRAÍN: In 1967, when my wife and I bought a loft in a building on the corner of Wooster and Grand, hardly anyone lived in the neighborhood. It was very, very empty. There were no traffic lights, only stop signs. The streets were dimly lit with maybe one streetlight per square block. In the winter, by five o'clock at night it would be dark; people walked around with flashlights.

The first ones to come to SoHo were the artists who needed the big spaces. They would get together with one another, have parties, and arrange showings of their works.

The only hangout in the neighborhood was the Broome Street Café on the corner of Broome Street and West Broadway, where you could play pool, have a hamburger and a salad.

For fifteen hundred we got a floor of twenty-eight hundred square feet. Our building was the first co-op in SoHo. It was nothing but walls and beams, no insulation, no bathrooms, not even a complete floor. You could overhear the most intimate conversations. But the sun shone through the front window, so I could grow my avocados, and the spaces were fantastic.

MARCIA TUCKER: The way SoHo grew was that little groups would hear about the spaces and that it was relatively inexpensive, and they would band together and buy a building.

Our group tried to get a building on Greene Street that fell through. Then my upstairs neighbor asked if I would be interested in this building on Sullivan Street that originally was a paint factory. It cost ten thousand.

We moved to Sullivan Street in 1970 when it was almost all Italian, with a few Portuguese starting to come in. The Mafia was very strong. There were two social clubs right on Sullivan Street. One was right next door, and it was really big. About four o'clock one morning, we heard a giant explosion; the whole front window of the club had been blown out. The next day I went over to the grocery store across the street. "What happened?" I asked.

And they said, "Nothing."

Still, it was a wonderful neighborhood. I grew up in Brooklyn, where my landlord and landlady were Italians, and I loved them to pieces. I gravitated to a place that was similar to the place where I had grown up. They had a tradition at Christmastime where all the merchants had little paper shot glasses and a bottle put out for their regular customers. The grocery store would give you stuff on credit, cash checks. It was like a small-town atmosphere. People looked out for each other; it was totally safe. By 1973, '74, it was clear that this area was going to provide the spaces that artists needed at relatively reasonable prices, and it began to fill up.

GILLES LARRAÍN: In 1973, I bought the six-story building at 95 Grand Street for ninety thousand dollars. Once it had been a warehouse for the Vanderbilts. By then, SoHo had been transformed from a rundown neighborhood of warehouses and small manufacturing companies to an exciting artistic community. People like Leo Castelli, who had opened up the art world uptown, began opening galleries in the area. Buildings had been cleaned, new windows installed. With their details now visible, one could see their simplicity and beauty.

But although the artists originally discovered the place, when it became popular, the money people came in back of them. And then the rents went up and up and up. People who are renting in SoHo today are from Wall Street. The kind of community SoHo was in the 1960s and '70s is gone. It's no longer the experimental human laboratory it used to be. All my friends, all the artists I knew, have moved. Today it's a tourist destination. I cannot get out of my house on the weekends; the crowds are tremendous.

There used to be so much space. Now there is not an empty square inch in the entire neighborhood. But it is all boutiques and high-class fashion stores. What they call galleries are in actuality boutiques. There are so many of them, but how many great artists are there? You may walk in the street and see broken glass. It's pretty, it sparkles, but it's not a diamond.

This kind of thing happens over and over again. For young people, maybe the East Village is the place to hang out, maybe that is the place for artists of the future. As for me, I had the best part of SoHo. I was here at the beginning when it was so wonderful because it was so free.

MARGOT GAYLE: I'm glad to see the buildings are still there. I'm glad it's rich and bountiful. If the current occupants move on, the buildings will remain and be put to some other use. I think saving SoHo is the best thing I did; I also raised a couple of nice daughters.

If You Live Long Enough . . .

MICKEY ALPERT: Manhattan used to be filled with all these ethnic enclaves. The West Village, Bleecker Street was home to all Italians. Yorkville, up to the middle 70s, had so many German delicatessens and restaurants—Café Geiger, the Bremen House, the Jaeger House on 85th and Lexington that had a live oom-pah band and seated a couple of hundred people.

MICHAEL GEORGE: On the Lower East Side, it was amazing to see the different alphabets—Hebrew, Chinese, Russian too. You'd see Catholic churches side by side, the Irish church and the Italian church.

I grew up in Hell's Kitchen—today they call it Clinton—just behind the garment district. It was a neighborhood where poor people lived. Yes there was crime, but you could grow up there, you could live there. You could eat cheap, you could sleep cheap.

A few blocks away, the Hudson River was all docks and ships and longshoremen loading and unloading. On the East River, the docks ended just below Sutton Place. What you saw were people working and lots of trucks moving about everywhere. If you look at Tudor City, which was built in the 1920s, you'll notice there are not too many windows facing the East River. At that time, the land was junk, soap factories. Tudor City faced into its own court, an island removed from everything else. This was very much an industrial city.

JOHN TAURANAC: There was quite a bit of light industry in Yorkville during the postwar years. The Fink Bakery on 76th Street was a commercial bakery that supplied restaurants. Their slogan was "Fink means good bread," but their smell was nothing like the aroma of baking bread. You could also get a whiff of beer when the wind was right, byproducts from the Ruppert Brewery up in the 90s.

There were sidings along the East River. The coal barges would tie up to the bank on 74th Street, scoop up great chunks of coal in a gigantic shovel, lift them up over the East River Drive, and dump them into the Con Edison plant. Coal was being burned in apartment houses, and the trucks went up and down the streets stopping to make coal deliveries through big chutes that went down into cellars.

The East River was at the end of our block. In the late forties, kids used to dive in and swim. On 78th Street, a ferry ran to and from Welfare Island. There's still a walkway over the East River Drive at 78th Street that leads to where the ferry used to dock.

ANDY BALDUCCI: The produce market used to be on Washington Street, which runs parallel to the West Side Highway in lower Manhattan. It was shut down in the 1960s when the city decided to upgrade the downtown West Side area, clean it up. Hunts Point took over, and the whole landscape, the entire mechanism of the produce business, changed. Today Washington Street is nothing but big office buildings.

Loading and unloading on the docks

But from where the Twin Towers were up to Canal Street—that all used to be part of the Washington Market. Most of the produce came by truck, but it also came up the Hudson in barges and boats. Rolling freight arrived from the New Jersey side; the trains would roll right onto the barges, which crossed the river and emptied out on the west-side docks. There were all these open warehouses on the Hudson River, where auctions took place of citruses and other fruit that came from California and Florida.

The main street was Washington Street, but all the adjacent side streets were part of the market as well. There were no fancy platforms, only stores off the sidewalks with basements that were used for bananas, tomatoes, and tropical fruits because they didn't need refrigeration. People came from throughout the metropolitan area, as far as Philadelphia. It was a real market, every inch of the way.

I remember like it was yesterday. Ten o'clock at night, my Uncle Frank would close the store in Flushing, and we would go up to the produce market. Even though I wasn't old enough to have a license, he let me drive his ten-wheeler, dark green Chevrolet with the canvas top while he slept.

Once we got to the market, my uncle would say, "You go downstairs to the banana house and sleep a couple of hours while I walk the street. When I'm done with most of the purchasing, I'll come and call you." That was how I began in the business, serving my apprenticeship with Uncle Frank.

SAUL ZABAR: There used to be a coffee district on Front Street. That's downtown on the East Side, south of the Fulton Fish Market, very close to the South Street Seaport. There were slips; the docks came right up to Front Street. When the boats came in, the brokers would go on the boats to see what their coffee looked like. The longshoremen would unload the coffee onto the docks. A broker bought your coffee. It would get shipped to a trade roaster who would roast it for you, and then a trucker

Waterfront seen from the other side of the river

The Fulton Fish Market was just north of where the coffee district used to be.

would pick it up and bring it to you. Zabar's used to buy coffee from a Front Street supplier called the Beacon Coffee Company.

All up and down Front Street were the coffee merchants' offices and small roasting operations. The brokers and importers met daily. They'd see each other on the street, exchange conversation, samples. This was thirty-five, forty years ago.

I have a letter dated 1973 from a company that did our roasting when we got into specialized coffees. It's a copy of my contract for them to roast my coffee and the prices they were going to get. But by that time, the coffee district no longer existed. The area had been razed to make way for high-rise and office buildings; the slips had been filled. The brokers' offices got moved to Wall Street, the trade roasters to Brooklyn. South Street Seaport was saved just by a fluke, and anyway it's only the façades of buildings. The coffee district was destroyed, and in the process, a whole piece of New York City history that was two hundred years old was destroyed as well.

LEONARD KOPPETT: In the years after the war, New York was still the major port. The Hudson River was lined with piers. Below 14th Street were a lot of ferries going across to Jersey and Staten Island. From 14th to 59th Streets were the piers for the ocean liners. I was on a lot of those ships saying good-bye to people who were going away to Europe. The custom was if you had your own stateroom, you had a little going-away party for two or three hours before they announced "All ashore who is going ashore." Until the jets came in regularly in the late sixties, the ocean liners were the way to go to Europe.

KEN LIBO: By the time I was living in Chelsea, the wharves were no longer used for ocean liners, and the piers were falling apart. I would walk down to the docks quite frequently and very much had the feeling of walking into a movie set of *Great Expectations*, particularly Miss Haversham's house.

The West Side Highway was still there. It was no longer used by cars as it was unsound, but it functioned as a pedestrian walk. You could walk for a mile or two and see the Hudson River from an elevated position, an advantage for residents of the area. It was a place where you could get away from the hustle and bustle of the city. I thought there was something very romantic about it.

Ocean liners were the
way to go to Europe.

JULIE ISAACSON: New York City used to be a manufacturing town. The garment industry once had seven hundred thousand workers; there was even a shoemaking industry in Manhattan. I watched as the scene changed.

After the war, I got a job putting eyes in dolls at the Imperial Crown Doll Factory for twenty-two dollars a week. It was unskilled work; you did it by the feel of your hand. The center of the toy and novelty industry was in New York, and it averaged about twenty-six thousand workers. Ideal Toy alone, for example, had seven thousand workers. The shops were mainly in the boroughs, but the showroom was in Manhattan at 200 Fifth Avenue. Every February there was a show for all the new toys, and every year they invented new dolls: League of Nations dolls, Shirley Temple dolls, Barbie dolls—all made in the USA. They tried to blame the unions for manufacturing dying out. It was really the imports.

MICKEY ALPERT: Fifth Avenue from 14th to 23rd was where they made men's clothing. Gone. The fur industry was south of where Madison Square Garden is now, buildings like 330 Seventh Avenue, 370 Seventh Avenue. No more. The garment district: you used to walk down Seventh Avenue and guys would be pushing racks of clothing—we called them Jewish airplanes. There are very few garment manufacturers here anymore.

Barney's was on 17th and Seventh Avenue. It was a fat boys' store: "short and portly." There were cheap men's clothing stores all over: Ripley, Crawford, Bonds, Howard Clothes—they had a singing ad: "I'm the little Howard label. . . ." Rogers Peet, Weber and Heilbrook were a little better. Union Square was Klein's, Orbach's, Franklin Simon. SoHo was warehouses and small factories where they made buttons and zippers and envelopes.

We used to have so much live television in New York. *The Tonight Show* was here, Merv Griffin broadcast from 44th next to Sardi's, Arthur Godfrey was here, and his program was the beginning of the talk show.

The movie theaters in the Broadway area were phenomenal palaces seating thousands of people. Radio City, the Roxy, Paramount, Capitol—they all showed first-run movies followed by live shows. A ticket cost a buck and a half. The movie would go on at nine o'clock in the morning. At 10:45 a band like Benny Goodman's would come out and play. At noon the picture would

The Roxy Theater— one of the phenomenal movie palaces on Broadway that showed first-run movies followed by live shows.

go back on. At 1:45 the band would play again. This went on till midnight. There were headliners: Frank Sinatra, Dean Martin and Jerry Lewis, Johnny Ray, preceded by an opening act. I remember Georgia Gibbs opening for Danny Kaye.

Movies would open in one of the big Broadway theaters. Then they would go to the big downtown Brooklyn theaters: the Albee, the Fox, the Brooklyn Paramount, and from there move out into the local theaters. This was true nationally as well. They'd use it in the advertising: "Direct from seven record-breaking weeks at Radio City . . ."

Radio City doesn't show movies anymore. The Roxy is gone; the Rivoli is gone. The Paramount closed with Sean Connery in *Thunderball*. It had stopped showing vaudeville long before that. The Capitol is now the Uris Building. Where the Victoria and Astor movie theaters and Ripley's Believe It or Not were is now the Marriott Marquis Hotel. Bertelsman owns the building across the street where the Loews State used to be. The Warner and Strand were where Morgan Stanley is now. To think such a company would be in that area.

When I came to Broadway as a kid, it was like going to the most magical place you could imagine. Today you could be in downtown Minneapolis.

Nothing stays the same. It used to be Ed Sullivan, now it's Regis Philbin. It used to be the fifteen-cent token, now it's the metro card. It used to be moving to the suburbs, now it's coming back at any price.

MARK FEDERMAN: I was always asked why I didn't move Russ and Daughters uptown to where my customers were. Sooner or later uptown will move downtown, I said. It's happening. The Lower East Side is becoming romantic.

KEN ARETSKY: Recently I got a phone call from a friend who had lived one floor above me in apartment 4D in the Amalgamated Houses. He told me there was a big cover story in *New York* magazine about gentrification on the Lower East Side. They listed the hot places to live, and one of them was the Amalgamated Houses. They have doormen now. "Can you imagine?" Jerry said. "Our parents did everything in the world to get out. Now they're fighting to get in." If you live long enough . . .

MICKEY ALPERT: The family that owns Ratner's has been there for a thousand years. Now they've opened up something on the side street, the back end of Ratner's, called Lansky's Lounge. It's a saloon where young people go. They've closed Ratner's and plan to expand Lansky's Lounge. The front will serve the old dairy food for lunch and that's it. They'll be open Friday nights and Saturdays—they won't be kosher anymore.

MARK FEDERMAN: Not long ago, people from the Smithsonian came to the store to discuss Russ and Daughters participating in an American food and folklore event. My thoughts turned to my grandfather. I could just hear him saying, "I told you we would be assimilating sooner or later."

ALVIN REED: One day in 1988, I saw an ad in the *Amsterdam News*: "Historical Place in Harlem for Sale." Wait a minute, I thought. Could it be Small's Paradise? I called the number and asked, "Where's it located at?"

"Lenox and 124th Street, the Lenox Lounge," they told me.

I was raised in Harlem. I knew this street. Our parents said, "Don't ever go down there." But now I thought, let me take a look, see what's going on.

Outside are drug addicts and dealers. There isn't a lot of dealing, but they're just starting their day out there, negotiating, deciding what they're going to do, where they're going to be. I go in. And it's like night and day. Outside was a mess, inside was something else.

I had been to the Lenox Lounge in the fifties as an eighteen-, nineteen-year-old. At that age, though, I didn't know the history of the place. I didn't know that Billie Holiday would come there to relax after she entertained downtown, that she had her own booth where no one could sit but her, that though she wasn't a paid performer, sometimes she'd get up and sing anyway.

The Lenox Lounge was still in the hands of one of the original owners. He was in his late seventies; his kids didn't want to take it over. I checked the books. The place wasn't really making any money, but the price was right.

I couldn't get any partners together. My wife was against it. I had to refinance my house. But I saw the future of Harlem and the future of this place, so I took it on.

The Lenox Lounge—"I saw the future of Harlem and the future of this place, so I took it on."

I had moved out of Harlem when I got married. It had become a much less stable environment. Drugs had started popping up everywhere, people coming in from we don't know where, a lot of transients in the community. Sanitation services, police services were dropping. Seemed like the better teachers left. Those who had a little bit of money moved out.

It got so I was embarrassed to say I lived in Harlem. When people asked, "Hey, Al, where you live?" I always said, "Upper Manhattan."

I purchased a house in Queens Village, where I still live today. I also have a house in Pennsylvania. But I never left Harlem. I may live over there, I may sleep over there, but Harlem is where I stay. All my friends are from Harlem. I still go to the restaurants: Sylvia's, M&G Diners, Charlie's—I know all the best places.

When I bought the Lenox Lounge, it was like everything came together for me. It was built in 1939, the year I was born. At that time El Morocco said they had a patent on the zebra material that is on the walls here. I don't know if they were in litigation or if there were strong-arm tactics, but because of that, the Lounge wasn't able to open up until November 11, 1942. November 11th is my wife's birthday. When we found out, we thought it was destiny.

BILL GALLO: My father died young so I needed to work. I would go to the theaters in the morning and ask the guy if I could sweep up. He would give me fifty cents. Doing that, I got to appreciate the theater. It is still the champ of the evening. The quality may change, but the feeling doesn't. The same is true of New York. It may change, but it's like that old dame. I still love it.

JOEL DORN: To me there is one story that defines the record business I knew. There was a very successful music publisher named Lou Levy who was married to one of the Andrew Sisters. He was a big gambler who went broke a couple of times, lost a million a couple of times. Then he married an Englishwoman and moved to England.

One day, another old-timer, Juggy Gayles, who was a music publisher and promotion man, called me up and says, "Listen, Lou's back in town. Hook him up because he doesn't know who the players are now."

We meet for lunch. Lou tells me he's got a big divorce pending and he's settling a property in England with his third or his fourth wife. He's gonna have money and start a publishing company and a record company. He's back in the game.

Two months later I'm walking up 61st Street crossing Madison toward Fifth. I pass one of those phone booths that were like gigantic hair dryers. If you made a call from inside one of those little acoustic domes, nobody could tell you were on the street; you couldn't hear the traffic. I see Lou in this phone booth. I tap him on the shoulder to say hello. He turns and sees me, and he says into the phone, "Harry, I gotta run. Somebody just walked in."

The last Tuesday of August 2001, we were in Manhattan having come down from our home in New Hampshire to return the many photographs people had loaned us to use in this book. It was a perfect summer day, rare in the New York of our memories, clear skies, no humidity. Around noon, we walked over to La Caravelle and Le Cirque, two restaurants that epitomize the level of haute cuisine New York is now renowned for, and took in the familiar midday, midtown scene: rushing pedestrians and pressing traffic, elegant emporiums and street vendors, glass and steel towers along Park Avenue, white brick buildings along Third.

That afternoon, we drove downtown along Second Avenue, catching a glimpse of Le Corbusier's optimistic vision: the UN building as we crossed 42nd Street. We passed tranquil Murray Hill and leafy Gramercy Park stopping at a few buildings in the area that once housed New York's china trade but now are home to public relations and advertising companies.

We went around stylish Union Square, where left-wing rallies used to be held while the hoi polloi shopped at S. Klein's and onto Fifth Avenue: Greenwich Village. Before us was the NYU campus where we'd met years ago as undergraduates writing for the school newspaper. Cars used to pass under the Arch back then and go right through Washington Square Park. Now the park is closed to vehicles and that beautiful day it was filled with children at play, students hanging out around the fountain, seniors taking in the sun.

At Houston Street, we stopped at Russ and Daughters, the eighty-year-old appetizing store that's part of the remarkable revival of the Lower East Side. Our great-grandparents were among the thousands of immigrants who had lived in this teeming neighborhood when they came to America around the turn of the last century. As soon as they could, they moved out. Now everyone wants to move back in.

Driving down Broadway through SoHo, we passed art galleries and high-end boutiques housed in the distinctive cast-iron buildings that were almost demolished to make way for a crosstown expressway. Our next stop was a building on Grand Street, once the warehouse for Vanderbilt treasures, now the home and studio of photographer Gilles Larrain.

At Canal Street, we turned west. Below us was TriBeCa, a distinctly nondescript downtown neighborhood until its transformation in the 1980s. From Greenwich Street, we could see all the way down to the World Trade Center. The flower-filled waterfront promenade that fronts Battery Park City, built on landfill dug up during the construction of the Twin Towers, beckoned. But our mission this day directed us back uptown.

Hudson Street became Eighth Avenue. Greenwich Village gave way to Chelsea. Upscale apartments and art galleries have replaced the rooming houses that once were home to retired stevedores and ship-workers. They are gone along with a New York whose ports were jammed with passenger liners and cargo ships.

We drove through the Garment District, still operative although hardly the manufacturing center it used to be, crossed 42nd Street for the second time that day but on the West Side now, and looked up to Times Square—still the heartbeat of the nation. After a few stops in fashionable Clinton—formerly Hell's Kitchen—we were before the fountained plazas and arcaded theaters of Lincoln Center for the Performing Arts.

This was our portico into the Upper West Side, the neighborhood that always seemed the most European in New York. There were stops to be made at a few majestic prewar buildings along the stately boulevards of West End Avenue and Riverside Drive. High on a bluff overlooking the Palisades, the Drive shimmered in the sunlight of this lovely afternoon. We passed the northern boundary of Central Park into Morningside Heights, home to Columbia University and Barnard College, and at 125th Street, we turned east. Harlem was just ahead.

We recalled how Laconia Smedley had sensed Harlem's rhythm when he first came to New York from Detroit in 1956. Apparently the rest of the world feels the beat as well, for Harlem is today a major international tourist destination. The legendary Lenox Lounge on Lenox Avenue where Billie Holiday hung out was our next stop. Since Alvin Reed bought and fixed up the place, it's been drawing the crowds once again.

Heading downtown once more, we drove along the upper reaches of Fifth Avenue to our final stop at a swanky building overlooking Central Park, home to Helen O'Hagan—who'd been vice president at Saks Fifth Avenue when Sophie Gimbel was designing clothes in her tenth-floor salon. And with that, our little circle tour of the isle of Manhattan was complete.

Driving around that day, we relived the exhilarating process of putting together the story of how a Manhattan that had come into its own during the Jazz Age changed to its very skyline in the postwar years. But at the same time, we were witnessing a story being born: twenty-first century Manhattan in all its glory.

New York was truly the Emerald City that beautiful end of summer afternoon. Everywhere people were out, walking the city streets, riding the buses, taking in the sunshine from a stoop or park bench, sitting with a cup of coffee in a sidewalk café. Formerly down-and-out neighborhoods were taking on new patinas. Even the traffic was manageable. All of New York seemed to be basking in the promise of this great city at the dawn of a new century.

The next morning we paid the de rigueur visit to Zabar's. Since moving from New York, we stop at Zabar's whenever we're in town and stock up on enough New York nourishment to last us until we come in again. This time was just a brief run-through; we didn't even fill the cooler in our car. Why bother, we thought. We'll be back again September 12th.

As it turned out, it was a while before we were able to return to New York. In the year following 9/11 we did return to witness a resiliency of the sort people described when recalling the 1970s when the city almost went broke. It's a resiliency that captures the very essence of New York. After all, once you've lived here . . .

HARVEY FROMMER: *Garry Schumacher, a true New York character and the publicist for the old New York Giants, had moved with the team to the West Coast where I met him in 1975 while I was in San Francisco interviewing for a baseball book. We went out for a few drinks, and I remember being amazed at what an incredible fund of baseball knowledge he was.*

Some years later, I read in the newspaper that Garry died. A short time after that, I dreamed about him. There he was, standing in my bedroom, big as life.

"Garry," I said, "great to see you. How are things? What's it like?"

"It's okay, Harvey," he solemnly said to me. "But it's not New York."

Photo Credits

Cover Photo Credits

Front cover (clockwise from top): Photofest, Photofest/Icon, Photofest, Photofest, Photofest

Background: Photofest

Back cover (counterclockwise from top): Photofest, Photofest, Mark Federman, Photofest, Photofest, Photofest/Icon

Interior Photo Credits

Kenny Allisburg: i, xiii, 38, 44 (large), 178, 180–1, 207, 211, 255 (bottom), 264 (top, bottom), 272–3, 276, 282, 289, 303, 304, 306, 313

Anonymous: 266 (third down)

Nina & Andy Balducci: 65

Jane Apt Bevans: 5, 7, 11–2, 33, 175

Martha Bushko: 39, 68–9, 117, 195, 286–7

Career Education Corporation: 51, 52

Mary T. Crabill: Endpapers, ix (bottom)

Sid Darion: ix (second down), xvi (second down), 30–1, 93, 125, 200, 244 (inset)

Mark Federman: 60–2, 64

Frommer Collection: vii (third down), ix (fourth down), xv (first, fourth down), xvi (top), xvii (third down), xix, xxi, 118, 124, 134, 205, 226, 227 (top), 231, 233–4, 271 (bottom), 277, 301

David Gahr: 165

Fiona Capuano Goldberg: Endpapers, 32, 120, 135–6, 146

André Jammet: 83, 85, 86–7

Jack Lang: 221

Gilles Larraín: 55, 78–9, 129, 244 (background)

Theodore Liebman: 265 (top), 266 (second down)

Alan Melting: 266 (top and bottom)

Sirio Maccioni: 89, 91–2

Helen O'Hagan: 105–6, 108–9

Robert Perron: 265 (top)

Photofest: Endpapers, iv–v, vi, vii (second, fourth down), viii (first, third, fourth down), ix (first, third down), xi, xvi (bottom), xvii (second, fourth down), xxi, 1, 4, 6, 24, 29, 35, 37, 42–3, 44 (in circle), 46, 48–9, 54, 76, 101, 121, 123, 132–3, 139, 141, 147 (top), 148–55, 157, 159, 160–4, 167–8, 171, 173, 175, 191, 198–9, 201–2, 209–10, 212, 217–9, 222–3, 228, 231, 237–8, 242–3, 245, 252–3, 256, 265 (bottom), 267–8, 269 (small), 270, 271 (top), 275, 284–5, 291, 292–3 (bottom left, background spread), 296–7, 299 (top), 300, 302

Photofest/Icon: Endpapers, ii–iii, vii (first down), viii (second, fifth down), x, xiv, xv (second, third down), 3, 8, 10, 23, 26–8, 34, 50, 73, 81, 100, 111, 113, 130, 147 (bottom), 176–7, 185, 187, 203, 211, 213–5, 241, 247–51, 255 (top), 258, 262–3, 264 (middle), 269 (large), 278–81, 283, 293 (top), 294–5, 298, 299 (bottom)

Barbara E. Pringle: 14–5, 18–20

Maurice Rapf: xviii (top), 182

Alvin Reed: xvi (fourth down), xvii (top), 13, 17, 206, 208

Paul Sinanis: xviii (second and fourth down)

John Tauranac: Endpapers, 21, 22

Sharon Telesca/St. Regis Hotel: 236

Dorothy Wheelock: xvi (third down), xviii (third down), 95–8, 235 (top)

Saul Zabar: xvii, 56–7, 59

Index

Page numbers in *italics* refer to speakers in this oral history.